The Orange Order

Studies in British and Irish Migration

Series Editors: T. M. Devine, University of Edinburgh, and
Angela McCarthy, University of Otago

Showcasing the histories of migration into and out of Britain and
Ireland from the seventeenth century to contemporary times and their
impact at home and abroad

From the 1600s to the current day, millions of British and Irish
migrants have sought new lives around the world. Britain and Ireland
have also received returning migrants and other newcomers of
diverse ethnicities. This series will examine the causes, consequences,
representations and legacies of these movements on the homelands,
the migrants and the destinations in which they settled. The series
incorporates the inward and outward movement not just of people,
but of ideas, products and objects. It specifically encourages
transnational and comparative cross-disciplinary approaches across
groups, space and time.

Titles available in the series:

New Scots: Scotland's Immigrant Communities since 1945
Edited by T. M. Devine and Angela McCarthy

Death in the Diaspora: British and Irish Gravestones
Edited by Nicholas J. Evans and Angela McCarthy

Gold Rush Societies and Migrant Networks in the Tasman World
Daniel Davy

*Forging Identities in the Irish World: Melbourne and Chicago,
c. 1830–1922*
Sophie Cooper

The Orange Order: A Global History
Patrick Coleman

edinburghuniversitypress.com/series/bims

The Orange Order

A Global History

Patrick Coleman

EDINBURGH
University Press

Edinburgh University Press is one of the leading university presses in the UK. Publishing new research in the arts and humanities, EUP connects people and ideas to inspire creative thinking, open new perspectives and shape the world we live in. For more information, visit www.edinburghuniversitypress.com.

© Patrick Coleman, 2025

Edinburgh University Press Ltd
13 Infirmary Street
Edinburgh EH1 1LT

Typeset in 10.5/13pt Sabon
by Cheshire Typesetting Ltd, Cuddington, Cheshire, and
printed and bound in Great Britain

A CIP record for this book is available from the British Library

ISBN 978 1 3995 1815 4 (paperback)
ISBN 978 1 3995 1814 7 (hardback)
ISBN 978 1 3995 1816 1 (webready PDF)
ISBN 978 1 3995 1817 8 (epub)

The right of Patrick Coleman to be identified as author of this work has been asserted in accordance with the Copyright, Designs and Patents Act 1988 and the Copyright and Related Rights Regulations 2003 (SI No. 2498).

This book is printed using paper from well-managed forests, recycling and other controlled sources

Contents

Figures and Tables

FIGURES

TABLES

Acknowledgements

This project first started as a PhD. My primary supervisor, Professor Angela McCarthy, encouraged me to get my research published. I owe an extraordinary debt of gratitude to Angela, who has guided and supported me from the start to the completion of my study and now this book. Professor Tom Devine, as co-editor in this series, has been very helpful in providing additional encouragement and editorial guidance. I am thankful to my examiners of the original thesis and the anonymous reviewers for the book proposal. Their comments informed my writing and editing. Many thanks to Becks Ireland who worked so patiently with me to produce a stunning book cover. The team at Edinburgh University Press have been fantastic in helping me negotiate the whole publishing process.

I am grateful to what was then the Department of History and Art History at the University of Otago, now a Programme, for funding research trips, conferences, workshops and postgraduate days. My research in the United States was funded through the John Main Research Fund. I am also thankful for funding from the University's Centre for Global Migrations for supporting my research. Many thanks to my former co-supervisors Dr Vanessa Ward and Professor Mark Seymour, who provided crucial input and editorial insight on the original thesis.

My research spans many countries and necessitated many research trips. This project was assisted by members of the Orange Order who gave time, hospitality and access to materials for my research. In New Zealand at Christchurch, Beverley Buist, the late Colin Buist and Sheryll Rodgers generously gave up time to help me access materials. The late Charles Ferrel in Wellington was a long-time supporter of my research. I was most grateful for his help and friendship. In Auckland, James (Jimmie) Crawford helped provide access to Orange materials there.

My first trip to 'Bonnie Scotland' was made memorable through the Grand Orange Lodge of Scotland. In particular, I wish to thank Jim McHarg, Robert McLean, and Malcolm and Isobel Campbell. The late David Bryce, Grand Orange Lodge archivist and historian, was always there to provide resources and help. In England, the late Michael Phelan was so generous with his resources and immense knowledge of the Orange Order. At the Museum of Orange Heritage in Belfast, Jonathan Mattison was incredibly helpful and generous. In Philadelphia, Walter Wilson helped with resources and sorely needed data. In Toronto, I wish to thank Jim Pyke and John Chalmers. Both helped me with resources at a time when their Orange archives were closed. Jeff Davis, Melbourne, the late Thomas Leary, Brisbane, Hilton Wickham, Sydney, and Ray Nolan, Adelaide, all provided materials and information about the Australian Orange Order.

Many libraries were repositories of material that I needed. I wish to thank the staff at the Alexander Turnbull Library and Archives New Zealand, Wellington. I am grateful for the assistance of the librarians at the University of Otago who helped me get access to materials. In Sydney, staff at the Mitchell Library, State Library of New South Wales, helped me with archival materials. In England, I am thankful to staff at the Central Library, Liverpool City Council. Thank you also to the staff at the Historical Society of Pennsylvania for assisting me in my visit.

Finally, I am thankful for the love, encouragement and support of my family and friends. My parents have supported me through the long research process. I dedicate this work to my children (now adults), who mean everything to me.

Series Editors' Introduction

Undertaking a global history is no easy task. It requires an ability to deal with many national frameworks and their various interactions and exchanges. Patrick Coleman's history of the Orange Order is therefore a welcome development in providing the first global study of the origins and operations of this Protestant organisation from the late eighteenth century right through to the present day. Charting the Order's evolution, spread and activities, Coleman effectively deploys examples from Ireland, Britain, Canada, the United States, Australia, New Zealand and Africa.

Situating the analysis within a comparative and transnational framework, and alert to existing studies of the Order in various locales, Coleman interrogates perceptions of the Order as a bigoted organisation and its efforts to promulgate a different view, particularly through its benevolent and charitable initiatives. But there are many other areas of interest traversed, including peaceful and antagonistic Orange parades and politics, the richness of rituals and material culture, and the drive to secure the Order's longevity through its Junior movement. Women's participation in the organisation also appears throughout the book to counteract studies that marginalise or overlook their engagement with Orangeism.

The Orange Order: A Global History is likewise notable in drawing on a vast array of sources, including newspapers, minute books, annual proceedings and reports, rules and regulations, websites, and interviews with Orange Order members. Coleman showcases to great effect many intriguing photographs, particularly in the chapter on material culture which features buildings, sashes, symbols, warrants, banners and ballot boxes. Especially striking is the Canadian First Nation beadwork technique on a crown showing King William on horseback. But so too do we see Orangemen marching with the Ku Klux Klan in Maine in 1924, while an image from New Zealand in the 1930s shows an Orange Order family.

Beyond its interest to scholars of the Orange Order, migration and ethnic associations, this book has widespread appeal for the global Orange Order family. How far they continue to operate in the face of ongoing decline, however, remains to be seen.

Angela McCarthy and T. M. Devine

Abbreviations

ALOI	Association of Loyal Orangewomen of Ireland
APA	American Protective Association
APDA	Australian Protestant Defence Association
DUP	Democratic Unionist Party
GOLE	Grand Orange Lodge of England
GOLI	Grand Orange Lodge of Ireland
GOLNZ	Grand Orange Lodge of New Zealand
GOLS	Grand Orange Lodge of Scotland
GPALO	Grand Protestant Association of Loyal Orangemen
JLOL	Junior Loyal Orange Lodge
JOAI	Junior Orangewomen's Association of Ireland
LLOL	Ladies' Loyal Orange Lodge
LOBA	Ladies' Orange Benevolent Association
LOI	Loyal Orange Institution
LOIE	Loyal Orange Institution of England
LOIGB	Loyal Orange Institution of Great Britain
LOIS	Loyal Orange Institution of Scotland
LOIUSA	Loyal Orange Institution of the United States of America
LOL	Loyal Orange Lodge
LOLIUSA	Loyal Orange Ladies' Institution of the United States of America
LTBA	Loyal True Blue Association
NSWPPA	New South Wales Protestant Political Association
OYA	Orange Young Americans
OYB	Orange Young Britons
PAFS	Protestant Alliance Friendly Society

PAFSA	Protestant Alliance Friendly Society of Australasia
PPA	Protestant Political Association
SNP	Scottish Nationalist Party
UUP	Ulster Unionist Party
WCTU	Woman's Christian Temperance Union
WM	Worshipful Master

Introduction:
Orange Histories, Sources and Methodologies

The day was overcast with a light wind. On both sides of the streets onlookers watched and took photos as line after line of marchers came down the city streets. The bands were in full flight with a mix of pounding drums and the shrill sound of the fifes. There were drum majors twirling their batons to show off their skills. The marchers were wearing Orange collarettes with a variety of badges. A couple of the older members were riding mobility scooters decked with union jacks. The men tended to wear black suits with some wearing blue. The women all wore dresses with some groups colour coordinating with blue and white. A police presence was evident as they walked alongside the parade. The marchers were marching in their lodge groups, so their distinctive banners were evident with pictures of Queen Victoria, King William. Others held bannerettes or flags. A few of the marchers interacted with the crowd shaking hands and smiling.[1]

To those with a vague idea of the Orange Order this may seem like Northern Ireland, but it is not. This is Glasgow in the 2020s. Why is this significant? The existence of a loyalist organisation that continues to maintain a presence on the streets of England, Northern Ireland and Scotland reveals the longevity of the Orange Order that has been in existence for almost 230 years.[2] How is this relevant in a post-Brexit United Kingdom? Issues around devolution, a united Ireland, and independence in Scotland are seen as threats to the Union.[3] The Orange Order sees itself as an upholder of the Union of Great Britain and Northern Ireland and has an established history of maintaining it. However, the Order's influence is not contained within the borders of the UK. Under the previous British Empire, the Orange Order planted lodges and established themselves as the empire expanded in such countries as Australia, Canada and even Ghana. The very existence of the Orange Order in these seemingly foreign contexts to the original Irish-founded Orange Order warrants investigation.

The origin story of the Orange Order exemplifies the prolonged negative image of the organisation. Ireland in the 1790s was a time of economic and political turmoil. France was in the throes of a revolution whose ideas were spreading through Europe. Ireland was under British rule, and there was always the threat that the French might invade and obtain support from the local Irish population. In County Armagh, there had been clashes between Catholics and Protestants. The Protestant Peep o' Day Boys were raiding and wrecking Catholic homes searching for guns as they illegally enforced the penal laws. The Catholic Defenders formed to protect Catholic homes. A significant clash – 'Battle of the Diamond' – occurred near a little town called Loughgall, County Armagh, on 21 September 1795. The 'battle' eventually settled on an inn owned by Dan Winter. The Protestants, better armed though smaller in number, won without loss of life while the Defenders suffered deaths and casualties. The events that followed proved to have far-reaching consequences. A small group of Protestants, some of whom took part in the 'battle', decided to form a new organisation. There were meetings in Dan Winter's home and the initial formation of the Orange Order was signed at the inn of James Sloan in the village of Loughgall. Many of these early men were Freemasons.[4] This story of the Orange Order has been retold with varying details and perspectives since it was first formed.

At this point, the story seems localised and best sits as microhistory. This was Ireland in the 1790s, and there would be more conflicts, and uprisings, and *An Gorta Mór*/the Great Irish Famine was still to come. The significance of these events does not therefore appear to be that great in comparison to the others. On the surface, this is true. However, the founding of the Orange Order was significant to its subsequent history since it rapidly spread across the British world. With its mix of loyalism and pan-Protestantism, Orangeism adapted to a variety of countries from Australia and Canada to Ghana and New Zealand. While its membership has significantly declined, its form of loyalism still plays a role in debates around national identity in the United Kingdom and Commonwealth countries.[5] In a post-Brexit United Kingdom, the Orange Order continues to maintain a highly public presence in the context of arguments of a united Ireland and Scottish independence.

HISTORIES

Despite the global nature of Orangeism, its history has taken a long time to attract the attention of historians. Early histories included a polemic by a Catholic priest and an Orange member's series of articles on the Orange Order for the *Belfast Weekly News*.[6] Both texts have been used as a starting point for many subsequent histories of the Orange Order. Outlining the historiography of the Orange Order is problematic because of the sporadic nature of the histories.

The most prominent social and political history of the Orange Order for many years was the work of Hereward Senior, who in the 1960s provided insightful research on the early phase of Orangeism in Ireland and later in Canada.[7] Senior covered the violent and political phases of early Orangeism well. He argued that the infiltration of Orangeism into the army and its extension to England demonstrated its adaptability and appeal to ultra-loyalists in the early decades of the nineteenth century. His account, however, stops in 1836 as he was drawing heavily upon the UK parliamentary inquiry into Orangeism in 1835. His next major book on Orangeism, published in the early 1970s, focused on Canada and was revisionist in intent. He drew on Orange source materials, particularly annual proceedings and contemporary newspapers, to demonstrate that the Orange Order was social in nature although it did have an interest in politics.[8] At that time the prevailing view was of the divisive nature of Orangeism within Canada. Decades passed before this research was updated through the work of Allan Blackstock. With access to more primary sources, Blackstock's focus was on a broader loyalism rather than the Orange Order itself. In other words, the Orange Order was one manifestation of Irish loyalism that developed in this period. The importance of his work is that it explores the 'multi-faceted' nature of Irish loyalism that laid the foundations for Irish conservatism and ultimately culminated in unionism.[9]

This 'divisive nature' of the Orange Order formed the focus of much of the later research on the conflict and sectarian character of the Orange Order. This was particularly noticeable in the work of Frank Neal writing about the Orange Order in Liverpool and Manchester and Scott See writing about Canada. Neal's main focus was on Orange-Catholic conflicts which drew their impetus from the street fights that comprised pub brawls through to conflicts at street parades. Competition for employment and the struggle for political power encompassed much of his focus. Neal drew upon the newspapers and government records in the absence of access to Orange archives.[10] See, meanwhile, investigated the New Brunswick Orange riots that occurred at Woodstock and Fredericton in 1847, and also at the York Point section of Saint John in 1849. He acknowledges that the impetus for Orangeism in this region of Canada came from Irish Protestant immigrants, but they were largely supplanted by locals. This finding, the result of meticulous research in identifying the backgrounds of the participants in the riots, exemplifies the ongoing value of See's body of work.[11]

A shift away from the usual focus on sectarian conflict was exemplified in the anthropological approach to the material culture of Orangeism in Northern Ireland by Neil Jarman and David Cairns. Their approach was informed by the emerging field of material culture studies that developed alongside the field of anthropology in the early 1990s.[12] In its simplest definition, the material culture approach is a way by which researchers explain the link or relationship between material objects and the people of the society surrounding them. Jarman focused on the banners and their symbolism in Orange parades and other religious groups in Northern Ireland. He studied several hundred banners that he photographed from 1990 to 1996 in which he sought to identify common themes.[13] Not surprisingly, he found that 69 per cent of the banners had 'King Billy', with a further 20 per cent dealing with biblical themes.[14] In a similar timeframe, 1993–96, David Cairns analysed the material culture of loyalism in Northern Ireland through an ethnographic investigation of four marching seasons.[15] His main findings were that material objects, such as flags, football strips and other political paraphernalia, 'comprise a "materialization" of sectarianism'.[16] He was trying to explain why the objects become offensive to others, in this case Irish Catholics, and also how they 'possess a certain social practicality', which meant linking the person or group to the wider loyalist community.

Alongside the work on material culture is a focus on Orange parades, moving beyond a sectarian focus to their impact and symbolism. This aspect has received excellent coverage from a mixture of individual studies and collections of work. Dominic Bryan provides one of the best analyses of Orange parades, not only dealing with historical and contemporary parades but unpacking their ritual and symbolism.[17] These studies, interdisciplinary in their approach to Orangeism, focus on the northern hemisphere variant.

The works of political scientist Eric Kaufmann have been an outlier compared to other standard histories of the Orange Order since he moved beyond microhistories to quantify the Order's strength and influence. Focusing initially on Orangeism from 1963 to 2005, he analysed the membership and the parades, especially Drumcree, but mostly from an economic and socio-political perspective.[18] Kaufmann then expanded his scope with a macro-social analysis, using a quantitative and comparative approach to examine ethnicity and membership in Newfoundland, Northern Ireland and the west coast of Scotland.[19] He found that the

Protestants in Newfoundland turned out to be more 'Orange' than anywhere in the world in the early to mid-twentieth century. He also noted that in terms of ethnicity the English-speaking part of Canada, together with Northern Ireland, the west coast of Scotland and north-west England, still considered themselves 'British-Protestant'. Closer to the present, Kaufmann produced a multi-site analysis of sectarianism in Canada, Ulster and Scotland.[20] His approach was to combine three discourses: social theory; social movements theory; and ethnicity/nationalism theory. In trying to analyse why Orangeism, which is central to Northern Irish society, was suddenly declining, yet stable in other regions, Kaufmann argued the drop in middle-class membership combined with the loss of Presbyterian clergy has accentuated a more rural and working-class form of Orangeism in Northern Ireland. One of the factors cited for the Presbyterian shift has been the rise of ecumenism within Presbyterianism with its softening stance towards the Catholic Church. Kaufmann was mostly posing questions and potential areas requiring further investigation such as attempting to demonstrate that a possible 'Orange decline (and a broader decline of sectarian conflicts) is a feature of post-industrial social organisation in the Anglo-Saxon West'.[21]

A further pivot in focus has scholars focusing on the Orange Order in new regions of the world, precipitated by changes in access to Orange records that started to influence even more historical enquiry in the Orange Order.[22] Now there were histories, particularly by doctoral students, about the Orange Order in nineteenth-century New South Wales, Wellington, New Zealand, and the United States, as well as Orangewomen in Ulster and Scotland.[23] The latter, especially, differed from other studies in adopting a timeframe that extended into the twenty-first century.

The emergence of women's history in the literature on the Orange Order has been influential in this book. While initial forays centred on Northern Ireland and specifically on the bands and parading culture,[24] the pioneering work of D. A. J. MacPherson and Donald MacRaild focused on female Orange lodges in Tyneside, England, as a result of access to rare Orange records, from the late nineteenth century until 1930.[25] Their focus is very much on a working-class association of which the men's attitudes towards women ranged from 'grudging acceptance' to 'outright hostility'.[26] MacPherson and MacRaild discovered the ways that Orangewomen contributed through fundraising and promoting Orangeism in public life in Tyneside.[27]

The previous study in collaboration with MacPherson was informed by MacRaild's unprecedented access to Orange archival material (mainly in northwest England).[28] Just like Neal's study of the 1980s, MacRaild found similar patterns to other researchers, particularly the Irish Protestant impetus for English Orangeism. In terms of the ethnic composition of Orangeism MacRaild found that, in contrast to the Liverpool experience of relying on the local English population to build the Order, the far north of England, along with Scotland, had a high proportion of Irish Protestants.[29] This also fits with the migration patterns of these groups, who developed a form of Orangeism that was essentially migrant inspired and maintained.

MacPherson's body of work continues to shed light on the experience of Orangewomen. In his study of Orangewomen in Scotland, he claimed that Orangewomen played a vital role in the migration process of other Orangewomen, mainly through maintaining a supportive network either through emotional support or sometimes with financial aid. Using terms such as 'diaspora space' and 'diasporic consciousness', MacPherson relates how the migration process is shaped not only by those who leave but also by those who stay behind.[30] He reaches some thought-provoking conclusions about Scottish Orangewomen who 'believed themselves to be part of an interconnected Orange world, which was shaped by the migration process, a strong belief in the British Empire and an overarching commitment to Irish Protestant culture'.[31] This demonstrates the importance of gender rather than just ethnicity as a crucial factor in the spread and maintenance of worldwide Orangeism. The main conclusion is that Orangewomen were not simply content to be helpers, but also assisted in the Order's ongoing activities and viability.[32]

More recently, MacPherson has adopted a comparative approach to Orangewomen focusing on Scotland and England, then adding Canada.[33] His work reveals that Orangewomen's activism created a sense of identity across the British world in the nineteenth and early twentieth centuries. In doing so, he built upon the work of other gender historians who looked at the temperance and suffrage activism of women in Scotland and more broadly the debate over whether women were able to shape an ethnic feminine public sphere.[34] My research on Orangewomen used a similar comparative framework but extended the coverage to all of the areas of the Orange world, finding, like MacPherson, that Orangewomen were active participants in the social and political activities of the Orange Order. The study also demonstrated the innovations of the Orangewomen of the Orange diaspora compared to their Irish counterparts.[35] These case studies illustrate the nuances of Orangeism as it became an outlet for women to participate in the public sphere.

This book builds upon many of these works by adopting a global context to analyse the spread, structure, rituals, activism and parades across the Orange world. In doing so it seeks to compare developments of the Orange Order in Ireland with the Orange diaspora, to overcome a focus on single countries. Secondly, it integrates female and male experiences. Thirdly, it addresses under-examined aspects of Orangeism such as material culture and the junior Orange movement. Some overarching themes demonstrate that through the use of transnational networks Orange members have supported and promoted Orange ideals for more than 230 years. It is this close fraternal bond that continues to maintain the global Orange network. The perception of the Orange Order as a male-dominated, bigoted and often violent organisation is an enduring image. This book demonstrates that despite the efforts of the Orange Order to transform this perception, it continues to persist.

CONCEPTS, APPROACHES, SOURCES AND METHODS

In conceptualising an Irish diaspora, I follow MacPherson in perceiving it as an invaluable tool to unpack the layered social world of these migrant groups who left their homeland to start a new life across the British world. MacPherson emphasises the connectedness of these migrants who deal with not only the locality of their destination but also their departing location and the various family and friends who never migrate. He argues that it is the Orange Order that holds 'a distinct diasporic function and mentality' and, in turn, helped to facilitate the migrants' awareness that they were part of a globally connected 'Orange world'.[36] Consequently, the concept of an Orange diaspora demonstrates the pivotal role that the Orange Order has had in the migration process of its members who are scattered across the world.

Investigating the Orange Order across centuries and in multiple countries requires a conceptual framework that captures the organisation's global character. As such, this book adopts a comparative and transnational framework since they are pivotal to examining the various Orange jurisdictions. In using the term 'transnationalism', I am careful not to be vague in its use as it needs to imply 'a sense of dynamic mobility and exchange, perhaps bilaterally, more commonly multilaterally'.[37] In this sense, transnationalism encompasses the idea of 'links and flows' in tracking 'people, ideas, products, processes and patterns that operate over, across, through, beyond, above, under, or in-between polities and societies'.[38] Orangeism involved dialogue and linkages between jurisdictions and in this book transnationalism encapsulates reciprocal links across the national borders of Ireland, England, Scotland, Canada, the United States, Australia and New Zealand. Hand in hand with this transnational approach, this book remains alert to identifying similarities and comparisons within the Orange world since Orange men and women resided within nation states. As Kevin Kenny has argued, the diasporic approach 'excels, capturing the fluidity, hybridity, and frequent ambiguity of transnational interactions. When diaspora and comparison are integrated, the result is a comprehensive and flexible framework of historical analysis.'[39]

The main sources used throughout this book are Orange Order-generated archives comprising minute books, annual proceedings, ritual books, photographs, banners, sashes and ritual objects. Each has benefits and drawbacks.

Minute books are generated from the meetings of the Orange Order and document the lodge meetings that were held regularly. Their existence owes just as much to chance as design since minute books could be destroyed by fire or water or thrown out – and often were. They also contain gaps in the record and sometimes the entries are not sufficient. For example, not all decisions are explained. The vagaries of the secretary writing the minutes may mean that sometimes the notes are detailed and other times they are brief. Despite this drawback, Orange minute books were used to cite evidence of activity at the lodge level. There was also the opportunity to link information noted in newspapers with evidence from minute books.

Other written materials of the Orange Order, such as annual proceedings, constitutions and laws, and ritual books, are important sources used in this book. Essentially, these provided insights into the beliefs, practices and internal world of the Orange Order across multiple countries. These were used not only for their varied content but as a means of exploring the differences and influences from one Orange jurisdiction to another. In particular, the ability to compare what messages were being told to members in annual proceedings was significant. These shaped the opinions of the membership and some of the internal issues, such as falling membership, were constant themes. The ritual books were useful in helping to inform the ritual practices that were only obliquely noted within minute books. As these were for members only there was the ability to see how they were structured, which in turn enabled good comparisons of other fraternal organisations like the Freemasons.

Newspapers provide insight into both the early and contemporary activities of the Orange Order. Wherever possible, major newspapers were used since they reflected a greater circulation and impact on society. However, newspapers with smaller runs also proved useful. For example, the *Fiery Cross*, although a newspaper of the Ku Klux Klan, was valuable for finding events and commentary on the Ku Klux Klan's links to the American Orange Order in the 1920s. The same is true of various Orange newspapers such as the *Watchman* from Sydney, which had extensive coverage of events of Orange lodges in Australia. The use of newspapers helped to provide a lot of useful content for the public life of the Orange Order including conflict or parades. Some newspapers were set up by or sympathetic to the Orange Order and these proved to be good sources of events not covered by other newspapers or analysed for comparison. Newspapers are ultimately a gauge of popular public opinion and, of course, newspapers could shape opinion.[40]

One of the more challenging groups of sources were those categorised as material culture. In this sense, material culture was used as a 'mode of inquiry' that investigates and 'uses artifacts (along with relevant documentary, statistical, and oral data) to explore cultural questions'.[41] This inquiry-based model is used in Chapter 5 to explore in a different way the ritual practices, both public and private, of Orange members. These physical objects were used to demonstrate the influence of the Irish Orange Order as its ideas were transferred to other countries. Provenance is an important part of beginning the process of decoding the use of a material object. The majority of the material culture objects were sourced from Orange members and visits to Orange lodges.

The use of emails and interviews formed an important verification stage in the research process.[42] All of the people chosen had positions of responsibility and a longstanding link to the Orange Order. Their information was used both to provide information that was not written and to check the various practices within the Orange Order. They were also generous providers of source material.

This book, then, is a macrohistory of the Orange Order that moves beyond the narrower focus of previous studies. The following chapters examine the Orange Order in many key areas: its spread across the world, structure and rituals, activism, parades, material culture and junior Orange movement. Its key aim is to analyse the differences and similarities of the Orange Order through its transfer from Ireland to other countries in the British world. This raises questions as to the extent of transnational influences and diasporic connections between the various Orange jurisdictions. The exploration of such issues informs studies of migration more broadly and the role of the Orange Order in the expansion of the British Empire and its maintenance of loyalist ideals in the present day.

NOTES

1. Generalised description of a recent parade in Glasgow, Scotland.

2. While there have been a handful of Welsh lodges, the most recent, formed in 2012 (Rawlings White Memorial LOL, Cardiff), comes under the jurisdiction of the English Grand Orange Lodge.

3. For a recent perspective on these issues see Joseph Webster, 'From Scottish independence, to Brexit, and back again: Orange Order ethno-religion and the awkward urgency of British unionism', *Social Anthropology/ Anthropologie Sociale*, 30:4 (2022), pp. 18–36.

4. David W. Miller, 'The origins of the Orange Order in County Armagh', in A. J. Hughes and William Nolan (eds), *Armagh: History and Society* (Dublin: Geography Publications, 2001), pp. 538–608; 'The Armagh troubles, 1784–95', in Samuel Clark and James S. Donnelly (eds), *Irish Peasants: Violence and Political Unrest, 1780–1914* (Madison: University of Wisconsin Press, 1983), pp. 155–91.

5. The issue of loyalism and identity forms the basis of Allan Blackstock and Frank O'Gorman's *Loyalism and the Formation of the British World: 1775–1914* (Woodbridge: Boydell Press, 2014), pp. 1–2.

6. H. W. Cleary, *The Orange Society* (Melbourne: Bernard King & Sons, 1897). This went through a series of reprints. R. M. Sibbett, *Orangeism in Ireland and throughout the Empire*, vols 1–2 (Belfast: Henderson & Company, 1914).

7. Hereward Senior, *Orangeism in Ireland and Britain, 1795–1836* (London: Routledge & Kegan Paul; Toronto: Ryerson Press, 1966).

8. Hereward Senior, *Orangeism: The Canadian Phase* (Toronto: McGraw-Hill Ryerson, 1972).

9. Allan Blackstock, *Loyalism in Ireland 1789–1829* (Woodbridge: Boydell Press, 2007).

10. Frank Neal, *Sectarian Violence: The Liverpool Experience, 1819–1914* (Manchester: Manchester University Press, 1988; revised 2003); 'Manchester's origins of the English Orange Order', *Manchester Region History Review*, 4:2 (1990–91), pp. 12–24. A recent book that has both updated Neal's work and managed to access Orange Order archives is Mervyn Busteed's *The Sash on the Mersey: The Orange Order in Liverpool, 1819–1982* (Manchester: Manchester University Press, 2023).

11. Scott W. See, *Riots in New Brunswick: Orange Nativism and Social Violence in the 1840s* (Toronto: University of Toronto Press, 1993). See also his articles: '"Mickeys and demons" vs "bigots and boobies": The Woodstock Riot of 1847', *Acadiensis: Journal of the History of the Atlantic Region*, 21:1 (1991), pp. 110–31; 'The Orange Order and social violence in mid-nineteenth-century Saint John', *Acadiensis: Journal of the History of the Atlantic Region*, 13:1 (1984), pp. 68–92; and 'The fortunes of the Orange Order in 19th century New Brunswick', in P. M. Toner (ed.), *New*

Ireland Remembered: Historical Essays on the Irish in New Brunswick (Fredericton: New Ireland Press, 1988), pp. 90–105.

12. Ian Woodward, *Understanding Material Culture* (London: Sage Publications, 2007).

13. Neil Jarman, *Material Conflicts: Parades and Visual Displays in Northern Ireland* (Oxford: Berg, 1997).

14. Ibid. p. 172.

15. David Cairns, 'The object of sectarianism: The material reality of sectarianism in Ulster loyalism', *The Journal of the Royal Anthropological Institute*, 6:3 (2000), pp. 437–52.

16. Ibid. p. 449.

17. Dominic Bryan, *Orange Parades: The Politics of Ritual, Tradition and Control* (London: Pluto Press, 2000). For Northern Ireland, England and Scotland see T. G. Fraser (ed.), *The Irish Parading Tradition: Following the Drum* (Basingstoke: Palgrave Macmillan, 2000).

18. Eric Kaufmann, *The Orange Order: A Contemporary Northern Irish History* (Oxford: Oxford University Press, 2007).

19. Eric Kaufmann, 'The Orange Order in Ontario, Newfoundland, Scotland and Northern Ireland: A macro-social analysis', in David A. Wilson (ed.), *The Orange Order in Canada* (Dublin: Four Courts Press, 2007), pp. 42–68.

20. Eric Kaufmann, 'The decline of sectarianism in the West? A comparison of the Orange Order in Canada, Ulster and Scotland', in N. Singh and T. Vanhanen (eds), *Ethnic Violence and Human Rights* (Delhi: KIRS, 2002), pp. 1–19.

21. Ibid.

22. Patrick Coleman, 'Who wants to be a Grand Master? Grand Masters of the Orange Lodge of the Middle Island of New Zealand', in Brad and Kathryn Patterson (eds), *Ireland and the Irish Antipodes: One World or Worlds Apart?* (Sydney: Anchor Books, 2010), pp. 96–107; 'Orange parading traditions in New Zealand 1880–1914', *Australasian Journal of Irish Studies*, 10 (2010), pp. 81–104; David Fitzpatrick, 'Exporting brotherhood: Orangeism in South Australia', *Immigrants & Minorities*, 23:2–3 (2005), pp. 277–310; Dianne Hall, 'Defending the faith: Orangeism and Ulster Protestant identities in colonial New South Wales', *Journal of Religious History*, 38:2 (2014), pp. 207–23; David A. Wilson (ed.), *The Orange Order in Canada* (Dublin: Four Courts Press, 2007).

23. Eric Turner, '"Not narrow minded bigots": Proceedings of the Loyal Orange Institution of New South Wales, 1845–1895' (PhD, University of New England, 2002); Gerard Edward Horn, '"A Loyal, united, and happy people": Irish Protestant migrants to Wellington Province 1840–1930: Aspects of migration, settlement and community' (PhD, Victoria University of Wellington, 2010); Christi McCallum, 'Orangewomen show their colors: Gender, family, and Orangeism in Ulster, 1795–present' (PhD,

Southern Illinois University Carbondale, 2011); Deborah Butcher, 'Ladies of the lodge: A history of Scottish Orangewomen, c. 1909–2013' (PhD, London Metropolitan University, 2014); Cory Wells, '"Tie the flags together": Migration, nativism, and the Orange Order in the United States, 1840–1930' (PhD, University of Texas, 2018).

24. Katy Radford, 'Drum rolls and gender roles in Protestant marching bands in Belfast', *British Journal of Ethnomusicology*, 10:2 (2001), pp. 37–59; 'Red, white, blue and orange: An exploration of historically bound allegiances through loyalist song', *The World of Music*, 46:1 (2004), pp. 71–89; Linda Racioppi and Katherine O'Sullivan See, 'Ulstermen and loyalist ladies on parade: Gendering unionism in Northern Ireland', *International Feminist Journal of Politics*, 2:1 (2000), pp. 1–29.

25. D. A. J. MacPherson and Donald M. MacRaild, 'Sisters of the brotherhood: Female Orangeism on Tyneside in the late nineteenth and early twentieth centuries', *Irish Historical Studies*, 35:137 (2006), pp. 40–60.

26. Ibid. p. 41.

27. Ibid. p. 59.

28. Donald M. MacRaild, *Faith, Fraternity and Fighting: The Orange Order and Irish Migrants in England, c. 1850–1920* (Liverpool: Liverpool University Press, 2005).

29. Ibid. p. 14.

30. D. A. J. MacPherson, 'Migration and the female Orange Order: Irish Protestant identity, diaspora and empire in Scotland, 1909–40', *The Journal of Imperial and Commonwealth History*, 40:4 (2012), pp. 619–42.

31. Ibid. p. 636.

32. D. A. J. MacPherson, 'The emergence of women's Orange lodges in Scotland: Gender, ethnicity and women's activism, 1909–1940', *Women's History Review*, 22:1 (2012), pp. 51–74.

33. D. A. J. MacPherson, 'Personal narratives of family and ethnic identity: Orangewomen in Scotland and England, c. 1940–2010', *Immigrants & Minorities*, 32:1 (2013), pp. 90–114; *Women and the Orange Order: Female Activism, Diaspora and Empire in the British World, 1850–1940* (Manchester: Manchester University Press, 2016); 'Irish Protestant masculinities and Orangewomen in Scotland, Canada and England, 1890–1918', in Rebecca Anne Barr, Sean Brady and Jane McGaughey (eds), *Ireland and Masculinities in History* (Cham, Switzerland: Palgrave Macmillan, 2019), pp. 253–72.

34. MacPherson, *Women and the Orange Order*, p. 6; Megan K. Smitley, *The Feminine Public Sphere: Middle-Class Women and Civic Life in Scotland, c. 1870–1914* (Manchester: Manchester University Press, 2009); Marlou Schrover and Eileen Yeo (eds), *Gender, Migration, and the Public Sphere, 1850–2005* (New York: Routledge, 2009).

35. Patrick Coleman, '"In harmony": A comparative view of female Orangeism 1887–2000', in Angela McCarthy (ed.), *Ireland in the World:*

Comparative, Transnational, and Personal Perspectives (London and New York: Routledge, 2015), pp. 110–36.

36. MacPherson, *Women and the Orange Order*, pp. 7–8.
37. Malcolm Campbell, *Ireland's Farthest Shores: Mobility, Migration, and Settlement in the Pacific World* (Madison: University of Wisconsin Press, 2022), pp. 6–7.
38. Akira Iriye and Pierre Yves Saunier (eds), *Palgrave Dictionary of Transnational History* (London: Palgrave Macmillan, 2009), p. xviii.
39. Kevin Kenny, 'Diaspora and comparison: The global Irish as a case study', *The Journal of American History*, 90:1 (2003), p. 162.
40. Stephen Vella, 'Newspapers', in Miriam Dobson and Benjamin Ziemann (eds), *Reading Primary Sources: The Interpretation of Texts from Nineteenth- and Twentieth-Century History* (London: Routledge, 2008), p. 192.
41. Thomas J. Schlereth, *Material Culture Studies in America* (Nashville, TN: Rowman Altamira, 1982), p. 3.
42. All the material obtained through interviews and correspondence was done with consent. This was covered by the University of Otago Ethics Committee Ref: 14/139. The early interviews from 2005 were funded by a *Ngā Kōrero Tuku Iho*, New Zealand Oral History Award from the Ministry for Culture and Heritage. The project was Patrick Coleman, *Oral History of the Loyal Orange Institution in the South Island 2004–2005*. OHColl-0791, Alexander Turnbull Library, Wellington, New Zealand.

1

The Auld Orange Tree:
The Spread of Orangeism

Now the winter it is past, and the summer's drawing near,
Our Orange trees are budding in the spring-time of the year;
Our Orange trees are budding, and their roots are all alive,
And for every branch they cut off, we have engrafted five.[1]

The final verses from the song 'The Orange Tree' encapsulate some of
the elements in the spread of Orangeism. The use of a planting analogy
demonstrates an expectation of growth as the Orange tree embodies
the spread of Orangeism. The second is that Orangeism thrives in the
face of adversity. The catchcry of the Orange Order of 'No Surrender',
as shouted by the Protestant defenders in the Siege of Derry in 1689,
continues to the present day whenever the Orange Order feels under
attack. This militant element is also at issue when asking how did an
agrarian-based fraternal group that was formed in County Armagh,
Ireland, in 1795 spread so quickly across the British Empire?

This question around the expansion of the Orange Order from
its rural origins in Ulster to other parts of the world has attracted a
variety of scholarship but, generally, it has been localised in focus.
Early studies from the Canadian scholar Hereward Senior explored
the early history of the Orange Order in Ireland and then moved to
the Canadian context.[2] Senior's work was pioneering in the sense that
he was an academic, rather than an existing or ex-Orange member.
Probably the most systematic coverage of the spread of the Orange
Order, however, has come from historical geographers Cecil J. Houston
and William J. Smyth.[3] They mapped the spread of the Orange Order
across Canada and established some sense of the organisation's numerical and physical impact on Canadian communities. Recent scholarship
by Eric Kaufmann has also been insightful in providing a macro view of

the numerical spread of the Orange Order in Northern Ireland, Canada and Scotland in the early to mid-twentieth century. Key findings by Kaufmann reveal increased numbers in the pre-World War I period, and a decline in the Depression era, with World War II helping to bolster numbers before a final decline in the 1960s. Scotland was seen as the exception, with numbers not falling until the late 1980s.[4]

Missing from these studies is a comparison of Ireland and the Orange diaspora concerning the establishment of the Orange Order. So far historians have only superficially touched on this, and then only with a few countries. This chapter seeks to address this gap in the literature by focusing on the spread of Orangeism across the various regions of the world, and the reasons for it. The context of the wider British Empire and its spread are considered as the Orange Order grew alongside this imperial expansion. Key features of this spread are the military, migration and women. Possible reasons for the organisation's later decline will also be discussed. The transnational connections will be considered mostly in the context of the Grand Orange Lodges and the Imperial Grand Orange Council. These upper bodies both regulated and supported the growth of the Orange lodges across the world. An important aspect is the difference between lodges in Ireland and their diasporic counterparts. In this instance, the Orange diaspora proved to be more innovative than Ireland in terms of gender-inclusive lodges.

MILITARY ORIGINS

The Orange Order has had a long connection to the military. The very focus of the organisation is rooted in conflict. Their imagery and rhetoric particularly comes from the time of the Glorious Revolution of William III. All the various battles of the Jacobite-Williamite Wars (1689–91) and their subsequent collective memories have imbued an unshaken identity as Protestants defending against the encroachments of Catholics in every aspect of their lives. Even the catchcry of 'No Surrender', borrowed from the defenders in the Siege of Derry in 1689, is now synonymous with the Orange Order and the wider movement of unionism. The marching, the display of banners, and the bands all create an atmosphere of an army on the march. Tied to their Protestantism, this also evokes the army of God and its march to spread the Christian gospel. All of this culminates in an organisation that is fully immersed in a militaristic culture.

At the time of their founding in the 1790s, the Orange Order was surrounded by the threat of rebellion from the United Irishmen and possible French invasion. Militias were being formed by Protestants for the defence of Ireland against these threats. It was also a time of Catholics slowly getting more rights back and the lessening of these rights was seen by a frightened Protestant settler community as a foreboding of massacres to come, as they constantly reminded themselves of the 1641 massacres.[5] Secret societies abounded and so it was not surprising that the early Orange Order members took their cue from their experience of Freemasonry.

From an Orange Order perspective, the borrowing from Freemasonry proved to be fortuitous. A common feature in the spread of Freemasonry across the world at this time was the use of military lodges. If any Freemasons in the military were posted to other parts of the British Empire, warrants were issued by their respective Grand Lodges to give them the authority to form lodges within their regiments. This was a practice initiated by the Irish Freemasons who also had a system of travelling warrants.[6] The Orange Order borrowed this system when their members joined the military and they too, like their Freemason counterparts, were posted across the British Empire. These warrants meant that they were technically answerable to the Grand Orange Lodge of England or Ireland but in practice they were independent.[7] This independence fuelled the global growth of the Orange Order. By the end of the nineteenth century, the *Belfast Weekly News* had reported that while Ireland no longer had military lodges, they were flourishing overseas, where there were 'quite a number in India, China, and the colonies'.[8] What was true of the Freemasons was now true for the Orange Order – 'geographical flexibility'.[9] This allowed the Orange Order to spread its form of loyalism to countries it never would have dreamed of reaching. In history, timing is everything. The founding of the Orange Order coincided with an Ireland that had had a standing army since the 1690s. As the British Empire expanded, so did its capacity to wage war.[10] By the 1850s there was an increasing deployment of military and naval resources across the globe.[11] The loyalist Orange Order played a role in these deployments.

The military origins of the Irish Orange Order are echoed in aspects of their regalia but mostly in their regimented marching traditions. Many of these early members were in militias or the British army. David Fitzpatrick has emphasised the extent of this influence in the way that the Orange Order was a ubiquitous part of the British army from its origins until the Orange Order was nominally dissolved in 1836.[12] Some key aspects of this expansion are demonstrated in the statistic that there were 267 Orange military lodges formed in British and Irish units by 1835.[13] Fitzpatrick also noted that the soldiers who were assigned the marching warrants were mostly NCOs rather than commissioned officers.[14] In general, they were sergeants who had a close relationship with the ordinary soldiers. Fitzpatrick quite rightly emphasises the fraternal appeal of the Orange Order, as it gave the soldiers at the front end of any conflict a sense of order and purpose. Marching warrants were a useful tool that the Orange Order used to facilitate the opening of lodges wherever these regiments were posted. Essentially it was the transferable aspect of these warrants that ensured the ongoing spread of the Orange Order in a rather haphazard fashion.

Another feature was the borrowed Masonic lodge structure. This regimented system provided the structure that assisted in the initial set-up of lodges throughout the world (to be discussed in Chapter 2). Despite the initial setback of the suppression of the Orange Order with its dissolution in 1836, the military lodges continued to meet in defiance of this order. It seems that members believed the order of dissolution would eventually be rescinded, so they were not willing to let their organisation fade away in the meantime. This is a good example of 'loyalist' Orange members defying the very authorities they were supposed to support.

The early spread of the Orange Order came from the military lodges, and this pattern continued as subsequent regiments maintained growth. The marching warrant system also provided the impetus for the spread of Orangeism in Scotland and England. Scottish regiments involved in the brutal quashing of the Irish Rebellion of 1798 set up military lodges when they returned to Scotland. The Ayrshire Militia opened the first military lodge in Maybole, South Ayrshire, in 1799.[15] The spread of Orangeism to England, like their Scottish brethren, also began from regiments that returned from the 1798 Rebellion. In this case, it was the Manchester and Salford Militia that set up military lodges.[16] Just like their Irish counterparts, the English and Scottish regiments consisted of Protestants who were wary of the perceived constant threat of rebellious Catholics. In a climate of fear, having an ideology that gave meaning to the current situation and a means to band together as brothers had its attractions. Across the ocean and into the Americas, the advent of military lodges was a characteristic of the Orange Order. In Canada, there were military lodges in Nova Scotia in 1799. Like many other Orange jurisdictions, it was predominantly Ulster-born soldiers carrying marching warrants who set up lodges.[17] Orangeism was introduced to the United States in a similar time period to Canada, but the exact dates are uncertain.[18]

The expansion of the Orange Order often paralleled the British Empire's military deployments. In this respect, it was the Grand Orange Lodge of England (GOLE) that issued many of the military warrants. The case of South Africa is indicative of this since it is likely to have had a military lodge as early as 1821, set up by the 6th (or 1st Warwickshire) Regiment of Foot with warrant No. 181 from the GOLE. Members probably would have had lodge meetings, but no records appear to exist to verify this.[19] The regiment was based mostly in Cape Town and to a lesser degree in Grahamstown. By 1825 the regiment had to leave for India.[20] These early instances of military lodges were seen as temporary, and therefore 1852 is seen as the formal establishment of the first Orange lodge in South Africa. From this year onwards there was an ongoing military presence in the early establishment of lodges.[21] One of the few documented military lodges was the case of LOL No. 296 Maiden Cape Town. This lodge applied to the GOLE and received a warrant for LOL No. 114, which had previously been a Liverpool lodge. It first met on 15 July 1869.[22] By 1876 the lodge had grown to 132 members, most of whom were in the military.[23] They belonged to the 24th (2nd Warwickshire) Regiment of Foot, which lost twenty-six of its soldiers on 22 January 1879 at the Battle of Isandlwana.[24] This lodge was last noted in records in 1907. Between this time and 1910, they became defunct.[25] This South African example demonstrates the problematic nature of the initial establishment of military lodges. Trying to find some stability within a time of conflict and constant movement of regiments intensified the likelihood of these lodges disappearing unless they had civilian support.

The dual influence of the Grand Orange Lodges of England and Ireland was also apparent in Australia's first Orange lodge, even if there are a number of disputed claims to that title. The first origin story is set at the time of the dissolution of the Orange Order in 1835. The 50th Queen's Own Regiment arrived in Sydney in the same year and one of the soldiers, Private Andrew Alexander (1799–1893), smuggled in his lodge's warrant sewn into his tunic.[26] This warrant, No. 1780, was issued by the Grand Orange Lodge of Ireland (GOLI). The regiment, which had many Orangemen among their ranks, decided to hide the warrant as they believed the order would eventually be countermanded.[27] Members from this regiment formed the nucleus of the Australian Orange lodge that later claimed the 'title' of Sydney No. 1 in 1845. There was a counternarrative that in 1830 the 17th Leicestershire Regiment arrived in Sydney with their warrant granted by the GOLE.[28] This is corroborated by the Report from the Select

Committee investigating the Orange Institution in 1835, which included evidence from records in 1830 that the 17th Leicestershire Regiment did have warrant No. 260.[29] While this was technically the first, in terms of impact the regiment did not have the influence that Private Alexander's regiment had in their contribution of members to building the Orange Order in New South Wales.

The only other state in Australia where the Orange Order began with military lodges was Tasmania. Orangemen from the 63rd Regiment (West Suffolks) LOL 136, who were stationed in Hobart, briefly formed a lodge in 1832.[30] It was not long-lasting as the regiment was transferred. Since they did not connect with the civilian population it was left to other regiments and the local population to establish stable lodges.

Unlike the initial military dominance of Australian Orangeism, the origins of the New Zealand Orange Order followed a mixed model. It was County Wicklow-born James Carlton Hill (1798–1858), arriving in Auckland with his family on 31 March 1843, who used an Irish warrant to found the first Orange lodge.[31] Membership was drawn from both civilian and military personnel. However, this lodge did not last very long, as Hill emigrated to Australia, and many members were often away on military duty. It was the soldiers of the 58th and 65th Regiments who, when relocated around the North Island, began to open new Orange lodges. As more regiments came to New Zealand, especially during the period of the New Zealand Wars (1845–72), the lodges were reinforced by the large number of Irish-born soldiers who were Orangemen. Many of these men subsequently took pensions and stayed in New Zealand. A feature of the warrants issued after Hill was that they were brought out by military regiments, and generally issued by the GOLI.[32]

The situation of Orange lodges throughout Asia, particularly in Hong Kong, India and Singapore, is an interesting case study of military lodges that never transitioned to civilian lodges. India seems to have the longest history when it comes to Orange lodges in the Asian region. Tracing their early origins has proved to be problematic, but there were references to lodges based in India in the Parliamentary Committee investigating the Orange Order in 1835. There were questions about Orange lodges existing in the 2nd Battalion of the Royal Regiment. The committee had evidence that the regimental lodge had been suppressed by their commanding officer, Lieutenant-Colonel George Augustus Wetherall. He also gave evidence that there were 115 members in this Indian-based lodge when he dissolved it in 1829.[33] After the dissolution of the Grand Orange Lodge in February 1836, the Orange lodges in England eventually formed two separate movements: the Loyal Orange Institution of Great Britain (LOIGB), and the Grand Protestant Association of Loyal Orangemen (GPALO).[34] During this period of division, the two separate movements supported military lodges abroad, although these were technically illegal. The spread of the Orange Order in Hong Kong, India and Singapore has not been documented in the same way as the other Orange jurisdictions. This is due to a combination of factors ranging from the fact these lodges no longer exist to the lack of documentary records. Probably one of the most useful sources was the *Orange Standard*, the magazine for the GOLE. This magazine maintained diasporic connections as it provided updates throughout the First World War on its military members scattered across the world.

The GPALO had military lodges abroad such as the Grand Constitution Orange Lodge No. 859. It had previously been in Gibraltar in 1858 and then transferred to India in 1859.[35] They were stationed there at least until the 1860s.[36] Within the same period the LOIGB in 1854 reported Orange lodges LOL No. 75, the Loyal Lincoln, and No. 76, the True Blue, both in India.[37] There are no other details, but by 1861 there was another military lodge in Bareilly, India, called LOL No. 98. The reason for these particular regiments being stationed in India at this time was the Indian Rebellion of 1857. The Worshipful Master of No. 859 wrote, 'we are in India, surrounded by mutineers.'[38] Both English bodies had members represented in this region. After the merger in 1876 there were still more military lodges into the twentieth century, but many of these were simply temporary and many did not make the transition to civilian lodges.

The case of Hong Kong and Singapore demonstrated that although these military lodges had some longevity they ultimately became defunct. What can be established from the existing documentary record is that some of the early lodges in Hong Kong, like in India, were military lodges formed from soldiers who had been transferred from Gibraltar. Against the background of the Second Opium War (1856–60), a GPALO Orange lodge claimed they had difficulty meeting in the same place as they were scattered with their lodge Master 'at Canton, and several more of our brethren, and a great many in hospital'.[39] Their stay only lasted to the end of the conflict. Within a few months of the signing of the Convention of Peking on 24 October 1860, the Orangemen reported they were heading back to England.[40] By 1912, the next notable and sole military lodge in Hong Kong was LOL 802, Star of the East.[41] Reports of the lodge were common for the First World War years, and a sizeable proportion of the members were probably servicemen, particularly in the navy.[42] LOL 802 managed to survive both world wars, but after 1948 there is no further record of the lodge.[43]

As in Hong Kong, Singapore had a single military lodge, called LOL No. 615, Star in the Far East. There were reported meetings in 1893, but there must have been problems with membership because the lodge had ceased working by the early part of the twentieth century.[44] Its reopening in 1913 was aided by Sergeant William Neill, 1st Battalion, King's Own Yorkshire Light Infantry (KOYLI). He was noted in the *Orange Standard* as being a founding member of LOL 615 and its secretary.[45] The KOYLI had only been posted to Singapore in 1913, which coincides with the revival of the lodge there. It continued to be active throughout the First World War but by 1924 had been disestablished.[46]

All the Orange lodges noted in this discussion that began as military lodges made the shift to civilian lodges except for those in Hong Kong and Singapore. In the case of Hong Kong and Singapore there were a few salient circumstances that led to their demise. They had small European populations from which to draw. In 1911 Hong Kong had only 5,185 Europeans in a total population of 456,739, while Singapore had similar demographics with 5,711 Europeans out of a total population of 303,321.[47] An added problem for recruitment among the civilian population was that the European community in Singapore in the nineteenth century saw itself as social elites, and the predominantly working-class Orange Order would have struggled to attract socially like-minded members from within it.[48] Heavy casualties in the First World War, as well as many members returning to their home countries at the end of the war, contributed to weakening lodges. A contributing factor to the casualty rate was the degree of patriotism in Hong Kong's participation in the First World War. LOL 802 demonstrated their loyalism with all members volunteering.[49] While this example of loyalism to their country's war effort seemed admirable at the time, the casualty rate was high. It seems that the majority of these members were involved in frontline conflict. The *Orange Standard* documented numerous examples from 1915 through to 1918 of lodge members either dying or being wounded. The cases of Singapore and Hong Kong seemed to mirror one another in relation to membership problems, dependence on the military for members and leaders, and their lack of transition from a military lodge to a civilian one. There were other lodges established from the early nineteenth to early twentieth centuries, for example, in Brazil, Cuba and Trinidad. These were often a mixture of military and missionary-led efforts. None of them were sustained.[50]

MIGRANT GROWTH AND DECLINE

Besides the military lodges, which came at a time of unrest in Ireland, there was migration. The British world was pushing into new territories, and there were opportunities for settlers from the British Isles to own property and work in these newly appropriated lands. The catalyst for the Orange Order's growth tended to come from Irish Protestant migrants. Patrick Ireland's 2012 assessment of the legacy of Irish Protestant migration points to the problematic nature of extracting firm figures. From the colonial period through to the 1930s, the United States, Canada and Australia received 2 million, 50,000 and 50,000 Irish Protestants, respectively.[51] These nicely rounded figures are, of course, estimates, since defining an Irish Protestant is not a simple process. The various terms for Irish Protestants, such as Ulster Scots, Scots Irish, Scotch Irish, Irish Scots and even British, muddy the waters. Despite these difficulties, it is clear that this period was important in distributing migrants across the British world. In the case of the Orange Order in the nineteenth century, it also meant they were bringing not just their families but also their beliefs and associational cultures. In this case, an Irish Protestant ideology combined with the fraternal organisation of the Orange Order. The structure of the Orange Order will be covered more fully in Chapter 2. The following is an overview of the origins and spread of these migrants across the British world, and their connection to the Order.

England/Scotland

The spread of the Orange Order throughout England, despite receiving its impetus from military lodges, needed the influx of civilians to generate a lasting impact. In 1830 the number of English lodges before the dissolution of the Grand Lodge of Ireland in 1836 was 260. As noted earlier, after 1836, the English lodges divided into the LOIGB and the GPALO. It is clear that the dissolution did not harm the numerical growth of lodges. Just before the merger of 1876, lodge numbers for both institutions were relatively healthy, with 313 for the LOIGB and 320 for the GPALO.[52] In terms of lodge numbers, the overall figures combined seem to be greater at this point than at any time in the history of the English lodges. Included in the LOIGB figures were seventy-nine lodges from Scotland.[53] There were also military lodges scattered across the world that helped to inflate their numbers.

The context for the rise in membership of both Orange organisations was the increased numbers of Irish fleeing *An Gorta Mór*, or the Great

Irish Famine, flooding into England from 1845 to 1852. Liverpool and Manchester, traditional strongholds of the Orange Order, were the recipients of these new migrants.[54] For example, the proportion of Irish peaked in 1861 at 15.2 per cent of Manchester's population. After this point, the percentage declined not just for Manchester but for the whole of England and Wales. Despite this drop, there were still significant numbers of second- and third-generation Irish.[55] The continuing presence of a large body of Irish Catholics represented a perceived threat to the Protestants of England. The Orange ideology, which included guarding against the encroachments of Rome, was a core part of the Orange Order's belief. After the merger in 1876, the Loyal Orange Institution of England (LOIE) continued to flourish. The growth of its male Orange lodges continued well into the nineteenth century, with a peak of 537 lodges in 1882. Lodge numbers stabilised for a short period from 1887 until 1902, when the decline continued until 1950. Lodge numbers then flattened out into the early hundreds, dropping to ninety-four lodges by 1999.[56] Some possible factors may have contributed to this situation. The most prominent were the ongoing problems in Ireland. The Home Rule Crisis in 1886 consolidated membership through the Orange Order having a major issue to draw members. However, these new and potential members may have been dissuaded by the rioting that was endemic in Belfast during this period.[57] Another impact on membership was the longstanding tradition in some Protestant churches that were suspicious of the Orange Order because of its Masonic links. This objection to Freemasonry and by association the Orange Order would have limited membership.[58] The likely profile of membership has always been Reformation-style Protestants who identified with the anti-Rome stance of the Orange Order. The powerhouses of English Orangeism have tended to be Liverpool and Manchester. The bulk of the Orange lodges were, and still are, in these cities.

The Scottish Orange Order, just like their English counterparts, had the same pattern of military lodges followed by civilian ones. Scottish Orangeism was hampered by a lack of overall organisation following the dissolution in 1836. While there was an attempt at some unity, with the formation of a Grand Orange Association of Scotland that year, other lodges chose to join the Grand Protestant Confederation. Some waited and later in 1846 came under the Grand Lodge of Ulster. The year 1850 was important for both English and Scottish lodges as the Grand Protestant Association of Loyal Orangemen was formed. It seems that most Scottish lodges joined this. A major attraction for joining was that there was good organisation in the form of a Provincial Grand Lodge system. Later, in 1853, the Provincial Grand Lodge of Scotland became a Grand Lodge. The GPALO provided a stable system that helped the Orange Order in Scotland transition after the disarray caused by the dissolution of 1836. Another factor in stabilising the Scottish lodges was their first two Grand Masters, Robert Clements and John Leech, whose enthusiasm and organisational skills helped to consolidate and expand the Order in these early years.[59]

The early Scottish Orange Order was heavily reliant on Irish Protestants to bolster its membership. Many from the north of Ireland settled in Scotland in the 1820s and 1830s, and then later in the 1850s.[60] Since the Orange Order was seen as 'a foreign import among the native Scots population', Irish Protestants were the mainstay for membership.[61] However, there was some discontent as, in 1859, some lodges, mostly in Glasgow, seceded from the Grand Lodge of Scotland. These lodges sought warrants from the Orange Institution of Great Britain. The reason for the split is unclear. Orange historian David Bryce has speculated that it could have been a result of the reorganisation in the previous two years of the lodge's system and its rituals. The leadership had 'tightened up on standards and degrees'.[62] Another landmark year for Scottish Orangeism was 1876. Again, it was tied to the English lodges that amalgamated to form one Grand Lodge. The Scots also unified their separate lodges under one Loyal Orange Institution of Scotland.

The growth of Scottish male lodges followed a similar pattern to other organisations. From 1872 to 1900 the number of lodges increased to 385 before dropping to 347 in 1910. After that, the number of lodges peaked in 1920 before gradually falling and levelling off from the 1960s and declining to 284 in 2000.[63] These patterns of growth paralleled the so-called 'Putnam effect' that charted the rise and fall of many American chapter-based associations. The pattern was growth until 1929, then decline during the Great Depression, followed by significant growth after the Second World War until the early 1960s, and decline thereafter.[64] In the Scottish case, this pattern broadly applies, though the decline through the war period until the present is not as dramatic as in other Orange jurisdictions. This may be due, in no small part, to a membership that has maintained numbers and the issues around Scottish independence, exemplified in the 2014 Scottish referendum. The geographical impact of the Orange Order in Scotland has centred on the west coast of Scotland, particularly in the areas that had large Irish migration from the Irish Famine period in the 1840s onwards. Glasgow, therefore, is at the centre of Scottish Orangeism. Counties such as West Lothian and Ayrshire also had large influxes of Irish Protestants.[65] This pattern remains today.

North America

The expansion of the Orange Order in Canada has been well documented with quite specific studies charting its growth and spread.[66] While there is no clear evidence as to the exact date of the first Orange lodge, there were enough lodges for Ogle Robert Gowan (1803–76), who was Grand Master, to form the first Grand Orange Lodge of British America in 1830. A staggering statistic was that almost one in three adult Protestant men belonged to the Orange Order between 1870 and 1920. Despite large-scale migration by Irish Protestants to Canada, Orangeism was not an Irish Protestant organisation there. Instead, the dominant English Protestant majority combined with other ethnic groups to make up the membership. The regions with the majority of Orange members were Ontario, New Brunswick and Newfoundland.[67] The beginnings of Canadian Orangeism may have been Irish Protestant in their initial stages, but by the 1860s it had a 'native' outlook.

In his analysis of Canadian Orangeism, Kaufmann calculated that membership peaked in 1920. At this point, it made up about 60 per cent of worldwide Orangeism. Interestingly, members in Canada represented more than twice Northern Ireland's membership. An important aspect to note was the absence of the Catholic-Protestant sectarian divide in identifying membership growth. Irish Protestants were a minority, and it seems that close-knit rural communities provided the backbone of Orangeism in Newfoundland, which accounted for almost half of Canadian membership after World War II.[68] The peak of Canadian Orangeism occurred in the 1950s, and as its political influence waned, so did its membership. In 1955 it had 58,000 members and 4,000 lodges; by 1984 the membership size and number of lodges were 14,000 and 616, respectively.[69] Houston and Smyth documented the decline in 1980 and their later research only reinforced the demise of Canadian Orangeism, which reached 323 lodges by 2000. They also noted the difficulties in getting actual membership figures as these were not readily available. This was linked to the leadership not being forthcoming with these figures, especially as the Canadian Orange Order began to decline.[70] The heart of Canadian Orangeism is Toronto and the province of Ontario. While there were lodges scattered in the other provinces from cities to rural areas, the influence of Ontario has remained until the present day.

Orangeism was introduced to the United States in a similar period to Canada, but the exact dates are not clear. It probably began in New York. There were lodges in the United States around 1820 and their members were marching by 1824.[71] A mixture of Irish Protestants, either as military or as settlers, provided the bulk of the membership.[72] A lack of overall organisation did not help progress. This situation changed in 1870 when a group of Irish immigrants founded the Supreme Grand Orange Lodge of the United States. Having a central body to organise the lodges that were scattered around various states gave some stimulus to their growth. Five states provided the bulk of the lodges: Maine, Massachusetts, Michigan, New York and Pennsylvania.[73] Lodges in other states never really blossomed. Unsurprisingly, the eastern side of the United States, which had the greatest concentration of Irish Protestant migrants, accounted for the strength of the Orange Order. Pennsylvania stands out as a centre for Irish Presbyterianism in the United States.[74] This clustering of like-minded settlers may help to explain the strength of American Orangeism in this state. Conversely, this concentration could explain the weakness in other states as they did not have the same concentration of migrants.

Consistent figures for the early years of the American Orange Order are challenging to obtain. Even as early as 1883 the Grand Secretary was complaining of lodges failing to send in their returns.[75] Despite this, some early numbers reveal that there were only four lodges in 1868, forty-three in 1872, and then 120 by 1875.[76] From 1908's 237 lodges, the number generally fell, with a slight recovery in 1931 at 190 lodges. This was very close to the 1911 figure of 191. After that, the lodges continued to decline as increasing numbers of lodges began to close. The data for membership numbers is patchy but figures available show a rise from 1,351 members in 1938 to 2,500 by 1958. However, by 1988 this figure had fallen to 447.[77] In terms of lodges there were only twelve by 2010.[78]

There are a number of possible explanations for the lack of growth in the American Orange Order. A major flaw was the ongoing issue of maintaining a loyalist organisation in a republic. Also, there was competition from nativist organisations, which already provided a vehicle for anti-Catholicism. This hindered potential growth from American-born Protestants. Rioting at Orange parades in 1824 and most notably in 1870 and 1871 in New York could be seen as a driver of membership but also a reason for others not to join. Houston and Smyth's tough appraisal was that 'in the United States, Orangeism had always been anachronistic; it therefore never bloomed'.[79] The most significant reason for the lack of expansion may lie in the absence of intergenerational growth. This is likely to have been the result of the Orange Order being seen as an immigrant organisation rather than an American one. Another factor in the rise and fall of American Orangeism was the split that occurred in the early part of the twentieth century. It centred on two members, William Kirkland and George T. Lemmon, seeking to be Supreme Grand Secretary. This division led to the creation of two separate Supreme Grand Orange Lodges. Lemmon called his the International Orange Association.[80] After a series of legal battles, it was finally settled in 1930, with Lemmon losing and no longer taking part in Orange activities. This was also the year the organisations amalgamated. Despite this the American Orange Order never recovered their former numbers.[81] One of the factors that helped to stimulate the early growth of Orange membership was the dominance of Irish Catholic immigration to America. By 1870, 5 per cent of the American population was Irish-born. They were concentrated in five states: California, Illinois, Massachusetts, New York and Pennsylvania.[82] These were also the majority of areas where the Orange Order drew its membership. This concentration also accounted for the early conflict. However, as Irish Catholics were numerically superior and collectively well organised compared to their Irish Protestant counterparts, over time they gained more political influence.

Australia/New Zealand

In the southern hemisphere, Australia and New Zealand stand out as examples of mixed approaches to growth. Both had military lodges but were heavily reliant on migrants to establish their lodges. The context for growth was the expansion of the British Empire. The early nineteenth century saw a lot of movement of settlers, and this continued throughout the century. Military lodges were there because of the deployment by the British government as it used Australia as both a settler and a penal colony, while New Zealand was simply a colony. Pioneering colonies needed soldiers to both conquer the country and then be there as regiments and later militias to maintain the peace. The Orange Order, through their members, played a role in building and maintaining the British Empire as they helped to colonise 'new' lands.

The beginnings and the growth of the Orange Order in Australia were complicated by the early organisation of Australia into colonies. To further complicate matters some of these were initially part of another colony. For example, South Australia was originally part of New South Wales. This has created the situation of each state in Australia having its own Grand Lodge. Membership in the various states was helped by Ulster Protestant migrants who were either already an Orange member or open to becoming one.

Many of the Orange lodges were first formed in the early stages of the colonies as noted earlier by military lodges: New South Wales 1830 and Tasmania 1832. The others came later: Victoria 1843, South Australia c. 1849, Queensland 1865, and Western Australia 1886. New South Wales was the Grand Lodge with the largest membership in Australia. Their stimulus for growth was a mixture of Ulster Protestants and sectarian tension. This was particularly so in the late nineteenth century, especially after a boost in membership came with the assassination attempt on Prince Alfred in 1868 by the alleged Fenian Henry O'Farrell. This led to an upsurge in Orange membership as the 'Fenian scare' was capitalised on by the Orange Order. The event and causal links to this event were reported in a display of trans-Tasman camaraderie by Bro. J. W. McNeale speaking at the Imperial Grand Orange Council in London in 1882. He noted the 'very large influx of members' resulting from what the 'Fenian O'Farrell' had done.[83] For New South Wales, peak membership came in 1878 with 9,374 members, after which numbers fell. Up until 1893, there were about 350 lodges formed, but more than half had closed by this date.[84] These figures were based on returned reports and would have been a little higher. Getting reliable, or any, figures for the New South Wales Orange Order has been problematic. Annual reports in the twentieth and twenty-first centuries only comment on new members, not overall membership or the number of lodges. The geographical spread of these lodges centred on Sydney and then expanded to areas north of Sydney like the Hunter Valley, or further south to Kiama. Both are about 120 kilometres either way from Sydney.[85] The Orange Order in New South Wales was comparable to Ontario in Canada in its preponderance of Ulster migrants among its membership.[86]

Across Australia, from Perth to Brisbane, in the 1920s there was a rise in the Orange Order's membership.[87] However, World War I took its toll on the total membership in all states, and World War II continued this downward trend. Other factors contributing to the decline were the drop in church attendance and societal changes that led to the decline of the Orange Order across Australia.[88] By 1967, the Grand Lodge of Tasmania ceased to operate.[89] All of the other Grand Lodges have only a handful of lodges remaining. The only, albeit minor, reversal of this trend has been South Australia in the twenty-first century, with the influx of Northern Irish migrants. Now there is a new lodge, the Charlie Sands Memorial LOL 500.[90]

The struggle to build a sizeable membership base was also an issue elsewhere in the southern hemisphere. In New Zealand's case, the Orange

Order was divided by two islands. The North Island Orange lodges had their main catalyst for growth from military lodges. However, in the South Island (or Middle Island) of New Zealand, lodges were formed by civilians rather than the military. A simple reason was that the North Island had many militia, sent to protect British interests in that part of the country. This was not the case in the South Island, which was sparsely populated, and the number of migrants did not increase in any significant numbers until the 1860s and 1870s. In the South Island, a lodge was opened quite independently in Lyttleton in 1864 by a group of Ulstermen who obtained a private warrant.[91]

New lodges started popping up in the surrounding districts. However, a problem arose when they thought they could have the same powers as a Grand Lodge. A potential for disunity arose with the newly formed Grand Lodge in Auckland refusing to recognise their Canterbury counterparts. In response, the Canterbury brethren appealed to Ireland to open their own Grand Lodge.[92] A positive reply resulted in the Grand Lodge of the Middle Island being constituted in 1870.[93] It is important to note that although the Orange lodges in New Zealand looked to the Grand Lodge of Ireland for the authority to grant warrants, their Irish counterparts were content to have a laissez-faire approach to the Orange diaspora's attempts to set up Grand Lodges. Quite simply, if the establishment of a Grand Lodge furthered the cause of the Orange Order, they were not going to interfere.[94] These lodges were also keen for contact beyond this, since as early as 1890 the Grand Lodge of the Middle Island requested a visit from their Irish counterparts. This was politely declined.[95]

Progress for both was slow, with the North Island having fourteen primary lodges and 260 members by 1903, while the Middle Island had forty-three primary lodges and 1,020 members.[96] This was hardly spectacular growth given there had been enough migration of Irish Protestants to generate better figures. A possible reason for these poor membership returns for the North Island may well have been the instability of military lodges that did not integrate civilians into their lodges. The transient life of soldiers would also have had a detrimental effect on membership with constant turnover.

After much discussion, the two lodges amalgamated in 1908 to become the Grand Orange Lodge of New Zealand. This move certainly helped the overall organisation and was just in time for the lead-up to World War I, when patriotism among the general population was running high. Interestingly, the number of men's lodges peaked at ninety in 1948 before rapidly falling to only four by 2000.[97] The New

Zealand men's lodges peaked after World War II, at another time of patriotism, but also at a time of great loss from the war period. In 1968 there were forty-eight lodges, but by 1975 there were only twenty-nine. These sharp declines also coincided with the Troubles in Northern Ireland, which affected membership. New Zealand Orangeism's strength has been Auckland and Canterbury, with the main cities of Christchurch and Auckland long providing the bulk of the Orange lodges. These cities and provinces were the largest recipient of Irish Protestant immigrants, and therefore the strength of the Orange Order resides in these regions.

Africa

Another southern hemisphere country that struggled to maintain a consistent and sustained membership was South Africa. As noted earlier, the South African Orange lodges were indebted to the military for their beginnings. The impetus came from Irish soldiers in the British army, but their growth drew upon local Afrikaners. This was particularly so in the Transvaal where two-thirds of the membership was Afrikaner, and this became the power base for Orangeism in the country. There were even suggestions that all Orange rituals and regulations be translated into Dutch. Over time a combination of civilians and military made up their membership. However, their growth would have been hampered by the South African War of 1899–1902. This meant many members in the military were on active duty and therefore had difficulty having regular meetings. Despite this, there was some growth in numbers. The Transvaal was noted as being the strength of South African Orangeism in the early twentieth century, and, at this point, there were a significant number of Afrikaners in the Transvaal lodges.[98] The Imperial Grand Secretary James Rice's report at the meeting of the Imperial Grand Orange Council in Toronto in 1906 noted that the Orange Order in South Africa had been working under about four different Grand Lodges. This poorly administered situation was rectified by the announcement of the formation of one Grand Lodge of British South Africa.[99] Even though there were only seventeen lodges, Rice enthusiastically proclaimed, 'This, I believe, to be one of our grandest achievements in extension work.'[100]

The enthusiasm that greeted the announcement did not transform into subsequent large numbers or other lodges being opened. At the 1920 Imperial Grand Orange Council, despite the loss of members in World War I, all the jurisdictions had increased activity with one exception: South Africa.[101] There was a report on the progress of the Orange Order worldwide at the Imperial Grand Orange Council in 1958. The upbeat report finished with the regrettable announcement that the Grand Orange Lodge of South Africa had ceased to function.[102] The report was hopeful that the remaining lodges might come under another jurisdiction. This never eventuated and by the 1960s South African Orangeism ceased to exist. Politically this was a volatile time as the country became a republic in 1961 and what was left of the organisation decided to purge itself. That the members destroyed all their records is a testament to the erasure of their loyalist past in the face of a state that had removed the monarchy.[103] This adaptability of Orangeism again demonstrates its appeal beyond its Irish origins as it could not rely on Irish migration to sustain it. Therefore, there were common elements for other Protestants with no Irish allegiance to continue joining and maintaining the organisation.

In terms of other African countries, West Africa also had Orange lodges. The origins of the earliest Orange lodge in Nigeria, the Lagos Fine Blues LOL No. 801, is unclear. Some suggestions have attributed it to Irish missionaries, or even to the British soldiers posted there.[104] The last one is the most likely as GOLE records show the existence of this lodge under their jurisdiction in 1910.[105] LOL No. 801 managed to survive until the late 1960s before it folded. Although it was only one lodge, it managed to produce one member who had a great influence. John Amate Atayi found out about the Orange Order through British newspapers and then wrote to the GOLE to find out how to start a lodge.[106] They directed him to the lodge in Nigeria where he was initiated, and he then started the Defenders of Lome LOL No. 867 in Togo in 1915. In a similar vein, R. E. Sharlley, a post office worker in Ghana, after reading the *Orange Standard*, contacted the GOLE, which in turn advised him to contact the Orange lodge in Togo. He then started the first Ghanaian Orange lodge on 7 September 1917.[107] The proximity of Lomé and Keta probably helped in the formation of both West African lodges.[108] The Orange Order in Ghana and in Togo have not expanded beyond the coastal regions of their country; this Gold Coast area is still the centre of African Orangeism.

The transnational links of the GOLE were crucial in the ongoing survival of these African lodges. When the Ghanaian lodges were on the wane, they looked for support from the English Orange Order. The Rev. Dr Ferdinand Kwasi Fiawoo (1891–1969), a minister, educator and playwright, helped to revive Ghanaian Orangeism in the 1950s.[109]

He travelled to England to be a member as he needed to be initiated in the Orange ritual as well. By 1980 there were thirty lodges and almost 1,000 members. However, from 1982 onwards the push-back by evangelicals in the churches who saw the Orange Order as ungodly limited its expansion.[110] Another factor in the limited appeal of the Orange Order in Ghana was that its origins relied on membership of one tribe – the Ewe. They were the dominant tribe in this coastal region, and this may also explain why the Orange Order in Togo was also confined to the coast, as the Ewe were also the main tribal group in that area. This did not change until 1975 with the first non-Ewe Gershon Markwei, who founded LOL Pride of Labadi.[111] Both Ghana and Togo lodges have struggled to maintain membership numbers and even fight for their very existence. For instance, the coup in Ghana in 1981 by Flight Lieutenant Jerry Rawlings saw many fraternal societies such as the Freemasons, Odd Fellows and Orange Order deemed 'secret', and this led to the banning of parades and many lodge halls and temples being burnt or ransacked.[112] Togo also had severe internal political problems that drastically reduced members, as many became refugees.[113] Amid these setbacks, in 1985, Ghana and Togo lodges were elevated to Grand Lodge status. This meant they were able to issue warrants to begin new lodges, which had previously been done by the GOLE. Scottish and Ghanaian delegates at the 1985 Triennial Council established friendships that led to a mixture of financial and moral support.[114]

Like many parts of the Orange diaspora, for the Orange Order in Ireland there has been difficulty getting accurate and accessible membership data. The problem for the researcher is that so much information is held at the county level.[115] The lack of centralised information in this case accounts for the varied statistical data available for research. In 2006, the Grand Secretary Drew Nelson spoke freely about the significant drop in numbers. He identified the change with a more secular society with falling church attendance. The Orange Order had a peak membership in 1968 of 93,447.[116] This coincided with the advent of the Troubles in Northern Ireland. The same article noted that the Orange Order had claimed 100,000 members in 1990 when they in fact only had 47,084. This seems very similar to the claims made by the New South Wales Grand Master back in 1888. The most current figures show the slump to 34,650 that had occurred by 2013.[117] By way of comparison, the Irish ladies' lodges went from almost 8,500 members in 1951 to just over 2,500 in 2013.[118]

WOMEN'S IMPETUS

Ireland/England/Scotland

The Orange Order from its inception was male and this was also true of their Freemason counterparts. These were very much male organisations and yet women were a presence in them. As Ireland was where the Orange Order was founded, women were initially on the periphery in supportive roles. They were there watching and supporting the early parades. They were there in the home listening to their male family members talk about the various issues of the moment. When Irishwomen finally got directly involved, they had a very uneven development before finally gaining any form of stability. Appendix 2 illustrates quite clearly the stop-start nature of the Irish ladies' lodges. While Ireland did have the first ladies' lodges in Dublin, as early as 1801, they only operated for a few years.[119] An attempt to revive ladies' lodges in Dublin occurred in 1887. Again, this failed. The final attempt to revive the ladies' lodges in 1912, once again in Dublin, succeeded and it was named the Association of Loyal Orangewomen of Ireland (ALOI).

Similarly, the English and Scottish Orange ladies' lodges seemed to have had the same problem in maintaining any form of momentum. The reasons for these poor beginnings are far from clear, particularly in Ireland, as a lack of documentary evidence has made any possible explanation hard to identify. Possible explanations of the Irish situation have focused on the hiatus in the Home Rule debate. Another possible explanation is the fractured nature of the lodges after the 1836 dissolution. The lack of a centralised body did not help the growth of ladies' lodges in Ireland.

However, with the Ne Temere decree, ladies' lodges in Ireland underwent revival. This decree on mixed marriages was controversial because marriages between Catholics and Protestants were only valid if a priest officiated.[120] The spur for the revival of the ALOI was the tragic case of Belfast couple Alexander McCann, a Catholic, and his Presbyterian wife Agnes McCann. They had married in a Presbyterian church in 1908 before the decree. A dispute arose between the McCanns when Alexander wanted to validate the marriage with the local priest and Agnes refused. There are differing accounts as to who was applying more pressure. Alexander secretly took the children to Pittsburgh in the United States and Agnes was left without any knowledge of their location.[121] The result of Alexander McCann disappearing with the couple's children to bring them up Catholic caused an uproar in the

Protestant community.[122] A lot of the public attention came from Rev. William Corkey, a Presbyterian minister who took up Agnes's case.[123] The significance of Corkey's involvement was that he used this case to promote opposition to Home Rule in the general election in December 1910.[124] The McCann case also provided the impetus for the formation of the revived ALOI.[125]

Starting in 1919 with a base of twenty-five female Orange lodges (1,000 members), ten of these in Belfast, the ALOI extended its membership base in the face of successive crises.[126] Fears of a potential backlash on Irish Protestants provided the stimulus for membership in both the men's and women's lodges.[127] Other external factors, such as women's activism, particularly the temperance movement, as well as women's suffrage, fed into this growth. Essentially, the upsurge in female activism provided a stimulus that had not been evident in previous decades. The ALOI continued this momentum well into the middle of the twentieth century. There were 159 lodges (5,606 members) in 1935 leading into World War II, with growth continuing until 1967 with 238 lodges (6,829 members). Since this time membership has fallen rapidly, to 106 lodges in 2013 (2,544 members) and only ninety in 2020.[128] Causal factors in the fall have been identified as not political forces, but more subtle factors such as 'geographic mobility and changing cultural practices'.[129] Northern Ireland had previously been characterised as having close-knit communities, but with people becoming more mobile these previously close and often insular communities began to break down.

In stark contrast to Ireland, ladies' lodges in the Orange diaspora began well and steadily built on their solid foundations. For example, Canada and Scotland began strongly and are still active today. Their bright beginnings were linked to increased women's activism in the late nineteenth and early twentieth centuries. Indeed, the influence of the Woman's Christian Temperance Union (WCTU) can account for an increased interest in women forming their own organisations. The influence of the WCTU certainly helped in the origins and growth of the Orange ladies' lodges.[130]

The previously mentioned merger, in 1876, of the GPALO and the LOIE, stymied the growth of the ladies' lodges in England in the 1870s. Growth in lodges from the 1880s through to the eve of the Second World War parallels political issues such as Home Rule and societal shifts with the advent of the suffragette movement and women's activism. Significant growth occurred over this period. In 1903 there were forty-five female lodges, which jumped to sixty-seven only four years later. Lodge numbers continued to rise with a slight fall during the First

World War, peaking at ninety-one in 1938. The fall after that was not dramatic: there were still between seventy and eighty lodges throughout the decades from the 1940s to the 1980s. By 2003, however, there had been a significant drop to fifty-four lodges. The decline in membership of women's lodges resulted from a range of factors. These included a secularised society which was reflected in a decline in church attendance and the next generation being uninterested in joining the Orange Order.[131]

Scotland followed some similar trends to England with its growth occurring in the 1920s. Again, many of the same types of issues, such as increased public activism by women and political issues like Home Rule, boosted membership and led to the opening of more lodges.[132] Lodge numbers increased quite dramatically from seventy-two in 1921 to 183 by 1931. This growth was consistent until 1961, when lodge numbers reached their overall peak of 247. After this, numbers steadily fell to reach their lowest point since the 1920s at 148 in 2011.[133] The reason for the decline is presumed to be the same falling church attendance as in England.[134] However, by 2014 there had been a turnaround in lodge numbers with a new total of 152.[135] This seems to be a reverse of a trend that has been occurring elsewhere, with lodges closing and membership falling. With an air of defiance, the *Orange Torch* triumphantly declared in April 2015, 'the long mooted obituary notice of the Loyal Orange Institution has been shelved yet again with the formation of two new lodges!'[136] The main political factor for this change could well have been the 2014 independence referendum to decide whether Scotland should be an independent country or not. The Orange Order did figure prominently in this campaign, including doing a march, five days before voting, of approximately 15,000 members in full regalia with banners flying.[137]

North America

The growth of the Loyal Orange Ladies' Institution of the United States gained impetus from the migration of Irish and Scottish settlers. Cecil J. Houston and William J. Smyth have argued that the Orange Order in America was centralised in Pennsylvania as it had a strong Irish Protestant community.[138] This community had large numbers of migrants from as early as 1790, when about 100,000 people of Ulster birth or heritage lived in the state.[139] While Houston and Smyth were focused on the male lodges, there is a clear dominance of Pennsylvania for ladies' lodges too. The concentration of ladies' lodges is noticeable, with Massachusetts and Pennsylvania having the most lodges with ten each in 1911.

Two other states – Michigan and New York – had six and seven, respectively; by 1925 they had surpassed Massachusetts (eleven) and Pennsylvania (twenty-one) with twenty-three and twenty-four lodges, respectively. This was the high point of the American ladies' lodges as there followed a decline in lodges in all regions which resulted in only seven lodges left in the whole country by 2014. Pennsylvania was reduced to four lodges, while Massachusetts (two) and California (one) made up the remainder.[140] Internal tensions rather than any external changes accounted for the sharp decline in numbers, which occurred at a similar time as those in other parts of the Orange diaspora. There was tension in the 1920s between the male Orange lodges in Pennsylvania and Ohio, with both claiming Supreme Grand Lodge status. The eventual split saw the Pennsylvanian group renaming themselves 'The International Orange Association' in 1926.[141] While they reconciled with a merger in 1930, many lodges had members leave, or lodges became dormant. The damage had been done, and the ability to regain new members after this never gained momentum. This was true for both the men's and the women's lodges.

In Canada, the growth of the Ladies' Orange Benevolent Association (LOBA) was a success story in terms of numbers. In 1912 there were 1,907 members in the LOBA. There was an incredible jump in membership to reach 21,031 by 1925.[142] Reasons for this increase included the dynamism of the second Grand Mistress Mary Tulk, increased migration, the First World War and the Home Rule Crisis.[143] There was a fall in membership through the Depression and the Second World War before it peaked at 28,851 in 1955, before levelling off.[144] The data for numbers is incomplete, but celebrating their centenary in 1994, the LOBA reported total membership of only 6,790.[145] This was a shadow of their former glory days. In the same way, other Orange ladies' lodges grew. The reasons for this growth can be related to societal change, particularly women taking a prominent role in civic and religious organisations. Tracing a similar pattern to the other Orange diasporic countries, Irish Protestants initiated these early lodges before the arrival of English and Scottish migrants. This resulted in Canadian Orangewomen being more likely to be Irish-born or of Irish descent.[146]

Australia/New Zealand

The development of ladies' lodges in New Zealand took some time to gather momentum. Following the English model, numbers grew rapidly after 1916. This wartime period, with patriotism running high, seemed to spur on membership. It is likely that the loyalist organisation gave members a sense of purpose in times of uncertainty. In terms of numerical strength, lodge numbers peaked at fifty-five in 1936, before falling to forty-five in 1948 and then to thirty-eight in 1958. The advent of mixed lodges drew members away from exclusively female lodges, and by 2000 there were only three lodges.[147]

The spread of female lodges in Australia was complicated by the fact that each state had its own Grand Lodge. The ladies' lodges that first opened across the various Australian states appeared in the late nineteenth and early twentieth centuries. Queensland in 1890 and New South Wales in 1894 both saw dramatic growth. By 1912 the number of ladies' lodges in Queensland had increased to eighteen, and by 1933 to approximately fifty-three.[148] Ladies' lodges in New South Wales grew at a rapid rate. In the first two years there were forty-seven lodges with over 2,000 members.[149] The financial support these lodges provided was important as the debt on their Protestant Hall in Melbourne was reduced through money made by running a bazaar. After solid beginnings in the late 1890s, the New South Wales women's lodges experienced a dramatic increase in numbers to 104 lodges in 1911.[150] This may have been due to the political and social climate of female activism in society and the issues around Home Rule. While Ireland may have been half the world away, it was on the front pages of newspapers and ever-present in Orange rhetoric. Sydney, where many of these lodges were blossoming, was at the centre of heightened sectarian tension, as exemplified by the notorious attacks against Protestantism by Cardinal Moran and the infamous Coningham-O'Haran case.[151] Times of conflict have generally led to increased membership, and the timing of the increases is hardly surprising.

The other Australian states had their ladies' lodges founded in the early years of the twentieth century. South Australia had its first ladies' lodge in 1901 and increased to over forty lodges and about 2,000 members by 1914.[152] However, by 1991 only the Grand Lodge and a single private lodge remained.[153] Tasmania, which had founded its first ladies' lodges only a few months before, struggled to grow its female base. The Orange Order there was no longer operating by 1967.[154] Tasmania is the only Australian state not to have a current lodge. Each state had its own set of circumstances that affected their growth. In South Australia, the Great Depression and two world wars, coupled with low numbers of Irish-born migrants, could have contributed to the fall in Orange lodge numbers.[155] The ladies' lodges in New South Wales and Victoria were heavily reliant upon Irish Protestants for their membership.[156]

However, as these numbers fell, coupled with the falling of associational membership more generally, these states also experienced sharp declines in membership.

Ghana/Togo

While the majority of the ladies' lodges in the Orange diaspora owed their origins to the activism of organisations such as the WCTU, in Africa it was a different situation. Male leadership was integral to the establishment of ladies' lodges. In Ghana, the ladies' lodges were founded by Rev. Dr Fiawoo. Just like his initiation into the men's lodges, he again went to Liverpool, England, where he was given special permission to be initiated into a ladies' lodge. This was for the purposes of learning how to run them and learn the rituals. On his return to Ghana in 1959, the first ladies' lodge, Wycliffe LLOL No. 160, was formed. The impetus for Fiawoo's visit was that the wives and daughters of members had heard about ladies' lodges but needed to be a member first to create them. Fiawoo's direct connections with the GOLE visit facilitated the realisation of their wish.[157] He was transferring this knowledge back into the hands of the women. This demonstrates a willingness on the part of the male Orange leadership to support their female counterparts. For Togo, the first ladies' lodge is shown in GOLE proceedings in 1963 as the Morning Star LLOL No. 161.[158]

CONCLUSION

This chapter has sought to analyse and outline the spread of the Orange Order across the British world. Over the course of two centuries, the Orange Order transformed from a localised Irish male agrarian-based organisation to one that included women in rural and urban areas across the world. The shift was born out of conflict. Borrowing from the Freemasons, the Orange Order created military lodges that became pioneers in the dispersion of Orange ideology. David Fitzpatrick has argued that this ideology, exemplified in their pursuit of 'civil and religious liberty', included a call to defend the Protestant Ascendancy. This combative element in its ideology differentiated the Orange Order from the Freemasons and other fraternal groups.[159] Armed with a sense of purpose in the wake of the Irish Rebellion of 1798, the spread of Orangeism to England and Scotland began. The expansion of the British Empire provided the opportunity for the Orange Order's eventual advance. The infiltration of the British army by the Orange Order meant that its ideology ended up in countries quite by accident rather than by any grand plan.

While the military facilitated the Orange Order's expansion, this close relationship was never going to be sustainable. Conflicts come and go, as do military postings. The successful spread to many countries like Canada and New Zealand was the result of the transition from military lodges to civilian ones that occurred with new migrants. This process could only occur when there was a good supply of migrant settlers, generally Irish Protestants, joining their military brethren. Quite often, the military members may have initiated the lodges, but the civilians were needed to strengthen them and maintain longevity. In stark contrast, Hong Kong and Singapore had the problem of being military lodges that never made the transition to civilian ones. The lack of a suitable migrant base had a great deal to do with this. Africa provides some examples of both the traditional planting of military lodges, such as in South Africa, and transnational support by the English, in the case of Ghana and Togo.

Numerical growth across the Orange world has shown some diverse patterns. While the Putnam effect was evident in some countries, it did not apply in every instance. England peaked the earliest, in the nineteenth century, whereas Scotland and the Americas peaked in the early part of the twentieth century. New Zealand was the exception, peaking in the late 1940s. These peaks were generally due to wartime losses, other loyalist options and internal divisions. Ghana and Togo never really gained traction due to their political and religious contexts.

A notable factor across the Orange diaspora was the formation of separate Orange bodies in reaction to the dissolution of the Orange Order in 1836. While many eventually managed to amalgamate through a spirit of cooperation, this was not evident in later divisions. The formation of competing Grand Lodges in Queensland and the United States strikingly exemplified this. Both places were hampered by internal division. At this point, the international body of the Imperial Orange Council was seen as the arbiter of the disputes. The Council was transnational as it was a forum for discussion and in this case disputes between countries.

The advent of ladies' lodges in the nineteenth and early twentieth centuries changed the image of the Orange Order from a male-dominated organisation to one today that seems to be more gender-inclusive. However, this inclusive nature was not universal across the Orange world. This was mostly due to the way female Orangeism developed. This inclusiveness is evident in the positive support that the English and New Zealand lodges had in their establishment, whereas Australian, Canadian and Scottish women had to fight to start their own lodges. Essentially these conditions were due to the male leadership within the Orange Order. If the men could see the benefit of female inclusion, ladies' lodges were established, albeit with some opposition. Another difference was the fact that some jurisdictions like Canada and Ireland chose to form separate female associate organisations, whereas Australia and New Zealand were within the confines of the existing system. While patterns of growth varied, the inclusion of women helped to build the Orange Order's base membership. The following chapter discusses the inner workings of the Orange Order in terms of its organisational structure and its rituals. This twofold focus will help us to understand not only the appeal of the Orange Order but also how it was able to retain members.

NOTES

1. William Shannon, *The United Empire Minstrel: A Selection of the Best National Constitutional and Loyal Orange Songs and Poems* (Toronto: Henry Rowsell, 1852), p. 185.
2. Hereward Senior, *Orangeism: The Canadian Phase* (Toronto: McGraw-Hill Ryerson, 1972).
3. Cecil J. Houston and William J. Smyth, *The Sash Canada Wore: A Historical Geography of the Orange Order in Canada* (Toronto: University of Toronto Press, 1980).
4. Eric Kaufmann, 'The Orange Order in Ontario, Newfoundland, Scotland and Northern Ireland: A macro-social analysis', in David A. Wilson (ed.), *The Orange Order in Canada* (Dublin: Four Courts Press, 2007), pp. 42–68.
5. Allan Blackstock, *Loyalism in Ireland 1789–1829* (Woodbridge: Boydell Press, 2007), pp. 2–4.
6. Jessica Harland-Jacobs, *Builders of Empire: Freemasons and British Imperialism, 1717–1927* (Chapel Hill: University of North Carolina Press, 2007), pp. 32–3.
7. David Hume (ed.), *Battles Beyond the Boyne* (Belfast: Schomberg Press, 2001), pp. 9–10.
8. *Belfast Weekly News*, 28 January 1899.
9. Harland-Jacobs, *Builders of Empire*, p. 37.
10. Charles Ivar McGrath, *Ireland and Empire, 1692–1770* (London and New York: Routledge, 2016), pp. 2–3.
11. P. J. Marshall, *The Making and Unmaking of Empires: Britain, India and America c. 1750–1783* (Oxford: Oxford University Press, 2005), p. 58.
12. David Fitzpatrick, *Descendancy: Irish Protestant Histories since 1795* (Cambridge: Cambridge University Press, 2014), pp. 21–40.

13. Ibid. p. 24.
14. Ibid. p. 25.
15. Elaine McFarland, *Protestants First: Orangeism in Nineteenth-Century Scotland* (Edinburgh: Edinburgh University Press, 1990), p. 49.
16. Frank Neal, 'Manchester's origins of the English Orange Order', *Manchester Region History Review*, 4:2 (1990–91), pp. 12–24.
17. Kevin Haddick-Flynn, *Orangeism: The Making of a Tradition* (Dublin: Wolfhound Press, 1999), p. 393.
18. Samuel Ernest Long, *A Brief History of the Loyal Orange Institution in the United States of America* (Dromara, County Down: Samuel Ernest Long, 1979), pp. 5–6. The likely origins were in New York. There were documented lodges in the United States around 1820.
19. John Brown, 'Orangeism in South Africa', in Donal McCracken (ed.), *The Irish in Southern Africa, 1795–1910* (Durban: Ireland and Southern Africa Project, 1992), pp. 110–19.
20. Richard Cannon, *Historical Records of the British Army: The Sixth or Royal First Warwickshire Regiment of Foot* (London: William Clowes & Sons, 1837), pp. 93–9.
21. Brown, 'Orangeism in South Africa', p. 112.
22. W. Baker, *Orangeism in the Cape: A Resume* (Belfast, 1905), pp. 5–7. Changes to lodge numbers, in this instance, were due to the merger of the two institutions in England in 1876. The 114 warrant number was then transferred to another Liverpool lodge.
23. By 1878 it changed number to 296. It was not uncommon for lodges that became defunct to have their numbers reused.
24. Baker, *Orangeism in the Cape*, pp. 6–8. The lodge members donated money to the soldiers' widows.
25. Loyal Orange Institution of England, *Report of the Annual Meeting of the Grand Orange Lodge, 1907–1910* (Manchester: GOLE, 1907–10).
26. Alexander was born in County Derry, Ireland, and many in his regiment were also Irish. The regiment had been told by their Commander-in-Chief Sir Rowland Hill that all regiments had to surrender their warrants.
27. W. A. Stewart (compiler), *Early History of the Loyal Orange Institution N.S.W.* (Sydney: Grand Orange Lodge of New South Wales, 1926), pp. 7–8.
28. *Watchman*, 30 March 1916.
29. *Report from the Select Committee Appointed to Inquire into the Origin, Nature, Extent and Tendency of Orange Institutions in Great Britain and the Colonies; with the Minutes of Evidence, Appendix and Index* (London: House of Commons, 1835), p. xii.
30. Ibid. p. xv.
31. Joseph Carnahan, *A Brief History of the Orange Institution in the North Island of New Zealand from 1842 to the Present Time* (Auckland: Star Office, 1886), p. 6.

32. Joseph Carnahan, *Life and Times of William the Third and History of Orangeism* (Auckland: Star Office, 1890), p. 293.
33. *Report from the Select Committee*, p. 8.
34. These movements merged in 1876 to become the Loyal Orange Institution of England.
35. *Orange and Protestant Banner*, April 1859.
36. Ibid., May 1862.
37. Loyal Orange Institution of Great Britain, *Proceedings of the Grand Lodge held at the Green Man Inn, Bacup, 3rd July 1854* (Liverpool: Bro. T. Davies, 1854).
38. *Orange and Protestant Banner*, February 1859.
39. Ibid., June 1859.
40. Ibid., April 1861. The report was dated 12 December 1860, from the MacDuff transport ship in Hong Kong Harbour.
41. *Hong Kong Government Gazette*, 7 June 1912, p. 410; *Hong Kong Government Gazette*, 28 April 1913, p. 194. GOLE records note that LOL 802 existed in 1907.
42. David Hume, Jonathan Mattison and David Scott, *Beyond Banners: The Story of the Orange Order* (Holywood, County Down: Booklink, 2009), pp. 80–1. The GOLE magazine, the *Orange Standard*, reported meetings throughout the war period that included references to military personnel stationed throughout Asia.
43. Loyal Orange Institution of England, *Reports of the Annual Meeting of the Grand Orange Lodge, 1940–48* (GOLE, 1940–48).
44. *Straits Times Weekly Issue*, 16 July 1893.
45. *Orange Standard*, November 1915.
46. *The Straits Times*, 5 July 1924. The Colonial Secretary was satisfied they no longer existed.
47. *Hong Kong Blue Book for the Year 1911* (Hong Kong: Norontha & Co., 1912), N2; Carl A. Trocki, *Singapore: Wealth, Power and the Culture of Control* (London: Routledge, 2006), p. 64.
48. Trocki, *Singapore*, p. 46.
49. This was scaled back as some were still needed for the police and H. M. Dockyard. In the end eighty-eight were released to join the Army, Navy and Marines.
50. Hume, Mattison and Scott, *Beyond Banners*, pp. 71–85. In the case of Cuba, it was given Grand Lodge status in 1929.
51. Patrick R. Ireland, 'Irish Protestant migration and politics in the USA, Canada, and Australia: A debated legacy', *Irish Studies Review*, 20:3 (2012), p. 264.
52. Loyal Orange Institution of Great Britain and Grand Protestant Association of Loyal Orangemen of England Reports, 1811–76.
53. Grand Protestant Association of Loyal Orangemen of England, *Report of the Proceedings of the Association in Extraordinary Grand Lodge*

assembled, on Tuesday 4th July 1876 at the Guildhall Tavern in the City of London (Bradford: Squire Auty and Son, 1876).

54. John Belchem, *Irish, Catholic and Scouse: The History of the Liverpool-Irish, 1800–1939* (Liverpool: Liverpool University Press, 2007). Also see Donald M. MacRaild, *Faith, Fraternity and Fighting: The Orange Order and Irish Migrants in England, c. 1850–1920* (Liverpool: Liverpool University Press, 2005).

55. Mervyn Busteed, 'Resistance and respectability: Dilemmas of Irish migrant politics in Victorian Britain', *Immigrants & Minorities*, 27:2–3 (2009), pp. 178–93.

56. Grand Orange Lodge of England Reports, 1881–1999.

57. See Sean Farrell, *Rituals and Riots: Sectarian Violence and Political Culture in Ulster, 1784–1886* (Lexington: University Press of Kentucky, 2000).

58. Guy Liagre, 'Protestantism and Freemasonry', in Henrik Bogdan and Jan A. M. Snoek (eds), *Handbook of Freemasonry* (Leiden and Boston: Brill, 2014), pp. 162–87.

59. David Bryce, *The Undaunted: A History of the Orange Order in Scotland from 1799 to 1899* (Glasgow: D. Bryce, 2012), pp. 26–32. McFarland, *Protestants First*, p. 62. Technically the Earl of Enniskillen was the Grand Master, but this was more an honorary post as Clements was de facto Grand Master.

60. E. W. McFarland, 'The Loyal Orange Institution in Scotland, 1799–1900' (PhD, University of Glasgow, 1986); *Protestants First*, p. 108.

61. Kaufmann, 'The Orange Order in Ontario', p. 51.

62. Bryce, *The Undaunted*, p. 39.

63. Loyal Orange Institution of Scotland Reports, 1872–2000.

64. Robert D. Putnam, *Bowling Alone: The Collapse and Revival of American Community* (New York: Simon & Schuster, 2000).

65. Eric Kaufmann, 'The Orange Order in Scotland since 1860: A social analysis', in Martin J. Mitchell (ed.), *New Perspectives on the Irish in Scotland* (Edinburgh: John Donald, 2008), p. 177.

66. See, for example, Houston and Smyth, *The Sash Canada Wore*.

67. Kaufmann, 'The Orange Order in Ontario', pp. 42–68.

68. Ibid.

69. Eric Kaufmann, 'The demise of dominant ethnicity in English Canada: Orange Order membership decline in Ontario, 1918–1980' (full-length paper presented at the Institute of Commonwealth Studies conference on 'Canada and the end of empire', 26–28 April 2001), pp. 10–11.

70. Houston and Smyth, *The Sash Canada Wore*, pp. 162–3; 'The faded sash: The decline of the Orange Order in Canada, 1920–2005', in David A. Wilson (ed.), *The Orange Order in Canada* (Dublin: Four Courts Press, 2007), pp. 146–91.

71. Long, *A Brief History of the Loyal Orange Institution*, pp. 5–6.

72. Cecil J. Houston and William J. Smyth, 'Transferred loyalties: Orangeism in the United States and Ontario', *American Review of Canadian Studies*, 14:2 (1984), pp. 193–211.

73. Loyal Orange Institution of the United States of America, *Official Directory Recognized and Constitutional Lodges of the Loyal Orange Institution U.S.A., Inc. and the Loyal Orange Ladies' Institution, USA, Inc.* (Philadelphia: The Supreme Grand Lodge of the United States, 1911–2014).

74. Rankin Sherling, *The Invisible Irish: Finding Protestants in the Nineteenth-Century Migrations to America* (Montreal: McGill-Queen's University Press, 2016), p. 298, n. 50.

75. *Report of the Fourteenth Annual Session of the Grand Orange Lodge of the United States of America Held in a P. Hall, Pittsburgh PA. June 12th, 13th, 1883* (Philadelphia: Protestant Standard Print, 1883), p. 10.

76. Michael A. Gordon, *The Orange Riots: Irish Political Violence in New York City, 1870 and 1871* (Ithaca and London: Cornell University Press, 1993), p. 23.

77. *Report of the Forty-Seventh Session of the Supreme Grand Orange Lodge Loyal Orange Institution of the United States of America Inc. Held in Rochester, N.Y. August 13, 14, & 15, 1938. And the Forty-Eighth Session Held in Wilmington, Delaware August 16, 17 & 18, 1940* (Pittsburgh: LOI, 1938–40); *Report of the Proceedings of the Sixty-Seventh Biennial Meeting of the Supreme Grand Lodge of the Loyal Orange Institution of the United States of America Inc. Pittsburgh, Pennsylvania August 15 and 16 1978* (Pittsburgh: LOI, 1978), p. 28; *Report of the Proceedings of the Seventy-Second Biennial Meeting of the Supreme Grand Lodge Loyal Orange Institution of the United States of America Inc. Pittsburgh, Pennsylvania August 9 and 10 1988* (Pittsburgh: LOI, 1988), p. 28.

78. LOIUSA, Official Directory, 2010.

79. Houston and Smyth, 'Transferred loyalties', p. 209.

80. The American Orange Order newspaper the *Orange and Purple Courier*, owned by the winning faction under William Kirkland, documents the various issues.

81. Long, *A Brief History of the Loyal Orange Institution*, p. 25.

82. Kevin Kenny, 'Irish emigration, c. 1845–1900', in Thomas Bartlett and James Kelly (eds), *The Cambridge History of Ireland* (Cambridge: Cambridge University Press, 2018), p. 684.

83. Imperial Grand Orange Council, *Report of the Triennial Meeting of the Imperial Grand Orange Council. Held at the Westminster Palace Hotel, London, July 19th, and 20th, 1882* (London: LOI, 1882), pp. 10–11.

84. Eric Turner, '"Not narrow minded bigots": Proceedings of the Loyal Orange Institution of New South Wales, 1845–1895' (PhD, University of New England, 2002), p. 399.

85. Tony Laffan, *How Orange Was my Valley? Protestant Sectarianism and the Loyal Orange Lodges of Australia's Hunter Valley, 1869–1959* (Singleton, NSW: Toiler Editions, 2009). See also Dianne Hall, 'Defending the faith: Orangeism and Ulster Protestant identities in colonial New South Wales', *Journal of Religious History*, 38:2 (2014), pp. 207–23.

86. Ireland, 'Irish Protestant migration', p. 271.

87. *Daily News*, 3 January 1922; *The Telegraph*, 2 April 1923.

88. Ireland, 'Irish Protestant migration', p. 271.

89. Richard P. Davis, *Orangeism in Tasmania 1832–1967* (Newtownabbey, County Antrim: Institute of Ulster-Scots Studies, 2010), pp. 73–4.

90. 'Loyal Orange Institution of South Australia', <https://www.findglocal.com/AU/Adelaide/423984171071340/Loyal-Orange-Institution-of-South-Australia> (accessed 30 November 2023).

91. Carnahan, *Life and Times*, p. 293.

92. Ibid. This letter was written by the Grand Lodge of Ireland in December 1869 to the Canterbury lodge.

93. The Grand Lodge of the Middle Island consisted of the provinces of Nelson, Marlborough, Canterbury, Otago, Southland and Westland.

94. Patrick Coleman, '"A hotbed of Orangeism": The Orange Order in Canterbury 1864–1908', *Journal of Orange History*, 3 (2017), pp. 20–7.

95. Grand Orange Lodge of Ireland, *Report of the Proceedings of the Grand Orange Lodge of Ireland at the General Half-Yearly Meetings, Held in the Orange Hall, Lisburn, 1890* (Dublin: James Forrest, 1890), p. 9.

96. *Report of Proceedings of the Thirteenth Triennial Session of the Imperial Grand Orange Council of the Loyal Orange Association of the World (1903). Held in the city of Dublin, Ireland, July 15 and 16th, 1903* (Glasgow: Office of Imperial Grand Secretary, 1903), p. 40.

97. Grand Orange Lodge of New Zealand Reports, 1908–2000.

98. Brown, 'Orangeism in South Africa', p. 116.

99. Loyal Orange Institution of British South Africa, *Report of the Annual Meeting of the Grand Orange Lodge. Held in the Freemason's Hall, Jeppestown, Johannesburg on Friday, December 16th, 1910* (Johannesburg: The Lodge, 1910), p. 22.

100. *Report of Proceedings of the Fourteenth Triennial Session of the Imperial Grand Orange Council of the Loyal Orange Association of the World. Held in the city of Toronto, Canada, July 16th, 17th and 18th, 1906* (Toronto: The Sentinel Print, 1906), p. 16.

101. *Report of Proceedings of the Seventeenth Triennial Meeting of the Imperial Grand Orange Council of the World. Held in Belfast, Ireland, 15th–16th July, 1920* (Belfast: LOI, 1920), p. 33.

102. *Report of the Twenty-Sixth Meeting of the Imperial Grand Orange Council of the World. Held at Londonderry, Northern Ireland on the 16th July and 17th July, 1958* (Belfast: LOI, 1958), p. 20.

103. Donal P. McCracken, 'Odd man out: The South African experience', in Andy Bielenberg (ed.), *The Irish Diaspora* (Harlow: Longman, 2000), p. 268, n. 27.

104. Rachel Naylor, 'The Orange Order in Africa', *History Ireland*, 14:4 (2006), pp. 7–9.

105. Loyal Orange Institution of England, *Report of the Annual Meeting of the Grand Orange Lodge, 1907–1910.*

106. Atayi was also involved in politics in 1947 as President of the Parti Togolais du Progrès or Togolese Party of Progress. See D. E. K. Amenumey, *The Ewe Unification Movement: A Political History* (Accra: Ghana Universities Press, 1989), p. 181.

107. Naylor, 'The Orange Order in Africa'; Michael Phelan, 'Orange Order in Togo', 31 March 2014 (unpublished manuscript).

108. The distance between the two places is about 45km.

109. Amenumey, *The Ewe Unification Movement*, pp. 58–71.

110. Rev. Ian Meredith, *A Short History of the Orange Order in Ghana* (Glasgow, c. 1990s), p. 4.

111. Ibid. Markwei was from the Ga tribe, which was mostly in Greater Accra, Ghana.

112. Chris McGreal, 'Ulster-by-the-Equator', *The Guardian*, 6 November 1999, <https://www.theguardian.com/uk/1999/nov/06/northernireland. books> (accessed 9 May 2024).

113. *Report of the Thirty-Eighth Meeting of the Imperial Orange Council, 1867–1994. Held at Auckland, New Zealand, 26th, 27th, 29th & 30th September 1994.* There are reasonably detailed reports outlining the various difficulties for both Grand Lodges.

114. Meredith, *A Short History*, p. 5.

115. Eric Kaufmann, *The Orange Order: A Contemporary Northern Irish History* (Oxford: Oxford University Press, 2007), p. vii.

116. *Sunday Times*, 28 June 2009.

117. R. S. M. McClure Watters, *A Report on the Socio-Economic Impact of the Traditional Protestant Parading Sector in Northern Ireland* (Belfast: GOLI, 2013), p. 2.

118. Christi McCallum, 'Orangewomen show their colors: Gender, family, and Orangeism in Ulster, 1795–present' (PhD, Southern Illinois University Carbondale, 2011), p. 327; McClure Watters, *A Report on the Socio-Economic Impact*, p. 2.

119. McCallum, 'Orangewomen show their colors', p. 25.

120. Patrick Coleman, '"In harmony": A comparative view of female Orangeism 1887–2000', in Angela McCarthy (ed.), *Ireland in the World: Comparative, Transnational, and Personal Perspectives* (London and New York: Routledge, 2015), pp. 112–13. The decree by Pope Pius X was in 1908 but the implications of it were not apparent when it first came out.

121. Éamon Phoenix, 'Catholic unionism: A case study: Sir Denis Stanislaus Henry (1864–1925)', in Oliver P. Rafferty (ed.), *Irish Catholic Identities* (Manchester and New York: Manchester University Press, 2013), p. 303, n. 17.

122. D. A. J. MacPherson, '"Exploited with fury on a thousand platforms": Women, unionism and the *Ne Temere* decree in Ireland, 1908–1913', in Joan Allen and Richard C. Allen (eds), *Faith of Our Fathers: Popular Culture and Belief in Post-Reformation England, Ireland and Wales* (Newcastle: Cambridge Scholars Press, 2009), pp. 157–75.

123. Jesse Buck, 'The role of *Ne Temere* in the decline of an Irish custom regarding the religious affiliation of the children of mixed marriages', *Australasian Journal of Irish Studies*, 11 (2011), pp. 34–7.

124. Daithí Ó Corráin, '"Resigned to take the bill with its defects": The Catholic Church and the third Home Rule bill', in Gabriel Doherty (ed.), *The Home Rule Crisis 1912–14* (Cork: Mercier Press, 2014), pp. 189–92.

125. Approval for revival came from the Grand Orange Lodge of Ireland from a request by Mary Elizabeth Johnstone. She was an original member of the former ALOI.

126. These were the Partition in 1921 and later the Irish Republic declaration in 1948.

127. McCallum, 'Orangewomen show their colors', p. 145.

128. McClure Watters, *A Report on the Socio-Economic Impact*, p. 2; *Orange Standard*, March 2020.

129. Kaufmann, *The Orange Order*, p. 284.

130. Coleman, '"In harmony"', p. 112; D. A. J. MacPherson, 'The emergence of women's Orange lodges in Scotland: Gender, ethnicity and women's activism, 1909–1940', *Women's History Review*, 22:1 (2012), p. 67.

131. Peter Day, 'Pride before a fall? Orangeism in Liverpool since 1945', in M. Busteed, F. Neal and J. Tonge (eds), *Irish Protestant Identities* (Manchester and New York: Manchester University Press, 2008), pp. 277–81; D. A. J. MacPherson, 'Personal narratives of family and ethnic identity: Orangewomen in Scotland and England, c. 1940–2010', *Immigrants & Minorities*, 32:1 (2013), pp. 90–114.

132. MacPherson, 'The emergence of women's Orange lodges', pp. 58–9.

133. Grand Orange Lodge of Scotland Reports, 1911–2014.

134. Kaufmann, 'The Orange Order in Scotland since 1860', p. 177.

135. Grand Orange Lodge of Scotland Reports, 1911–2014.

136. *Orange Torch*, April 2015, p. 12.

137. *The Guardian*, 13 September 2014. See also Joseph Webster, *The Religion of Orange Politics: Protestantism and Fraternity in Contemporary Scotland* (Manchester: Manchester University Press, 2020).

138. Houston and Smyth, 'Transferred loyalties', pp. 203–4.

139. Kevin Kenny, *The American Irish: A History* (New York: Routledge, 2014), p. 24.

140. Loyal Orange Institution of the United States of America, *Official Directory*.

141. Long, *A Brief History of the Loyal Orange Institution*, pp. 24–5.

142. Eric Kaufmann, *Orange Order Membership Data, with a Focus on Ireland, Canada and Scotland, 1852–2002* (Colchester: UK Data Archive, 2004), SN: 4916.

143. D. A. J. MacPherson, *Women and the Orange Order: Female Activism, Diaspora and Empire in the British World, 1850–1940* (Manchester: Manchester University Press, 2016), p. 152.

144. Kaufmann, *Orange Order Membership Data*.

145. *Report of Proceedings of the Ninety-Seventh Session of the M.W. Grand Lodge Ladies' Orange Benevolent Association of Canada. Centennial Edition. June 14, 15, 16, 17, 1994 Saint John, New Brunswick* (Toronto: LOBA, 1994), p. 31.

146. Houston and Smyth, *The Sash Canada Wore*. See chapter 5 for an analysis of male Orange membership.

147. Grand Lodge of New Zealand, Annual Reports 1908–2000.

148. A. S. Russell, *Loyal Orange Institution of Queensland History 1865 to 1932* (Brisbane: Loyal Orange Institution of Queensland, 1933); *Watchman*, 12 September 1912.

149. *The Age*, 13 July 1905.

150. Turner, '"Not narrow minded bigots"', p. 420.

151. Ian B. Waters, 'The first Australasian Catholic Congress: A mirror of the Australian Catholic Church in 1900', *Journal of the Australian Catholic Historical Society*, 21 (2000), pp. 18–19; Anne Elizabeth Cunningham, *The Price of a Wife: The Priest and the Divorce Trial* (Spit Junction, NSW: Anchor Books Australia, 2013).

152. David Fitzpatrick, 'Exporting brotherhood: Orangeism in South Australia', *Immigrants & Minorities*, 23:2–3 (2005), p. 302, n. 39.

153. Ibid. p. 284.

154. Davis, *Orangeism in Tasmania*, p. 73.

155. Ibid. p. 285.

156. Tas Vertigan, *The Orange Order in Victoria* (Melbourne: Loyal Orange Institution of Victoria, 1979).

157. Meredith, *A Short History*, p. 3.

158. Phelan, 'Orange Order in Togo'.

159. Fitzpatrick, *Descendancy*, p. 22.

2

The Heart of Orangeism: Structure and Rituals

On a chilly night on 20 May 1915, the usual monthly meeting of True Blue LOL No. 17 was held in the red brick Orange Hall in Southbridge, Canterbury, New Zealand. The Worshipful Master of the lodge, County Armagh born, Joseph Henry Hampton (1888–1937) opened the lodge meeting, and then the Lodge Chaplain gave a devotional by reading a portion of scripture. Next, the order of business proceeded with the minutes being read and confirmed. Hampton then read the 'Qualifications of an Orangeman'. After that the correspondence was read and various matters dealt with. After this, the gathered brethren had to decide on the upcoming July celebrations. Different members proposed the Anglican, Reverend Henry George Hawkins (1867–1957) and the Wesleyan, Reverend William Grigg (1862–1951) as to who would conduct the service. Hawkins was the preferred preacher for the day. For the parade, they selected the local Ellesmere Brass Band. They agreed that all proceeds from the social that followed the parade should go to the Red Cross. A visitor from another lodge was 'accorded a hearty welcome', and then Hampton declared the meeting closed. A time of socialising then ensued.[1]

This description of an Orange lodge meeting in the early twentieth century was quite typical of meetings, not just for the New Zealand Orange Order, but also for other parts of the Orange world. Orange lodge meetings tended to be either more or less formal depending on the country. Despite this, the essential elements were generally the same. The only aspect missing in these recorded minutes were the ritual instructions but, when noted, these were very brief and did not give any exact detail other than who was initiated.

General histories of the Orange Order in Ireland have acknowledged the social bonding of its rituals and commented on the overall structure in passing.[2] Other more academic histories have identified the link between rituals and violent Orange processions. Private rituals have been seen as reinforcing sectarian belief, particularly concerning Catholic conspiracy theories.[3] Other researchers have investigated how the Orange Order's structure, in the context of Northern Ireland, is used to influence its members, mainly through their ritualised behaviours, such as the Twelfth of July parades. They point to the hierarchical structure of the Order, albeit recognising the 'semiautonomous character' of local lodges.[4] Still others have highlighted the borrowings from Freemasonry.[5]

Generally, two issues have emerged from the historiography. First is the degree to which the Orange Order borrowed Masonic structures and how this organisational framework was adapted to both unify and discipline its members. The second issue is the extent to which the rituals have helped to build cohesion among members as believers in an Orange narrative of history.

The purpose of this chapter is to understand the lodge system and its inner workings. This is important because it was this structure that the Orange Order used to adapt and successfully spread throughout the British world and which formed the basis of its lodge practices. This chapter is divided into two main sections. The first section will outline the origins of the Orange Order's organisational patterns, particularly the extent to which it borrowed these structures from Freemasonry. The similarities and differences between the Orange Order's structure in Ireland and the Orange diaspora will be explored. Attention will be paid to the way these structures were used to decide who was eligible to join. The second section will focus on the strengths and weaknesses of rituals, their practices and their significance.

STRUCTURE

Origins

Any discussion of the organisational structure of the Orange Order inevitably begins with the origins of the organisation. While various Orange associations, clubs and societies arose following the rise to power of King William III in 1688, the present organisation began in 1795. The oft retold story is of the meeting of a small group of Protestants who, following the Battle of the Diamond in 1795, formed the first Orange lodge. The early founders, James Wilson, Dan Winter and James Sloan, were Freemasons and appropriated Freemasonry organisational patterns, emblems and passwords. However, the extent of Freemasonry's influence needs clarification. Petri Mirala, in his study of

Freemasonry in Ulster, outlines the concentrated nature of Freemasonry in the region.[6] The first documented warrant for a Masonic lodge was in 1733, although Freemasonry was more informally in existence in the region before this date.[7] In particular, Mirala argues for time and place being factors that influenced the shape of the early Orange Order, since it was founded between 1793 with the disbanding of the Volunteers and 1796 with the raising of the yeomanry.[8] During this interim period, the loyalists of County Armagh had been denied by the government the means to band together as military or even paramilitary units. The guise of a semi-secret fraternity was, according to Mirala, the next best option for loyalists to be organised to defend themselves when needed. The location of Loughgall was also significant as it had almost a third of the Masonic lodges within the surrounding area.[9] These were undoubtedly factors in the early Orange Order choosing some of the trappings of Freemasonry. The process of trying to mobilise like-minded Protestants needed a framework, and using a Masonic-style system made sense as the early founders were familiar with it.

Before we move to a discussion about the organisational structure of the Orange Order, a brief overview of Freemasonry is needed. As already noted, not only were the original founders of the Orange Order Freemasons but Freemasonry was a known fraternal organisation, with its rituals and structures familiar to many Irishmen in the late eighteenth century. The Orange Order, not surprisingly, shared many of the same aspects in its early stages as Freemasonry. Freemasonry was originally an exclusively male fraternal organisation. This brotherhood was a means for men to meet and have a shared sense of purpose. The use of the term 'brotherhood' in a Masonic sense meant that all mentioned were part of a 'universal family'. This is important as now, wherever a Mason travelled, they could feel at home anywhere in the world. This meant 'Freemasonry displayed both cosmopolitan and universalizing tendencies'.[10]

Freemasonry claimed a link to medieval stonemasons and even the builders of King Solomon's Temple. In the Irish context, Freemasonry became better organised in 1725 with the formation of the Grand Lodge of Ireland.[11] The description of the march and subsequent installations of the Grand Master and his officers took place on St John's Day.[12] The Masonic historian Robert Freke Gould claimed, '*After* the formation of a Grand Lodge there was centralization; *before* it there was none.'[13] This bold statement had more to do with the way Freemasonry was able to spread across other countries with a transnational system that encouraged and nurtured the formation of lodges.

The lodge system came first and was an essential means of organising Freemasons, and there was a certain amount of autonomy. The publication of various constitutions and regulations through Grand Lodges specified the types of rules that regulated practice. One of the early publications was *The Constitutions of the Free-Masons* (1723) by Scottish-born James Anderson (1679/1680–1739). In it lodges were defined:

> A LODGE is a Place where Masons assemble and work: Hence that Assembly, or duly organiz'd Society of Masons, is call'd a LODGE, and every Brother ought to belong to one, and to be subject to its By-Laws and the GENERAL REGULATIONS.[14]

Some significant aspects of lodges are encapsulated in this definition. Firstly, it claims a lodge is where the members meet but does not specify it has to be a particular type of building. Although Freemasons did later build various halls or temples, they also met in rented premises such as public houses. Secondly, the members, called 'brothers', had to abide by the rules of the lodge. This sense of order and obedience to the rules of the society regulated both the running of the lodge and also the behaviour of members. In this lodge, there were various roles or officers that included Worshipful Master, Warden, Secretary, Treasurer, Deacon, Steward, Inner Guard, Tyler and Chaplain. Each of the lodges managed its own affairs, and the Grand Lodge was the governing body. Each country had its own Grand Lodge and there could only be one. Sometimes there were Provincial Grand Lodges, depending on the size of the country. This was to help in the organisation of various regions. While the lodges were essentially in charge of their own affairs, it was the Grand Lodge that helped to frame and amend any rules. In the early years, starting a lodge required the permission of the Grand Master.[15] This permission was referred to as a 'warrant'. Around 1731 the Irish Grand Lodge moved from verbal recognition to physical documentation that had to be displayed as evidence of this approval.[16]

Significant research by Jessica Harland-Jacobs outlines not only the local to global scale of the Freemasons' lodge structure but also the bold comment that 'the growth of the global network would not have been possible without the establishment of metropolitan grand lodges'. These Grand Lodges in England, Ireland and Scotland facilitated growth through a centralised system of collecting fees, printing principles and regulations.[17] Having an organised administrative structure helped spread Freemasonry through military lodges and civilian ones.

The formation of the Orange Order benefited from the existing Freemasonry structure. The initial leaders were able to utilise the Irish

Freemasons' structural system to their advantage. It gave them the means to organise their membership in a unified and structured way that would, in turn, be used for their expansion. This borrowed structural system would be invaluable as the Orange Order exported their organisation to other countries. As with the Freemasons, lodges were established with physical warrants. The only difference in the formative years was the lack of a Grand Lodge. This would come later.

In Figure 2.1, we can see the basic structure that the Orange Order chose to follow in Ireland. This model has the primary or private lodge at the bottom. Here there were initially five members who then, in turn, admitted or rejected prospective members. With the formation of at least five lodges a district lodge could be formed in an area. Once there were three districts, a county or city Grand Orange Lodge was instituted. The Grand Orange Lodge of Ireland presided over all of these lodges.[18] This organisational structure helped in the growth of the Orange Order as the patterns had been set very early.

The fact that the Grand Lodge formed in 1798, the year of rebellion throughout Ireland, was not by chance. The gentry sought to control what was an agrarian organisation that had the potential to be quite a sizeable militia when needed. For the early Orange Order in Ireland, the Grand Orange Lodge was formed in Dublin. They elected Thomas Verner as Grand Master.[19]

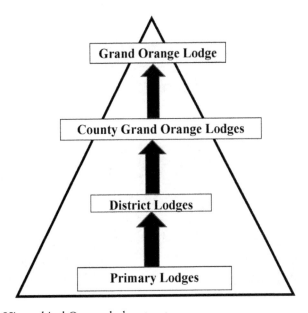

Figure 2.1 Hierarchical Orange lodge structure

On the surface, the structure of the early Orange Order does seem very hierarchical with a Grand Orange Lodge overseeing the various lodges. It gave the appearance of the leaders at the top being in control. However, this proved to be far from the reality on the ground. Just like their Masonic counterparts, the Orange Order similarly used the humble lodge. It had greater autonomy than one might expect if an outsider was simply to look at the rules. The lodge was the entry point for all members, and it was here that new members first came into contact with other members and went to monthly lodge meetings. The concept of a Grand Orange Lodge for Ireland mimicked the Masons. This situation meant having the Grand Orange Lodge in Dublin just like their Masonic counterparts. While there were attempts to portray this Grand Orange Lodge as gentrified, this was not the case. Even the newly appointed Grand Master Verner realised that 'as a "brother" Orangeman he was under a fraternal obligation to afford them respect and treat them as brethren, irrespective of their humble social rank'.[20] This form of egalitarianism within the fraternal Orange Order is an important concept that is still maintained today. The dissolution of the Orange Order's Grand Lodge in Dublin in 1835 eventually led to its return to the north of Ireland with Belfast the new seat of the Orange Order. Looking at Figure 2.2, the concept of the primary lodge being at the centre is the essence of the Orange Order structure. This is also the same for Freemasonry, and in this respect they are aligned.

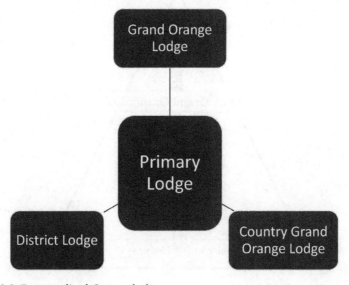

Figure 2.2 Decentralised Orange lodge structure

The Orange diaspora generally followed the Irish Orange Order's example of having one Grand Lodge in a country with some exceptions. The only variations on County Grand Lodges were regionally specific with Provincial or State Grand Lodges in the case of Canada and the United States. These groupings reflected localised circumstances, and Freemasonry also has Grand Lodges that reflect this in these same countries. Otherwise, there was uniformity in the use of the structure. The Australian Orange Order has a Grand Lodge for each state and keeps the same structure below this with districts and primary lodges.[21] It was at this level that the various Grand Lodges kept in contact and sent as a matter of courtesy to each other annual proceedings, making note at these annual events anything significant that happened in other jurisdictions.[22]

Membership

The early Orange Order not only borrowed and adapted the structure of Freemasonry but did the same with their membership criteria. Freemasonry outlined the character of their potential candidates under the concept of 'charges'. A candidate had to agree to these sets of charges in order to become a member. When it came to 'God and Religion' there was flexibility. While acknowledging the history of Christian Masons, it was accepted that Masons were 'To be good Men and true, Men of Honour and Honesty, by whatever Names, Religions, or Persuasions, they may be distinguish'd'.[23] This liberality in terms of belief opened the doors to theists and pantheists alike. In this sense, Freemasonry was a product of the Enlightenment.[24] As such, it tried to promote itself above religion. This was also reflected in the behaviour expected of members, ranging from not bringing quarrels of religion or politics to meetings to being good husbands and not slandering other people.[25] This moral code of conduct was secular in expression as it did not invoke Christian doctrine but instead humanist concepts. A further requirement for membership was that the candidate 'must be free-born (or no Bondmen) of mature Age, and of good Report; hail and sound, not deformed or dismembered, at the Time of their making; But no Women, no Eunuch'.[26] The Enlightenment principle only went so far since those with disabilities were excluded. The adding of 'no Eunuch' may have been to emphasise the brotherhood of Freemasonry, with eunuchs not seen as 'real' men.

Superficially, the differences between the rules for membership of Freemasonry and the Orange Order are quite marked. However, the similarities are more in the structure of the rules rather than the detail. It is in this that the Orange Order used what would nowadays be called a template. The framing of the rules and the logical order it followed are very similar to Freemasonry. For instance, the Freemasons' constitutions began with the historical background of Freemasonry and then moved to their beliefs, membership criteria with inclusions and exclusions, and, finally, the rules for organising private lodges and Grand Lodges.

Freemasonry and the Orange Order were fraternal organisations of brotherhoods. The brotherhood aspect was true for many years for Freemasonry but only true in the early stages for the Orange Order. Each organisation was religious but for Freemasonry this religious aspect was generalised. The Orange Order, however, was very clear and specific on this issue. They were 'exclusively a Protestant Association' that existed to 'support and defend' the British monarch and their successors conditional on them being Protestant. This mixture of militaristic, political and religious allegiances was a departure from the apparently apolitical and religiously diverse Freemasons. The Orange Order, with its conditional loyalty, was, in essence, a defence organisation. It was formed at a time of unrest and a resurgent Irish Catholic population pushing for greater civil rights. This 'defensive spirit' is evident in the atrocity literature used by the Orange Order such as the 1641 Rebellion and its massacre of Protestants.[27] These memories are used on banners and in their speeches and writings and demonstrated a marked difference from Freemasonry despite the ritual borrowings.

In the same way, Freemasonry had its 'charges' to guide members' behaviour; the Orange Order had its own version of this called 'qualifications'. It was split into two parts. The first qualification was originally called 'Qualifications requisite for an Orangeman', which changed after the dissolution of the Orange Order in 1836 to the 'Qualifications of an Orangeman'.[28] This statement of belief for all Orangemen and later Orangewomen emphasised members' faith in Jesus Christ and various comments about the virtues they had to uphold. Besides, they also 'should strenuously oppose the fatal errors and doctrines of the Church of Rome ... by all lawful means, resist the ascendancy of that Church, its encroachments, and the extension of its power'.[29] For the later ladies' Orange lodges, these 'qualifications' were adjusted to reflect a 'sisterhood' rather than 'brotherhood'.[30] This sisterhood reflected the shared fraternal ideals of the Orange Order regardless of social class. The standard seemed quite high and reflected the strong Reformation Protestant tradition, both Lutheran and Calvinist, of its early members.

It was Lutheran in the sense of emphasising the role of personal faith and the Bible, while Calvinist in the right to resist unjust authorities.[31]

The second qualification was called 'Obligation of an Orangeman', which was later renamed 'Particular Qualifications'. A new member had to state: 'I do further swear, that I am not, nor ever was a Roman Catholic, or Papist; that I was not, am not, nor ever will be an United Irishman; and that I never took the Oath of Secrecy to that or any other Treasonable Society.'[32] This very early example of the rules emphasises the fear of any members having been associated with the very groups they were mobilising against. The language is very strong and the pro-scribed statement is a way of demonstrating loyalty to the British Crown as opposed to the Catholics and other disloyal groups.[33] The use of the term 'Papist' is common in the Irish context. For example, the Irish rules in 1872 and 1896 still have the dual terms 'Roman Catholic or Papist'.[34] Despite the 'no Roman Catholics' rule, Catholic converts to Protestantism were allowed if approved by the Grand Lodge.

In contrast, in Melbourne, Australia, as early as 1854, in Canada and New Zealand in 1883, and in the United States in 1889 there is no mention of the word 'Papist'.[35] This derogatory term for Catholics was either not seen as acceptable or even not needed by the Orange diaspora, but lodges in Ireland still kept using it.[36] This was prob-ably more to do with the ongoing sectarian tensions that continue in present-day Northern Ireland whereas the other parts of the Orange diaspora have become more multicultural and secular. Membership criteria, then, rather than merely following the original template, reflect the societies in which the various Orange lodges operate. In some jurisdictions, there have been additions and deletions in refer-ence to unacceptable churches. For the early female Orange lodges in New Zealand in the 1880s, they included the 'Greek Church' with the Catholic Church as an exclusion for membership.[37] Moving quickly to present-day England, the Orthodox Church is mentioned in a similar context. Still, it goes further by asking members to swear they will not marry or 'cohabit' with Catholics or Orthodox churchgoers.[38] While the Orange Order in England and Ireland maintain their 'no Roman Catholic' stance, the Loyal Orange Ladies' Institution of the United States allows 'Protestant women of good moral character' to join. This also includes those married to someone of another faith.[39] In the case of New Zealand in 1978, as the Orange Order there became a charitable society, they removed any references to marrying Roman Catholics. They emphasised the Protestant nature of the organisation instead.[40] There is a general principle in all of this membership eligibility: whether male or female, members had to be Protestant and of good report or good character.

The issue of members marrying Catholics was always a difficult one, and the rules, regardless of the country, stipulated that a member would be expelled for doing so. Implementation of this rule proved challenging at times, as members may have been accused of this but the circumstances were not always so clear. In one example from Dundas, Sydney, Australian-born Orangeman Elijah Eyles defended himself against the accusation that he had married a 'Roman Catholic'.[41] He was not at the meeting and sent a letter. There was no formal charge, but the Worshipful Master of the lodge laid a charge that he had a suspicion that this had taken place. This was referred to a committee, which could not sustain the charge.[42] Eyles had married Australian-born Margaret Fitzgerald of Irish descent.[43] While she had an Irish Catholic background, they were married in a Wesleyan Church.[44] This was an instance where the accused did marry a Catholic but somehow was not expelled. He, later on, became Mayor of Orange in 1889 and also switched from being an Orangeman to being a well-known Freemason.[45] There are numerous cases recorded in annual proceedings around the Orange world of others who were expelled for marrying Catholics and other breaches of the rules.

The only other difference in terminology for membership occurred in the United States. Their criteria for male membership included that he be 'a white male, over the age of 18 years, free born, sound in body and mind with no defect calculated to shorten life'.[46] The reference to mental and physical attributes harks back to the early Irish Masonic rules of membership, but being white reflected the American situation. In no other Orange jurisdictions was there a membership requirement that was race-based. This rule took until 1992 to be changed, when the Supreme Grand Lodge of the Loyal Orange Institution of the United States of America removed all references to race as well as to physical and mental health.[47]

Female Lodges

Just like Freemasonry, the Orange Order is seen as a male entity. However, unlike Freemasonry, there were already women active in 1801, forming ladies' lodges in Dublin.[48] While the ladies' lodges were seen as a separate organisation, they were still part of the 'Orange family'. This early inclusiveness by the Orange Order was in stark contrast to the exclusiveness of Freemasonry. Unfortunately, the fleeting nature of these Dublin-based ladies' lodges meant they were unable to contribute to the overall organisational structure of the Orange Order.

Nevertheless, it was the spread of the Orange Order to other countries that generated some structural changes. The Orange Order in England in the 1850s and Scotland in the 1870s had ladies' lodges that were attached to male lodges. This attachment was formulated in the biblical concept of oversight. According to this concept, men had authority over women in the religious sphere. In this case, it was the nearest local male lodge that had this authority over the female lodges.

Breaking this traditional model was the Loyal Orange Ladies' Institution of the United States of America (LOLIUSA). Founded in 1876 in Philadelphia, Pennsylvania, it established a new organisational structure.[49] The LOLIUSA was established as a separate organisation from its male counterparts and followed the organisational structure of male lodges. It had a Supreme Grand Lodge, State Grand Lodges and Subordinate Lodges (another term for private lodges). The same organisational system still exists today.[50] Across the border, in Canada, the Ladies' Orange Benevolent Association (LOBA) formed in 1894 and was a separate organisation from its male counterparts. Just like its American sisters, it had a Grand Lodge but followed the English model by having Provincial Grand Lodges and primary lodges.[51]

The innovations in membership criteria came from the female branches of the Orange Order in Canada and the United States. While the Association of Loyal Orangewomen of Ireland was entirely separate from its male counterparts, the organisation remained exclusively for women. It was the LOLIUSA that allowed men to be members, and this rule still stands. The only admitted men were Royal Arch Purple Marksmen of the Loyal Orange Institution of the United States. This innovation came at the LOLIUSA's beginning in 1876 as men were also present at the formation of the first lodge. However, the men had a limited role as only women could hold office.[52] The LOBA in Canada had a similar requirement in its membership. Since the LOLIUSA was formed before the LOBA, this was a borrowed concept. In the LOBA men could be members as long as they had been admitted to the Royal Arch Purple degree in the men's lodge first. Just like its American counterparts, the LOBA was a separate institution but, of course, was a part of the Orange family.[53] No reasons have ever been given as to why the Americans and Canadians made these allowances.

Countries like Australia and New Zealand initially followed the English model of having ladies' lodges attached to the men's. Australia had separate Grand Orange Lodges for each state so that the women did not have a central organisation of their own. As numbers grew, there were calls for changes in representation so that in 1905 in Queensland, Australia, the ladies' lodges were allowed representation at the Grand Lodge by delegates from the male lodges. This still meant the men represented them in person but voiced the ladies' lodges' views. It was proxy representation. By 1914 at the annual sessions, the ladies' lodges were allowed direct representation.[54] In the New Zealand context, the auxiliary nature of ladies' lodges meant in real terms that there was always male 'oversight' in any ladies' lodge activities and decision making. Again, it was following the biblical model as noted in Genesis 2.18 that women were created as the 'helper' or 'helpmeet' (King James Version) for men. This is best exemplified by the fact that although the ladies' lodge officers were women, in the early days they still had to be represented at the annual Grand Orange Lodge sessions by men.[55] Not only were delegates for the annual sessions men, but ladies' lodge instructors who were required to be present at elections of ladies' lodge officers were also elected.[56] By 1923 a Ladies' Conference was formed but was directly under the control of the all-male Grand Executive.[57] Progress was slow and it was not until 1982 that the Grand Lodge became mixed. Up until then only the male members of the Grand Lodge could nominate women.[58] These examples from Australia and New Zealand demonstrate the conservative nature of the Orange Order, which only changed through lobbying by women. This, in turn, was symptomatic of wider society, where women called for change in organisations where men dominated leadership positions and women wanted greater representation.

Mixed Lodges

The inclusion of women in the Orange Order tended to be dealt with either by women forming their own organisation or through ladies' lodges attached to the men's lodges. The separation by gender was also common in other fraternal organisations. However, having mixed lodges was not common in most Orange jurisdictions. The case of the American and Canadian Orange lodges having some mixing was different; in those cases, the men were joining a female-dominated and -led organisation. It was in the southern hemisphere that mixed lodges flourished.

The Australian Orange Order had mixed lodges in the early twentieth century. As early as 1909, a Chaplain from LOL No. 58 Victory in Sydney made a case for mixed lodges and welcomed open debate on the topic. His arguments for the ladies' inclusion included their enfranchisement, difficulty in country areas for women to travel alone to 'an unmixed lodge', increased numbers, and for the women to be educated so that in turn they could instruct their children 'as to the dangers and seductions of Rome'.[59] The response from other writers from New South Wales and Victoria was positive; this included a comment that the Independent Order of Rechabites already had successful mixed lodges.[60] South Australia took up the challenge and formed mixed lodges. By 1915 the Federal Grand Orange Council of Australasia strongly requested that the South Australian Grand Lodge stop this practice and get the ladies to form their own lodges.[61] The Grand Lodge suggested doing away with mixed lodges in 1919 but by the following year they decided to leave things as they were with extra rules about members applying to join these lodges.[62] At the same time, other friendly societies such as the Protestant Alliance Friendly Society of Australasia (PAFSA) were also dealing with this issue. Its Federal Council met in 1922 and included a discussion on the vexed issue of mixed lodges. Queensland and New South Wales had them, but they wanted Victoria not to oppose them.[63] What happened in the PAFSA was relevant as it was a friendly society founded in 1868 by a former Orange Grand Master in Victoria.[64] The crossover in membership meant that what happened in one organisation could affect the decisions made in the other.

The one region in the Orange diaspora that created a structure that made mixed Orange lodges prominent was New Zealand, albeit much later (1953) than their Australian brethren. The main driver for change was the downturn in numbers and increasing numbers of lodges going into recess. It was seen as a solution to a problem rather than as a progressive or innovative move. The then Grand Master, C. P. Harris, believed that to deal with closing lodges 'they would also overcome many financial and social problems'.[65] However, when the opportunity to have a mixed lodge in Christchurch arose, the all-male Grand Lodge would not allow a mixed adult lodge. Many members were lost, as this decision meant young people having to join lodges with much older members. In particular, many of the young men were not made welcome, and, as a result, many left. The 1960s were notable for lodges amalgamating. This was 'all done through necessity'.[66] Faced with falling numbers, the New Zealand Orange lodges had to adapt or die. Nowadays, there are more mixed lodges than male or female ones. Falling numbers also affected the overall structure, leading to a mixed Grand Lodge in New Zealand. Again, this was necessary as the Orange Order had such low numbers it needed to streamline its structure. In Australia, this also occurred in the states that still have Orange lodges.

RITUAL

Strengths of Rituals

Fraternalism, expressed as a shared brotherhood or sisterhood, formed the basis of the Orange Order. This concept of 'family' through people not blood related needed something to tie them together. This was achieved through the use of rituals. To help us understand its importance within the Orange Order, some explanation of how rituals were expressed in Freemasonry needs to be outlined.

In its original form, Freemasonry was clearly defined as a men's only fraternity, as stated in the membership of their organisation. To create a sense of brotherhood for men who had no blood ties to each other, there was a need for some form of initiation. This was where the three degrees of Freemasonry were created, called 'the Craft' or 'blue lodge'. These degrees were the Entered Apprentice, Fellow Craft and Master Mason. The content of the degrees is derived from the medieval masons' guilds and the Old Testament story of the building of King Solomon's Temple. A candidate was initiated into each of these degrees through a series of formularised dialogues and re-enactments of the various stages. This included in the first degree being blindfolded and stripped of clothing (candidates often reduced to wearing only trousers) and having a noose put around their neck.[67] The purpose was to create a sense of mystery and vulnerability, which culminates in the candidate being given various passwords and information only known to the members.

Once the candidate progressed through the degrees, they were part of a brotherhood where the members had common beliefs but also could trust one another. Other branches of Freemasonry would add further degrees to heighten the mystery and create additional opportunities to build their fraternal bonds.[68] Now initiated, the candidate was part of a large fraternity that shaped their life. To recognise another Mason, they had secret handshakes and passwords. These rituals also served a broader societal function of knowing who to trust in business and in life generally. This is also why some lodges were wary of members being readmitted, as there were claims that some had gained access to lodges to steal their 'secret' rituals and the passwords.[69]

The rituals that the Orange Order adopted grew out of a time of political and social unrest in the north of Ireland in the late eighteenth century. Knowing whether to trust someone was necessary with the pro-liferation of secret societies espousing competing nationalist and loyalist ideals.[70] The early Orangemen therefore decided to appropriate much of the structure of Freemasonry. As a loyalist organisation, Orange members felt the need to band together, and having a structure and set of agreed rituals was deemed a necessity.

The Orange degree system, while following the original Irish Orange Order's example, did allow for some variations. In the early years of the Orange Order, there were a range of different degrees as the early Orangemen appropriated from Freemasonry and possibly James Wilson's Orange Boys.[71] Wilson, one of the early founders of the Orange Order and a Freemason, had his own Orange organisation that pre-dated the Orange Order. In its bid to maintain order within the organisation, the newly formed Grand Orange Lodge of Ireland (GOLI) declared on 24 October 1801 that 'all other colours or names of Black, Scarlet, Blue or any other colour are illegal and injurious'.[72] These colours referred to the various degrees being practised within Orange lodges. The GOLI fol-lowed up with more resolutions.[73] Only two degrees within the Orange Order were accepted: the Orange and the Purple. Besides asserting control over its members, the GOLI was also symbolically distancing itself from Freemasonry. Many within the Orange Order had dual membership, so they wanted to maintain a point of difference in the two organisations. The other degrees found another outlet, particularly in the Black lodges, which have eleven degrees.[74] While the Royal Black Institution is made up of members from the Orange Order, even their degrees are biblically based with the emphasis on Old Testament imagery, with the notable exception of the Red Cross degree.[75]

As the Orange Order spread across the world, clear differences emerged between the men's and women's rituals. All lodges in all coun-tries have the Orange as their first degree. This serves as a transnational connection, meaning that regardless of the location, any Orangeman and later Orangewoman would have a similar bonding ritual. The only exception is the American Orange Order, which has a combined Orange and Blue degree for women. Where the complications lie are in the subsequent degrees. In Table 2.1, we can see that the Royal Arch Purple is used as much as the Orange degree. The only difference is Ireland, where this is a separate institution affiliated to the Orange Order. What makes this remarkable is that the Royal Arch Purple was one of the degrees denounced by the Grand Lodge of Ireland on 11 November 1811. It was included with the Black, Scarlet and Blue.[76] Yet it was not until 1911 that the Royal Arch Purple was organised as

Table 2.1 Degrees in men's Orange lodges

	Orange	Blue	Purple	Royal Arch Purple	Royal Scarlet
Australia	✓			✓	
Canada	✓	✓		✓	✓
England	✓		✓	✓	
Ghana	✓		✓	✓	
Ireland	✓		✓	✓	
New Zealand	✓			✓	
Scotland	✓			✓	
Togo	✓		✓	✓	
United States	✓			✓	

the Grand Royal Arch Purple Chapter of Ireland. The situation is still the same today, with this degree being a separate one in Ireland but part of the other Orange lodges elsewhere. In this sense the Orange diasporic connections seem resolute in being different from the 'home' country of Orangeism.

The Canadian Orange Order is an aberration when it comes to the Orange system of degrees. Their degree system had five degrees: the Orange, Purple, Blue, Royal Arch Mark (later Royal Arch Purple) and Royal Scarlet.[77] The constant rejigging of the degrees resulted in the Purple being removed. Currently, the Canadian Orange Order has just four: Orange, Blue, Royal Arch Purple and Royal Scarlet.[78] The Scarlet always ran as a separate chapter or branch, similar to the way the Arch Purple is used in other jurisdictions. The Canadian Orange Order claimed the Scarlet degree was brought to Canada by the British military in the nineteenth century. Speaking at an annual session in 1950, the Grand Master, R. Hardy Small, claimed that the Royal Scarlet Order or Grand Lodge Degree 'originated from the fertile brain of Ogle R. Gowan, our first Grand Master'.[79] When the Grand Lodge of New Brunswick became part of the Grand Lodge of British America they brought with them the Scarlet degree. By 1849 the Chapter of Royal Scarlet was formed. The Grand Master's title was changed to Sovereign Grand Master of British America. The Royal Scarlet Chapter was not legally part of the Orange Association but had its own constitution.[80] In this regard, the Canadian Orange Order seems to have been influenced by the ritual and ceremony of Freemasonry, as the extra degrees attest. As shown in Table 2.1, however, the most common degree format was the Orange and Royal Arch Purple degrees. Maybe the simplicity of only offering two degrees was enough for most members. The dual membership of the Orange Order and Freemasonry by some members meant that those who wanted to delve into more ritual could do so. Of course, there was the Royal Black Institution with its Masonic-like degrees that could also satisfy members' desires for this.

When it came to the various degrees offered to Orangewomen, there are only two degrees, regardless of what the degree is called. Probably the most prominent aberration is with the degrees from America which seem to be an amalgamation of the Canadian men's degrees in terms of the names. Despite the differences in name and sometimes practice, these degrees were part of the social cohesion within the lodges. Just like the Freemasons and other fraternal societies, the Orange Order used these degrees to give members a sense of both accomplishment and identity. To further understand the degrees beyond the names, an explanation of the practice is needed.

The early Orangewomen's degrees tended to follow a pattern similar to their male counterparts in form but not content. Over time the female degrees in the Orange diaspora changed and became reasonably standard across jurisdictions. It was the degree work of the Canadian Orangewomen who led the way. For instance, in 1909, the LOBA gave advice to their Scottish counterparts in the formation of the revived Scottish Orangewomens' lodges. By 1920, the Scottish ladies' lodges were instructing their English and Irish counterparts by providing sets of rituals and advice on them. These transnational links demonstrate it was the Orange diaspora that was leading the way, not the Irish Orangewomen.[81] However, despite this apparent amicable situation the differences became noticeable at the Triennial Orange Council of the World in July 1937. There was a push for uniformity in the practice of the ritual work across the world, but the ALOI would not agree. They wanted to be different as they claimed to be the only Grand Lodge not under male rule. What aspect was disputed? It was the stronger sectarian language in the Irish Orange ritual.[82] The Orange diaspora was softer and more focused on their Christian faith than the Irish Orangewomen's criticisms of the Catholic Church.

So, what exactly was the focus of the rituals performed in the degrees by women of the Orange diaspora? An example from the degrees undertaken by the early Australian Orangewomen reveals that the rituals performed within the degrees were a mixture of role-playing that included Bible verses and biblical truths. The officers of the lodge played various parts in reciting these, and hymns were also sung. At initiation, the candidate had to swear allegiance and 'solemnly promise that I will not in any manner communicate, or reveal, any of the proceedings of my Sisters in Lodge assembled'. This obligation was sealed by kissing

Table 2.2 Degrees in women's Orange lodges

	Orange	Orange & Blue	Second degree	Purple	Blue	Purple & Scarlet
Australia	✓				✓	
Canada	✓		✓			
England	✓			✓		
Ghana	✓		✓			
Ireland	✓				✓	
New Zealand	✓		✓			
Scotland	✓					
Togo		✓				✓
United States		✓		✓		

the Bible.[83] In the ladies' lodges, there were two degrees: the Orange and the Blue. The Blue or Second degree is heavily focused on the story of Ruth and her mother-in-law Naomi.[84] At the heart of the original story from the Old Testament Book of Ruth is trust. The two women, though not blood related, are bound initially through marriage, then, through a shared journey of uncertainty, they support one another to be ultimately rewarded with a happy life. The function of using this biblical story is to reinforce the sisterhood for Orangewomen, that even though they are not blood related they have a shared Christian faith. The main differences between Orange jurisdictions tend to be in the application of these rituals, often referred to as 'floor work'. It is a type of choreography in which specific movement and gestures may be modified and different passwords used. The challenge for members is to improve application of these aspects of the ritual. Orangewomen, through a kind of diasporic transference, have learnt from one another not just through members migrating, but from international meetings like the Imperial World Councils where Orangewomen also meet and share. These transnational connections helped to reinforce the bonds of sisterhood for Orangewomen as they had a shared experience, albeit with differences in practice.

Weaknesses of Rituals

The Masonic rituals, whereby candidates pass through degrees in their initiation, seem rather innocuous. This is also true of the Orange Order that borrowed and adapted the content of the Masonic rituals. However, it is these same rituals that have been heavily criticised, particularly by former members. The most stunning are allegations of the Masonic rituals containing satanic elements. The Orange Order, by association, has also had this accusation. The previously mentioned descriptions of role-playing various biblical texts and satanic or even pagan rituals are at odds with reality. How did this occur?

The main impetus for the anti-Masonic rhetoric can be traced to the papal condemnations that were first issued in the eighteenth century. Beginning with Pope Clement XII's *In Eminenti*, this papal bull not only referred to Freemasons as 'depraved and perverted' but also warned Catholics to stay away from Freemasonry and other societies 'under pain of excommunication'.[85] In the context of the time, the Pope was literally saying that if you became a Freemason, you would go to hell. For extra emphasis, the papal bull also noted you could only get 'absolution' at 'the hour of death'. More papal bulls were issued, but it was Leo XIII's *Humanum Genus* in 1884 that associated Freemasonry with Satan. He also claimed Freemasons wanted to 'bring back . . . the manners and customs of the pagans'.[86]

Against this backdrop of anti-Freemasonry and Leo XIII's papal bull entered Frenchman Léo Taxil (born Gabriel Jogand-Pagès). Taxil was originally known for his anti-Catholic and often pornographic literature.[87] He converted to Catholicism in 1885 and then wrote a series of anti-Freemasonry texts. In these, he wrote about Freemasons being involved in rituals that included devil worship and various sexual encounters by initiates. Some of these included multiple meetings with Satan and an assortment of demonic creatures, including a winged crocodile. Taxil then announced a press conference on 29 April 1897. In this briefing, he proclaimed that it was all a hoax and all of the characters and information were utterly untrue. The inspiration for all of this was the papal bull of Leo XIII. Taxil also stated that his 'conversion' was fake as well.[88] Taxil had played on the anti-Masonic feelings of the Catholic Church. While not all Catholics believed him, he was able to fool enough people to fuel anti-Masonic feelings.[89]

The primary outcome of this anti-Masonic literature, both official and imagined, was to create the idea of Freemasonry being anti-Christian and even satanic. This, in turn, has had a flow-on effect to the Orange Order. There have been various attempts to either ridicule or imply a malevolence of members of the Orange Order in their ritual practice. The early-nineteenth-century examples were from Henry Cleary, later Catholic Bishop of Auckland, and Edward Lewis, a former Orangeman from Australia.[90] Their books exclusively refer to the male lodges and reveal the rituals within the lodge meetings. The background for Lewis's revelations was the visit of ex-priest and ex-nun Joseph and Mary Slattery.[91]

Ex-religious preachers, genuine or 'sham', were a common staple in the nineteenth and early twentieth centuries. They made money from their lurid tales, more imagined than real, of their time in the Catholic Church. These visits resulted in trouble and often riots but also helped to increase Orange membership for a time.[92] In this instance, the Slatterys had been invited by the Australian and New Zealand Orange Order for a lecture tour of their respective countries.[93] Their visit polarised both Catholic and Protestant communities since the Slatterys criticised the Catholic Church in a sensationalist way. This included Mary Slattery dressing up as a nun to deliver her women's-only lectures.

Lewis's exposé of the Orange rituals was in response to the Slatterys' Australian leg of the tour. In this, he gave a detailed exposition of the Royal Arch Purple degree. For good measure, he included sketches of various parts of the ritual. His motivation was his encounter with Slattery, whom he found to be a liar and a fraudster. Lewis described the Royal Arch Purple degree and its ceremonies as 'a wretched and disgustingly stupid travesty of incidents narrated in Scripture history' and called it 'blasphemous tomfoolery'.[94] In tandem with Lewis's revelation, the Catholic paper the *New Zealand Tablet* published extracts from Cleary's book on the Orange Order, which also condemned the Orange rituals. Just like Lewis, the *New Zealand Tablet* denounced the Royal Arch Purple degree as 'a compound of coarse horse-play and of blasphemous travesties of incidents narrated in the Sacred Scriptures'. The paper then claimed the candidate for this degree does so 'in a state of ALMOST COMPLETE NUDITY'.[95] The use of capitalisation only served to titillate readers and emphasise the allegedly lurid nature of the rituals.

The early criticisms of Cleary and Lewis have been noted, but criticisms of the Orange rituals have never gone away.[96] In the late twentieth century Rev. Ian Meredith, Grand Chaplain from Scotland, and Rev. Brian Kennaway, a Deputy Grand Chaplain from Ireland, wrote a rebuttal of the claims that the Orange Order was too close to Freemasonry and therefore not Christian.[97] While they acknowledged the Masonic-like nature of the Royal Arch Purple degree, they argued it was non-Masonic in theology. They cited the non-biblical accounts in the Masonic third degree. They went even further in distancing Orange ritual practice from Freemasonry by making the claim: 'if the Orange Order were stripped of all its ritual it could continue to exist. Ritual is not basic to its principles or motivation.'[98] Despite this attempt to deflect criticism of their ritual activities, the accusations failed to go away. In 1999, yet another book, called *Behind Closed Doors*, focused on the Orange Order was published.[99] This time the allegations cut

Figure 2.3 Front cover, *Orangeism Exposed* (Lewis, *Orangeism Exposed*, p. 1)

into the heart of the rituals, particularly the Royal Arch Purple. The author, W. P. Malcomson, makes the following striking claim: 'The Royal Arch Purple Order is, in reality, paganism in disguise. Only Satan could devise a ceremony, which could so commonly be shared throughout the world by Protestant Arch Purple men, Masons and Witches alike.'[100]

Likening the rituals to satanism and witchcraft prompted a response from the Grand Chapter of the Royal Arch Purple Chapter of Ireland in the form of a book.[101] Rev. Ron Johnstone, a Free Presbyterian minister, and a member of the Grand Royal Arch Purple Chapter of Ireland, distanced the Orange Order from Freemasonry and addressed the 'absurd' allegations of Malcomson. Despite this attempt to meet Malcomson's claims head-on, there were serious consequences. Malcomson alleged in the same year his book was published that hundreds of born-again Christians had left the Orange Order.[102] He also launched a website that 'exposed' Freemasonry, the Orange Order, the Royal Arch Purple and the Royal Black.[103] Some of Malcomson's claims are similar to the early papal bulls and even Taxil's hoax. The Royal Arch Purple degree seems to be the one Orange degree that gets the most criticism. It is probably because the Royal Arch Purple degree is the most known Orange degree associated with Freemasonry. Again, as Freemasonry continues to receive similar accusations of links to satanic practice and witchcraft, so too does the Orange Order.

Public revelations by former members are nothing new to religious organisations: the Catholic Church has had scandals for centuries with former nuns and priests exposing ill-treatment within the Church. There have long been elements within Christianity that abhor anything other than a pure form of Christianity. This has often been labelled fundamentalism, but it also could be seen as a form of traditionalism as adherents want a faith that harks back to the time of Jesus. The Orange Order has upheld itself as a Reformation Protestant organisation and made great use of the literature that pillories the traditions of the Roman Catholic Church as originating in paganism. Common examples include the imagery of the Madonna and Child as originating in Babylonian worship, and the various symbols that were used by the Church as also being pagan.[104] Given that Orange members are drawn from across various Protestant churches, this strong traditionalist element was bound to eventually question the 'non-biblical' practices within the Orange rituals. Ultimately, many of these traditionalists would see the Catholic Church and anything aligned to Freemasonry as being the same. Therefore, their rejection of the Orange Order was a natural outflow of their evangelical belief.

CONCLUSION

The shadow of Freemasonry has long been cast over the Orange Order. From its inception until the present, the Orange Order has had to deflect criticisms of its ritual and practice. In reality, the Orange Order made changes to both the borrowed structure of Freemasonry and the rituals being all biblically based. Some apparent similarities with Freemasonry included having mostly gender-exclusive lodges. But the clear difference lay in the early involvement of Orangewomen in forming ladies' lodges. Also, there was the exception of the American and Canadian women who allowed some male membership, but under certain conditions, and with women still in leadership roles. A feature of the Australian and New Zealand Orange Orders is the use of mixed lodges, which was introduced to include family and as a solution to falling membership. The structure, adapted from Freemasonry, helped to stabilise the Orange Order in its tumultuous early years as it was founded in a climate of civil and social unrest in Ireland. The replication of this system helped Orange members who migrated to other countries and founded lodges there. Once a critical mass was achieved, the move to establish Grand Lodges was one inevitable outcome. Having a strict set of regulations was a way of maintaining discipline. It also reinforced the ideals of a Reformation Protestantism.

The rituals of the Orange Order have been both a strength and a weakness to the organisation as a whole. The power lay in building a sense of identity and as a form of social bonding. Members in the Orange diaspora created competitions that helped maintain not just a high standard of ritual practice, but also pride in their sense of accomplishments. The weakness lay in the secretive nature of the rituals. Any organisation with 'secret' rituals has had to deflect criticism of something sinister in its intentions. Again, Freemasonry and the plethora of fraternal organisations that also have 'secret' rituals have had to deal with claims of paganism, witchcraft and satanism, particularly by former members within the Evangelical movement. They see such practices as contrary to their view of Christianity. The rituals as they applied to degrees were fairly homogeneous across the Orange world, except for Canada. Despite this, the degrees themselves were mainly Old Testament based, with the men focusing on the trials of the journey from Exodus. In contrast, the Orangewomen had more maternal bonding from the Book of Ruth. While each reflected masculine and feminine sensibilities, they also provided biblical role models for members to aspire to.

The structure of the Orange Order laid the platform for growth, and the ritual provided the means to maintain membership by giving some 'colour' to the daily grind of life. The Orange Order, like other fraternal organisations, through a clearly defined structure and the lure of an inner brotherhood or sisterhood, was able to build and maintain its membership for a couple of centuries across the British world. Building on the strength of its structure and fraternal bonding, the Orange Order could influence the wider society. They did this through their activism, mostly in the public spheres of politics, education and benevolence.

NOTES

1. *LOL No. 16 and LOL No. 17 True Blue, Southbridge, Minute Book, August 1892–February 1916* (Orange Hall, Christchurch, New Zealand), 20 May 1915. The description above was based on this minute book. Griggs was from Cornwall while Hawkins hailed from Norfolk.
2. Tony Gray, *The Orange Order* (London: The Bodley Head, 1972); Ruth Dudley Edwards, *The Faithful Tribe: An Intimate Portrait of the Loyal Institutions* (London: HarperCollins, 1999), pp. 51–80. Also, see chapter 3 of Mervyn Jess, *The Orange Order* (Dublin: O'Brien Press, 2007).
3. Sean Farrell, *Rituals and Riots: Sectarian Violence and Political Culture in Ulster, 1784–1886* (Lexington: University Press of Kentucky, 2000), pp. 115–16.
4. Jennifer Edwards and J. David Knottnerus, 'The Orange Order: Strategic ritualization and its organizational antecedents', *International Journal of Contemporary Sociology*, 44:2 (2007), pp. 179–98.
5. Petri Mirala, *Freemasonry in Ulster, 1733–1813: A Social and Political History of the Masonic Brotherhood in the North of Ireland* (Dublin: Four Courts Press, 2007).
6. Ibid. pp. 224–5.
7. Ibid. p. 56.
8. The Volunteers were originally raised to fight any foreign threats to Ireland, notably from France and Spain, when the regular British soldiers were called to fight overseas. The yeomanry had a similar function, except this time the threats were mostly local, with the Catholic group called the Defenders and the United Irishmen. See Allan F. Blackstock, '"A dangerous species of ally": Orangeism and the Irish Yeomanry', *Irish Historical Studies*, 30:119 (1997), pp. 393–405.
9. Mirala, *Freemasonry in Ulster*, pp. 226–7.
10. Jessica Harland-Jacobs, *Builders of Empire: Freemasons and British Imperialism, 1717–1927* (Chapel Hill: University of North Carolina Press, 2007), pp. 68–9.
11. *Dublin Weekly Journal*, 26 June 1725.
12. St John's Day, 24 June, was celebrating not just the biblical St John the Baptist but also the date when the Grand Lodge of England was established, on 24 June 1717.

13. Robert Freke Gould, and revised by Frederick J. W. Crowe, *The Concise History of Freemasonry* (London: Gale & Polden Ltd, 1920; revised 1951), p. 55.

14. James Anderson, *The Constitutions of the Free-Masons: Containing the History, Charges, Regulations, &c. of that Most Ancient and Right Worshipful Fraternity* (London: William Hunter, 1723), p. 51.

15. Ibid. p. 60.

16. R. E. Parkinson, *History of the Grand Lodge of Free and Accepted Masons of Ireland, Volume 2* (Dublin: Lodge of Research, CC, 1957), pp. 268–9.

17. Harland-Jacobs, *Builders of Empire*, pp. 23–4.

18. Grand Orange Lodge of Ireland, *Rules and Regulations for the use of all Orange Societies. Revised and corrected by a Committee of the Grand Orange Lodge of Ireland; and adopted by the Grand Orange Lodge, January 10, 1800* (Dublin: Printed by an Orangeman, 1800), pp. 7–14.

19. James Wilson, 'Orangeism in 1798', in Thomas Bartlett (ed.), *1798: A Bicentenary Perspective* (Dublin: Four Courts Press, 2003), pp. 345–62.

20. Ibid. p. 360. See Ogle R. Gowan, *Orangeism; Its Origins and History* (Toronto: Lovell & Gibson, 1859).

21. The main reason for the separate lodges was that pre-Federation (1901) Australia comprised six different self-governing colonies. For more information on the situation pre and post Federation see Helen Irving (ed.), *The Centenary Companion to Australian Federation* (Cambridge: Cambridge University Press, 1999).

22. Copies of other jurisdictions' proceedings can be found in Orange-owned archives across the world.

23. James Anderson, *The New Book of Constitutions of the Most Ancient and Honourable Fraternity of Free and Accepted Masons* (Dublin: Edward Pratt, 1751), p. 137.

24. See Margaret C. Jacob, *Living the Enlightenment: Freemasonry and Politics in Eighteenth-Century Europe* (Oxford: Oxford University Press, 1991).

25. Anderson, *The New Book of Constitutions*, pp. 140–1.

26. Ibid. p. 138.

27. Naomi McAreavey, 'Building bridges? Remembering the 1641 Rebellion in Northern Ireland', *Memory Studies*, 11:1 (2018), pp. 100–14; 'Portadown, 1641: Memory and the 1641 depositions', *Irish University Review*, 47:1 (2017), pp. 15–31.

28. Grand Orange Lodge of Ireland, *Rules and Regulations*, 1800, p. 4.

29. Orange Institution of Ireland, *Laws and Ordinances of the Orange Institution of Ireland. Revised and Adopted by the Grand Orange Lodge of Ireland* (Belfast: News Letter, 1872), p. 12.

30. Loyal Orange Institution of Ireland, *Laws and Ordinances of the Association of Loyal Orangewomen of Ireland* (Dublin: Brother James Forrest, Printers, 1888).

31. David A. Roberts, 'The Orange Order in Ireland: A religious institution?', *The British Journal of Sociology*, 22:3 (1971), p. 276.

32. Grand Orange Lodge of Ireland, *Rules and Regulations*, 1800, p. 5.

33. Ibid. p. 6.

34. Orange Institution of Ireland, *Laws and Ordinances of the Orange Institution of Ireland. Revised and Adopted by the Grand Orange Lodge of Ireland* (Belfast: News Letter, 1872); Orange Institution of Ireland, *Laws and Ordinances of the Orange Institution of Ireland. Revised and Adopted by the Grand Orange Lodge of Ireland, June 3rd, 1896* (Dublin: Br. James Forrest, 1896).

35. Loyal Orange Association of Australia Felix, *Laws and Regulations of the Provincial Grand Lodge of the Loyal Orange Association of Australia Felix, on the registry of the Grand Lodge of Ulster* (Melbourne, 1854); Loyal Orange Association of British America, *Constitution and Laws of the Loyal Orange Association of British America* (Toronto: The Sentinel Print, 1883); Loyal Orange Institution of New Zealand, *Laws and Ordinances of the Orange Institution of New Zealand* (Auckland: Free Press, 1883); Loyal Orange Institution of the United States of America, *Constitution and Laws of the Loyal Orange Institution of the United States of America* (Philadelphia: Protestant Standard Print, 1889).

36. It is used in some Scottish rules and there is an instance in the North Island Orange lodges in New Zealand in 1906, but after this it disappeared with amalgamation in 1908.

37. *Female Orange Association Laws and Ordinances in Connection with The Grand Lodge of the Middle Island of New Zealand* (Christchurch: Caygill and Co., 1888), p. 2.

38. Loyal Orange Institution of England, *Laws and Constitution Enacted by the Grand Lodge of England at Corby 15 September 1995* (London: GOLE, amended 2015), p. 41.

39. Loyal Orange Ladies' Institution, Supreme Grand Lodge (U.S.), *Constitution and By-Laws of the Supreme Grand Lodge of the Loyal Orange Ladies' Institution, Inc. Also Constitution for Subordinate Lodges with Rules of Order, 1996* (Philadelphia: LOLI, 1996), p. 19.

40. *Constitution of the Loyal Orange Institution of New Zealand. Adopted by the Grand Orange Lodge of New Zealand March 1978* (Wellington: LOI, 1978), pp. 1–2.

41. Eyles was born on 15 September 1848 in Field of Mars, Parramatta, New South Wales, and died on 11 March 1892 in Orange, New South Wales.

42. *Victorious Loyal Orange Lodge, No. 40, Dundas, N. S. W. Minute Books, 1870–1936*, MLMSS 2064 (Mitchell Library, State Library of New South Wales, Sydney, Australia), 3 April, 8 May 1876.

43. Her father John Fitzgerald (1816–99) was born in County Cork. Her mother Mary Murphy (1824–1905) was born in County Galway.

44. Certificate of Marriage, Elijah Eyles to Margaret Fitzgerald, 4 March 1876, Registration No. 1876/003779. Births, Deaths and Marriages, Sydney, New South Wales. When Margaret died in 1934, she was buried in a Catholic cemetery in Australia.

45. *Newcastle Morning Herald and Miners' Advocate*, 14 March 1892.

46. Loyal Orange Institution, Supreme Grand Lodge (U.S.), *Constitution–General Laws, Regulations and Rules: Supreme Grand Lodge of the Loyal Orange Institution of the United States of America, Inc. Adopted at 48th Session of the Supreme Grand Lodge August 1940* (Philadelphia: LOI, revised 1964), p. 35.

47. Loyal Orange Institution, Supreme Grand Lodge (U.S.), *Constitution–General Laws, Regulations and Rules: Supreme Grand Lodge of the Loyal Orange Institution of the United States of America, Inc. Adopted at 74th Session of the Supreme Grand Lodge August 1972* (Philadelphia: LOI, revised 1992), p. 35.

48. D. A. J. MacPherson, 'Migration and the female Orange Order: Irish Protestant identity, diaspora and empire in Scotland, 1909–40', *The Journal of Imperial and Commonwealth History*, 40:4 (2012), p. 623.

49. Loyal Orange Ladies' Institution United States of America, *History of the Loyal Orange Ladies' Institution United States of America* (Philadelphia: LOLI, 1944).

50. Loyal Orange Ladies' Institution, *Constitution and By-Laws*.

51. Ladies' Orange Benevolent Association of British America, *Constitution and Laws of the Ladies' Orange Benevolent Association of British America* (Toronto: W. E. Johnston & Co'y Limited, 1920).

52. Loyal Orange Ladies' Institution, *Constitution and By-Laws*, p. 20.

53. LOBA, *Constitution and Laws*, 1920, pp. 27–8.

54. A. S. Russell, *Loyal Orange Institution of Queensland History 1865 to 1932* (Brisbane: Loyal Orange Institution of Queensland, 1933).

55. Grand Orange Lodge of New Zealand, Middle Island, *Report of Proceedings of the Thirty-Ninth Annual Session, 1905* (Christchurch: James Caygill, Printer and Binder, 1905), p. 6.

56. Ibid. p. 12.

57. *Report of Proceedings of the Fifteenth Annual Session of the Grand Orange Lodge of New Zealand. Held in Dunedin, March 31, April 2 and 3, 1923* (Palmerston North: Watson & Eyre, 1923), p. 9.

58. Loyal Orange Institution of New Zealand, *Grand Orange Lodge. Report of Proceedings of the Fifty Fourth Session and 39th Session of Ladies' Conference of the Grand Orange Lodge of New Zealand, Wellington, April 4, 5 and 7, 1980* (Wellington: LOI, 1980); *Report of Proceedings of the Fifty Fifth Session and 40th Session of Ladies' Conference of the Grand Orange Lodge of New Zealand, Hastings, 9–12 April 1982* (Hastings: LOI, 1982).

59. *Watchman*, 19 August 1909.

60. Ibid., 16 September 1909. The Rechabites were a fraternal and friendly society founded in England in 1835. They were in Australia as early as 1843.
61. *The Register*, 22 September 1915.
62. Ibid., 20 September 1919; 20 March 1920.
63. *The Age*, 22 November 1922.
64. Brian Stevenson, *'Stand Fast Together': A History of the Protestant Alliance Friendly Society of Victoria* (Brisbane: Boolarong Press, 1996).
65. Loyal Orange Institution of New Zealand, *Abridged Report Book for the year ended 31st January 1953 and containing Resume of Grand Executive Meetings, Wellington, 10–11 April 1953* (Napier: Swailes Print, 1953), p. 7.
66. Beverley Buist, interview by Patrick Coleman, 11 January 2005, transcript, OHA-5201. Patrick Coleman, *Oral History of the Loyal Orange Institution in the South Island 2004–2005*. OHColl-0791, Alexander Turnbull Library, Wellington, New Zealand. Buist was a former Grand Master of New Zealand.
67. Harland-Jacobs, *Builders of Empire*, p. 18. For a detailed breakdown of Masonic degrees see Jeremiah How, *The Freemason's Manual; or, Illustrations of Masonry, containing, in addition to the rites sanctioned* (London: Simpkin, Marshall & Co., 1862).
68. For a discussion of Freemasonry and brotherhood see Stephen C. Bullock, *Revolutionary Brotherhood: Freemasonry and the Transformation of the American Social Order, 1730–1840* (Chapel Hill: University of North Carolina Press, 1996); Mark C. Carnes, *Secret Ritual and Manhood in Victorian America* (New Haven and London: Yale University Press, 1989); Mary Ann Clawson, *Constructing Brotherhood: Class, Gender, and Fraternalism* (Princeton: Princeton University Press, 1989).
69. Loyal Orange Institution of New South Wales, *Grand Lodge Report for the Year 1880* (Sydney: Samuel E. Lees, 1881), p. 6.
70. *Minutes of Evidence Taken Before the Select Committee of the House of Lords Appointed to Inquire into the State of Ireland: More Particularly with Reference to the Circumstances which May Have Led to Disturbances in that Part of the United Kingdom* (London: House of Commons, 1825), pp. 334–43. This was the evidence by former Orangeman Rev. Holt Waring.
71. David Cargo, 'Part III: The Royal Arch Purple degree', in Cecil S. Kilpatrick, David Cargo and William Murdie (eds), *History of the Royal Arch Purple Order* (Belfast: Royal Arch Purple Order Research Group, 1993), pp. 171–3. Wilson also founded the Protestant Orange Boys in 1792.
72. Cecil S. Kilpatrick, 'Black, Scarlet, Blue, Royal Arch Purple or any other colour', *Ulster Folklife*, 42 (1996), p. 23.
73. *Report of the Proceedings of the Grand Orange Lodge of Ireland at a Meeting Held at No. 3, Stephen's-Green, North Dublin, on the 14th, 15th, 16th, 17th, 18th and 20th November 1848* (Dublin: LOI, 1848).

74. Their degrees are Royal Black, Royal Scarlet, Royal Mark, Apron and Royal Blue, Royal White, Royal Green, Gold Crown, Gold Star and Garter, Crimson Arrow, Gold Link and Chain, and Red Cross.

75. *Forms to be Observed by Dominion Grand Chapter and Private Preceptories for Invitation, Dedication, Installation of Officers and Diagrams of Halls* (Christchurch: Cyril E. Rose, Printer, 1928), pp. 159–66. The Red Cross degree focused on the death and resurrection of Jesus, whereas all the previous degrees had their foundation in the Old Testament.

76. Ibid.

77. *Constitution and Laws of the Loyal Orange Association of British North America* (Toronto: Sign of the Golden Sun, 1859), p. 8.

78. *Constitution and Laws of the Loyal Orange Association of British North America Including the Act of Incorporation. Assented to, April 24th 1890 By an Act of the Parliament of Canada. Amended 1st Session 15th Parliament 16–17 George V, 1926. Laws and Rules relating to real Property of the Association* (Toronto: Grand Lodge, revised 2015), p. 22.

79. Loyal Orange Association of British America, *Report of the Proceedings of the One Hundred and Twentieth Meeting of the Grand Orange Lodge of British America: Held at St John's, Newfoundland, 22nd and 23rd June 1950* (Toronto: Grand Lodge, 1950), p. 18.

80. Ibid. p. 19.

81. Patrick Coleman, '"In harmony": A comparative view of female Orangeism 1887–2000', in Angela McCarthy (ed.), *Ireland in the World: Comparative, Transnational, and Personal Perspectives* (London and New York: Routledge, 2015), p. 127.

82. Ibid. p. 129.

83. Loyal Orange Grand Council of Australasia, *Ritual–Female. For the Opening and Closing of Lodges and the Initiation of Members into the Orange Degree* (Adelaide: L. J. McBride Print, 1913), p. 22.

84. Grand Orange Lodge of Scotland, *Ladies' Loyal Orange Association: Ritual of Introduction/Ritual Second Degree* (Glasgow: George Watt, Printers, 1955); Ladies' Orange Benevolent Association of British America, *Ritual: First Degree. Second Degree* (Toronto: The Sentinel Print, 1894).

85. Clement XII, *In Eminenti Apostolatus Specula* (Papal Bull) 28 April 1738, *Papal Encyclicals Online*, <https://www.papalencyclicals.net/Clem12/c12 inemengl.htm> (accessed 1 December 2023).

86. Leo XIII, *Humanum Genus* (Papal Bull) 20 April 1884, *Papal Encyclicals Online*, <https://www.papalencyclicals.net/leo13/l13human.htm> (accessed 19 May 2023).

87. One book focused on the sex life of Pope Pius IX. Léo Taxil, *Pie IX Devant l'Histoire: Sa Vie Politique et Pontificale Ses Débauches, Ses Folies, Ses Crimes* (Paris: Librairie Anti-Cléricale, 1883).

88. David Allen Harvey, 'Lucifer in the city of light: The Palladium hoax and "diabolical causality" in fin de siècle France', *Magic, Ritual, and Witchcraft*, 1:2 (2006), pp. 177–206.

89. Ruben van Luijk, *Children of Lucifer: The Origins of Modern Religious Satanism* (New York: Oxford University Press, 2016), p. 226.

90. H. W. Cleary, *The Orange Society* (Melbourne: Bernard King & Sons, 1897); E. Lewis, *Orangeism Exposed* (Melbourne: Advocate Office, 1900). Lewis was Chaplain of Loyal Campbell Orange Lodge, No. 130, Collingwood, Melbourne.

91. For more detail on Slattery see Patrick J. Coleman, 'Transplanted Irish Institutions: Orangeism and Hibernianism in New Zealand 1877–1910' (MA, University of Canterbury, 1993), pp. 103–7.

92. Donald M. MacRaild, 'Transnationalising "anti-Popery": Militant Protestant preachers in the nineteenth-century Anglo-world', *Journal of Religious History*, 39:2 (2015), pp. 224–43.

93. *Victorian Standard*, 30 June 1899. There was anticipation in Australia of this tour boosting Orange Order membership.

94. Lewis, *Orangeism Exposed*, pp. 7–14. According to Lewis he was expelled from the Orange Order in Victoria.

95. *New Zealand Tablet*, 29 March 1900.

96. W. J. McK. McCormick, *Christ, the Christian and Freemasonry* (Belfast: W. J. McK. McCormick, 1977).

97. Ian Meredith and Brian Kennaway, *The Orange Order: An Evangelical Perspective* (Meredith & Kennaway, 1993).

98. Ibid. p. 12.

99. W. P. Malcomson, *Behind Closed Doors: The Hidden Structure within the Orange Camp* (Banbridge: Evangelical Truth, 1999).

100. Ibid. p. 129.

101. R. Johnstone, *Behind Closed Minds: An Examination of the Book 'Behind Closed Doors'* (Grand Royal Arch Purple Chapter of Ireland, c. 2000).

102. *The Observer*, 24 October 1999.

103. 'Evangelical Truth', <www.evangelicaltruth.com> (accessed 5 November 2023).

104. *Popery Proved Paganism* (New Plymouth, NZ: Taranaki Daily News, n.d.).

3

Orange Activism:
Politics, Propagation and Benevolence

I would advise the delegates to get in touch and study some of our Political and Educational questions at the present time. Our opponents and enemies to our Flag and Freedom are ever busy and use every means and every opportunity to gain a controlling hand in our Government and in the Education of our children. The alteration of the English Prayer Book is in the interest of the Roman Catholic Church, and is certainly a menace to our Protestant Faith. I would urge every member of the Ladies' Lodges to use all her influence, all her power, and every vote in placing the right men on your local government bodies, on your school committee, and in our Parliament.[1]

This call to action, from Scottish-born Grand Master Isaac McFarlane (1870–1953) at the New Zealand Ladies' Grand Chapter Annual Conference in 1927, exemplified the type of activism that both Orangemen and Orangewomen engaged in: strategic voting in local and national elections.[2] The loyalism espoused here, to be actively involved in politics with an anti-Catholic stance, was shared across the Orange world. The threefold call, to loyalism for the country, guarding against the encroachment of the Catholic Church and the action required to maintain the place of reformed Protestantism in society, is evident. The missing components from McFarlane's call were the platforms to propagate their message and their involvement in benevolence.

Research on the Orange Order's forays into activism primarily focuses on the political realm and benevolence. Within the political realm is a focus on two common threads: Home Rule and unionism, especially in Ireland and later Northern Ireland. The issue of Home Rule has produced many studies. Often the focus has been on the Orange Order's contribution as a staunch opponent to Home Rule. Tied to this were the political meetings and sometimes riots that ensued. However, the Orange Order was feeding into a broader debate to such an extent that other Protestants who shared their anti-Home Rule stance did not feel the need to join the Orange Order. The Orange Order figures prominently in the Home Rule narrative, with Ulster and Canada being the focus of many studies.[3]

The second political issue with which scholars of the Orange Order concern themselves is unionism, particularly concerning Northern Ireland. Research has generally focused on the forging of links between the Orange Order and the Ulster Unionist Party (UUP), and the subsequent separation of the two.[4] There have been some histories on unionism that have tried to redress the balance by including the role of women.[5] However, this has generally focused on Ireland and has meant that the Orange diaspora has been largely ignored except for Canada and New Zealand. Outside of this, the impression is of a male-dominated Orange Order heavily involved in maintaining the Protestant hegemony in Ireland.

The second key area of activism within the Orange Order is benevolence, but most scholars have only mentioned this in passing. This is notable in research into Protestant orphan homes or orphanages but the influence and focus has not been on the Orange Order.[6] The most striking exceptions are in the work of Donald MacRaild and D. A. J. MacPherson. Together they have noted the activism of ladies' lodges in England, particularly in the Tyneside area, while MacPherson also focuses on Scotland and Canada.[7] MacPherson has emphasised Orangewomen's diverse public activities such as fundraising and involvement in political campaigns against Home Rule. He has argued that this activism helped Scottish Orangewomen to fulfil their desire to be fully active within the Orange Order and to justify the formation of ladies' lodges. MacRaild, meanwhile, devoted an entire chapter to money and mutualism in northern England, but only briefly mentioned the charitable aspects of the Orange lodges.[8] Instead, he argued that the Orange Order had tried to compete with the other friendly societies in offering benefits to their members, but were never as successful. He also views these attempts as a 'craving for respectability' due to the Orange Order being seen as bigoted and violent.[9] In aligning themselves with the activities of organisations offering benefits, the Orange Order sought to deal with their 'image problem'.

Another key area of activism within the Orange Order that scholars have largely neglected is the propagation of the Orange Order's message. Generally, the focus has been on the activities of the Orange Order, not how they disseminate their message.[10] This chapter will seek to fill this gap in the research and provide a broader overview of change over time in the methods the Orange Order used to promote their message. Moving to the present day and the use of digital platforms by the Orange Order demonstrates their adaptation to changes in modern society. The use of benevolence is argued as a form of activism. This activism was how members activated their Orange-tinged Protestant faith by looking after orphans or fundraising for 'suitable' causes tied into these beliefs.

The overriding focus of this chapter is to examine how the Orange Order was and still is actively involved in society. The first section deals with how the Orange diaspora used Protestant associations as a conduit to broaden their anti-Catholic message. There is also a discussion of the 2014 Scottish referendum as the most recent and public display of activism by the Orange Order in recent years. The second section delves into the methods of propagating the Orange message. These include the transition from the use of old-fashioned meetings or print media to digital platforms to promote the anti-Catholic message and to showcase Orange activities. Finally, private and public aspects of Orange benevolence are examined, encompassing benefits to members locally, charitable giving to members transnationally, and altruism within wider society. The emphasis in this chapter is to discuss the attempts by the Orange Order to bring its core beliefs, forged in the privacy of the lodges, into the public realm.

POLITICS

The Orange Order's involvement in political issues harks back to its origins as a fraternal movement formed out of the sectarian conflict in 1790s Ireland. While the Orange Order's day-to-day focus is on its fraternal activities, its ideology is by nature political. The very basis of the Orange Order is enshrined in its *Laws and Ordinances*:

> The Institution is composed of Protestants, united and resolved to the utmost of their power to support and defend the rightful Sovereign, the Protestant Religion, the Laws of the Realm, the Legislative Union, and the Succession to the Throne in the House of Brunswick, BEING PROTESTANT; and united further for the defence of their own Persons and Properties, and the Maintenance of the Public Peace.[11]

This conditional loyalty to the British Crown being Protestant might seem to be simply about religion, but this is not solely about passively supporting the monarchy. The clear statement that they do not just support but also defend implies united activism on the part of members. In their 'Qualifications of an Orangeman', they further stipulate that

> An Orangeman should ... uphold, and defend the Protestant religion ... he should strenuously oppose the fatal errors and doctrines of the Church of Rome ... he should, by all lawful means, resist the ascendancy of that Church, its encroachments, and the extension of its power.[12]

This last point about opposing 'the fatal errors and doctrines of the Church of Rome' and resisting it meant more than simply having a set of stated aims or, in this case, qualifications for members. It is framed as 'active' participation. This type of political and religious rhetoric was not exclusive to the Orange Order. The origin of these beliefs lies in the Reformation and the rise of Protestantism. In England, Protestant associations have played a role in politics since Elizabethan times. They were later resurrected in the eighteenth century and were active in Scotland.[13] Each time one was formed the focus of the political association was on opposing the political changes that gave Roman Catholics more rights under the law. This, in turn, sparked the forming of these pressure groups to reverse the legislation. While these early Protestant associations pre-date the Orange Order, they also shared some of the concerns that some Protestants had against possible Roman Catholic or other external threats. This defensive aspect of these Protestant associations laid the foundation for the Orange Order to feed into a historical narrative that many Protestants were familiar with. When the Orange Order in Britain and Ireland was dissolved in 1835, Protestant associations were resurrected in these same countries.[14] These new associations had a definite 'Orange' flavour as they were formed to replace the disestablished Orange lodges. Often the leadership came from the recently dissolved Orange Order. This demonstrates the pan-Protestant aspect of the Orange Order that attracted members and sympathisers to the cause.

The United States also had a similarly named Protestant Association, which was mostly anti-Catholic in focus. On 8 November 1842 in Philadelphia, a group of Protestant ministers formed the American Protestant Association.[15] This organisation was quite defiant in declaring 'we believe the system of Popery to be, in its principles and tendency, subversive of civil and religious liberty'.[16] The use of 'civil and religious liberty' echoed the catchcry of the Orange Order, who used this as one of their foundational principles. Their focus was on upholding the principles of the Reformation and promoting the 'open Bible' as a means of educating the public against the 'errors' of the Roman Catholic Church. While these claims seem more religious than political, the group tapped into the same concerns that the Orange Order espoused. These included the fear of the Roman Catholic Church gaining power within the United States. The American Protestant Association also shared the American Orange Order's whites-only policy. At a meeting in 1873 of the Grand Lodge of the American Protestant Association, there was a case of two 'colored men' being illegally initiated into the organisation who needed to 'peaceably withdraw, and establish an Order of their own'.[17] The Orange links to the American Protestant Association weakened in the 1880s as the American Orange Order grew in strength and helped to develop the newly formed American Protective Association (APA).[18]

The APA was formed in 1887. This new organisation, while nativist in focus, did not bar membership to the foreign-born. A contemporary description of its membership claimed it was 'very cosmopolitan' since it was made up of Canadians, English, Germans, Irish Orangemen and many other Europeans.[19] Orangeman William J. H. Traynor led the APA from 1894 to 1896.[20] He had the perfect blend of the so-called Scots-Irish identity with Scottish paternal and Irish maternal lineage.[21] At the time he assumed the role of Supreme President of the APA, he was still Grand Master of the State Grand Orange Lodge of Michigan. While in this dual role he sent a report to his fellow Orangemen in Michigan. His report encapsulated the spirit of the American Orange Order at the time. He believed that many native-born Americans wanted to join the Orange Order as they knew it was 'neither an English nor an Irish organization – as our enemies would have them believe – but a cosmopolitan institution'. Interestingly, this last comment echoed the contemporary observer's description of the APA. He added that although the Orange Order was 'not nominally a political organization' it had to get involved as there were 'issues' where the objects of their institution could be furthered.[22]

Traynor's involvement in the APA was an outworking of the political involvement to further the aims of both organisations. There was a visceral hatred of Catholics by Traynor that included his references to keeping the 'scum of Europe' out of America and also blocking former Catholics from joining lodges in Michigan.[23] The 'scum' were Catholic immigrants to America. At their Grand Lodge, it was asked if they could initiate a man who was raised as a Catholic but renounced that faith thirty years ago. The curt answer was 'No. Not eligible if ever a Romanist.'[24] This was not the norm anywhere in the Orange diaspora as a potential candidate could always be admitted on the proof of their regular attendance at a Protestant church. The APA was a vehemently anti-Catholic nativist organisation and had a political agenda to promote Protestantism and deal with the perceived Catholic threat. The involvement in politics by the APA was notable in the national and local election campaigns.[25] The link between the APA and the Orange Order lay in much of the leadership and membership of the APA coming from the Orange Order.

In other Orange jurisdictions, the Orange Order took an active part in political issues both locally and nationally. Sometimes the apparatus of the Orange Order was not suited to the complexities of the local situation. A more straightforward path to activism was either partnering with other political movements or individual Orange members being the catalyst for these movements. A good transnational example of this was the Orange Order in Canada and the United States who continued their partnering with other prominent nativist organisations, particularly, in the 1920s and 1930s, the Ku Klux Klan. The Ku Klux Klan and the Orange Order had shared ideals of anti-immigrant and anti-Catholic rhetoric. There was cross-border cooperation within and between these organisations. Maine and New Brunswick stand out as examples of push-back against perceived Catholic influence in education and society. While the claim of a 150,000 Ku Klux Klan in Maine at its peak is likely to be an inflated figure, it does demonstrate that the Orange Order was looking to partner with a substantial nativist organisation so that they could promulgate the loyalist Protestant message.[26] There was also the campaign to stop bilingualism in New Brunswick as speaking French was seen as undermining the 'British heritage' and culture of this region. New Brunswick had a large population of American loyalists who fled after the War of Independence and they wanted to create an ideal society with their British Empire roots within a colonial context. There was crossover membership between organisations that helped to fuel their respective organisations and agendas.[27] This cooperation ceased once this version of the Ku Klux Klan no longer operated.

In Australia, particularly Sydney, there was a strong base of Orange involvement in political issues. One of the sparks for this was the attempted assassination of Queen Victoria's son, Prince Alfred, on 12 March 1868 at Clontarf in New South Wales. The perpetrator, Dublin-born Henry O'Farrell, initially made the false claim that he was acting under orders from Australian-based Fenians. Although found to be mentally unwell and an alcoholic, he was hanged on 21 April 1868. This led to a wave of anti-Irish and anti-Catholic hysteria. In the same month as the assassination attempt, the New South Wales Protestant Political Association (NSWPPA) formed, with members drawn from the Orange lodges.[28] The NSWPPA's primary objective was to help get 'gentlemen of known liberal Protestant principles' into parliament and also to seek the abolition of state aid for 'religious purposes'. It was in their manifesto that the true nature of this political association revealed itself. The NSWPPA drew heavily on Orange rhetoric to state their overarching aims of 'undying hostility to Romanism; fearless action in the exposure of its designs; inflexible resistance to its encroachments [and] support of the British throne and Constitution'.[29] Despite what should have been a potent political platform, they had still lost their impetus by the late nineteenth century.

Sometimes there were transnational links in the formation of political entities with an Orange impetus. In June 1901 Irish-born William Marcus Dill Macky (1849–1913), who was both a Presbyterian minister and Grand Chaplain of the Orange Order in New South Wales, founded and was the first President of the Australian Protestant Defence Association (APDA). Dill Macky acknowledged the defunct NSWPPA in his opening speech.[30] A key plank in the APDA's objectives was 'to preserve and defend the general interests of Protestantism against the encroachments of Roman Catholicism in matters religious, political, social, and commercial'.[31] The APDA had around 135 branches across Australia and claimed a membership of 22,000 by 1904. Across the Tasman Sea, a Protestant Defence Association was established in Dunedin, New Zealand, in May 1903.[32] There was a reference to it being 'somewhat on the lines of those founded by the Rev. Dill Mackey [sic] in New South Wales'.[33] To further emphasise the need for the Association, there were comments on the 'disturbances' Dill Macky encountered at his meetings in Australia.[34] The founding members were drawn heavily from the local Orange lodge, with local Protestant ministers who were also Orange chaplains and other Grand Masters.[35] This Orange influence was reflected in the Protestant Defence Association's membership despite its claims to be a separate entity. While the organisation spread to the main centres in New Zealand, by 1907 there were only disparaging remarks in some local newspapers, which asked, 'was there not some such Association down here?'[36]

The transnational influence of the APDA is evident in it providing the impetus for its New Zealand counterpart, along with visits to New Zealand by Dill Macky to promote the organisation.[37] Yet ultimately it did not last. Likely reasons for its failure were the lack of public appetite for sectarianism before World War I and the reliance on the existing Orange Order for membership. Once circumstances changed with a world war, New Zealand had their Protestant Political Association (PPA), backed and supported by their Orange Order. However, despite the PPA's rise it also inevitably petered out after the end of World War I.[38] The social and political climate had changed. These associations fed on fear and anti-Catholic sentiment in the general population. Once these conditions were absent, the Orange Order likewise failed to maintain membership, and their associate organisations ceased to function.

The examples of political activism by the Orange Order in Canada, the United States, Australia and New Zealand have so far focused on upholding their Protestant belief with a strain of anti-Catholic rhetoric. However, activism from these other organisations, like the Protestant associations, failed to outlive the Orange Order. In contrast to this, the Orange Order in Northern Ireland has had a longer-lasting political impact. It held significant political influence in the period from 1921 through to 1972 when all six Prime Ministers were members of the UUP and the Orange Order.[39] Once the 100-year ties between the groups were severed in March 2005, this influence lessened.[40] This was notable in the following months with the UK general election in 2005 that saw the rise of the Democratic Unionist Party (DUP). The *Orange Standard* opined that 'for Orangemen . . . the great desire is still for a single Unionist party'.[41] In recent years, numbers in the Orange Order have plummeted to such an extent that their political sway is no longer as important as it was in the past. With the loss of many UUP seats in Northern Ireland, the DUP are now the leading unionist party. Despite the split, ordinary Orange members provide roughly 35 per cent of the membership for each party.[42] Therefore, while the Orange Order's overall membership has reduced, they still provide significant support for both parties.

Across the sea in Scotland, the political influence of the Orange Order remains significant, as shown by the Scottish referendum on independence in 2014. One of the prime backers of the referendum was the Scottish Nationalist Party (SNP), which is seen as a more radical party by those on the right of politics. While the result of the vote on 18 September 2014 was to keep the status quo, the role of the Orange Order in Scotland on this issue is noteworthy. In the lead-up to the referendum, the *Orange Torch*, the main news platform of the Loyal Orange Institution of Scotland (LOIS), fed members a diet of articles against Scottish independence and exposed what they felt were the inadequacies of the 'Yes' vote.[43] The main target was Alex Salmond, leader of the SNP and leading proponent of independence.[44]

In a move to try and be contemporary, the LOIS promoted stickers in the shape of hearts with 'love the UK' designs. Their purpose was to show the separatists that they were proud to be 'Scottish and British'.[45]

The combination here is vital as LOIS members identified as Scottish but also emphasised their British identity, thereby affirming their commitment to the Union and, in turn, to the British Crown. They also displayed posters on walls and windows declaring 'Scotland Says No to Separatism'.[46] In the lead-up to referendum day the LOIS held an anti-independence march in Edinburgh to demonstrate their 'pro-unionist' strength. Some newspapers claimed that up to 15,000 Orangemen from Scotland, Northern Ireland and particularly England took part.[47] The media coverage had a gender bias as it often noted 'Orangemen' and yet photographs featured Orangewomen too. The Orangewomen were relegated to the role of 'supporters' in many reports, or described simply as 'a group of women in white dresses'.[48] Yet, in all cases, the Orangewomen were identifiable wearing their Orange collarettes. The march attracted a large crowd, but the Better Together campaign leader Alistair Darling disowned them, saying, 'They are nothing to do with us.'[49]

This distancing from the Orange Order by the leader of the 'No' campaign, which the Orange Order supported, prompted a response from the *Orange Torch*. It ran an article entitled 'Better Together: Unless You're Orange, of Course'.[50] This article pulled no punches in noting how the Better Together campaign organisers ignored advice and even dissuaded any volunteers from the LOIS. The article outlined the army of Orange volunteers who continued to help despite the snub and how their efforts through the Edinburgh march brought the campaign to life. David Bryce, Orange archivist and historian, claimed Orangemen and Orangewomen carried out their activities 'in a quiet but enthusiastic and efficient manner, against a backdrop of an aggressive campaign by the "Yes" camp, which on occasion was intimidating and threatening'.[51] The article continued: 'Who saved the Union? It surely wasn't Better Together, whose lacklustre efforts looked pathetically amateurish against the glossy appeal of the "Yes" campaign.' The Orange Order claimed the victory and noted at the end, 'Don't expect to be thanked, just quietly satisfied.'[52] In an expression of transnational support, the *Orange Torch* received letters from supporters in Scotland as well as England and Australia maintaining that the Orange Order had saved the Union.[53]

Events such as this demonstrate that the Orange Order considered itself a much-maligned institution that receives little credit for its actions but manages to get results regardless of opposition. In the political arena, whether fighting the encroachments of the Catholic Church, local and national elections or activity around the referendum, the Orange Order views its actions as maintaining liberty for all, even if others do not share its particular worldview. Overall, the Orange Order in Scotland had little influence on the referendum. Their strength and influence are not as they once were. There is the added factor of Protestant churches, particularly the evangelical ones, not supporting them. Also, Scottish society in general is no longer as religious and the focus is on being a civic society. The sectarianism in Scotland was often associated with the Orange Order and there was a low tolerance for it.[54]

PROPAGATION

Public Lectures/Meetings

Just like politics, propagation of their message is a fundamental aspect of the Orange Order. Their core beliefs of 'civil and religious liberty', as outlined in their *Laws and Ordinances*, necessitate the dissemination of their ideology to like-minded members of the public. The idea of propagation is to promote and educate members from young to old in the beliefs of the Orange Order: 'An Orangeman should ... sincerely desire and endeavour to propagate its doctrines and precepts ... and diligently train up his offspring, and all under his control, in the fear of God, and in the Protestant faith.'[55]

The message of propagating doctrines was espoused through the Imperial Grand Orange Council, a platform for delegates from around the Orange world to share and discuss matters of importance to the Orange Order. John J. Bond, Grand Master of the Loyal Orange Institution of the United States of America, speaking at the Council in 1873, urged members to recommend that a 'course of lectures upon the principles of Orangeism be delivered under the auspices of the various Orange lodges universally'.[56] This was supported at the next Council in 1876 with a resolution from Rev. Gustavus Carson, who proclaimed 'many good men who wished well to the Order, kept aloof from us through misconceptions of our principles or erroneous impressions'.[57] This last point is crucial as it encapsulates the image problem that has dogged the Orange Order since its inception. The perception of the Orange Order as a bigoted or even hate group akin to the Ku Klux Klan has never been far from public view. Educating Orange Order members and the wider community by a variety of mediums was therefore essential.

The Order's medium of dissemination could take many forms from instruction in their private lodge meetings to publishing and distributing their beliefs through the print media. The simplest method in the early years, particularly in the nineteenth and early twentieth centuries, was to hold public meetings. Besides the annual July and November celebrations, there were other times when the Orange Order made use of the public meetings or special lectures to broadcast their message. There were political public meetings such as those seeking to influence the issue of Home Rule for Ireland. For example, in 1893 in Belfast, the Orange Order held a large meeting to protest against Home Rule. In the same year, in Sydney, Australia, Orangemen held similar meetings.[58] These meetings drew crowds of non-members, which provided the Orange Order with the opportunity to inform potential members of the Order's principles.

One of the many ways to promote Orange beliefs about the 'encroachments' of the Catholic Church was through the stories of escaped nuns and former priests. There are numerous examples of these former Catholic religious clergy, some real and some fraudulent. Stories of their lives proved a popular form of promoting Orange ideas during lecture tours by these individuals around England, Canada, the United States, Australia and New Zealand.[59] They had a chance not only to present the reason why Catholicism was a tyrannical form of Christianity but also to bolster membership of Orange lodges in the countries where these 'lecturers' visited. Among the many examples of these former Catholic clergy was Irish-born Edith O'Gorman (1842–1929). She famously 'escaped' from the confines of a convent in the United States before converting to Protestantism and writing an exposé of convent life.[60] O'Gorman initially lectured in America and Canada, and then toured England from 1881 to 1885.[61]

While in England O'Gorman was promoted by the English Orange Order, who used her 'experiences' as a platform for their anti-Catholic rhetoric. Her tour met with resistance from the local Catholic Irish, who heckled and attacked those at her meetings. The Orange lodges acted as enforcers with the police in dealing with the crowds.[62] In this sense, they were fulfilling their Orange duty to uphold the civil and religious liberty of Protestantism. Nearing the end of her English lecture series at Coventry, in 1885, O'Gorman attempted to speak several times before the crowd rushed the platform, with O'Gorman 'dexterously escaping by the platform door'.[63] Depending on the perspective at the time, her meetings were seen as either vindicating the violent and problematic nature of Roman Catholicism or simply stirring up sectarian strife.

Her tour of England and the trouble that followed it were not a deterrent to the Orange Order in Australia and New Zealand. They saw her lecture series as a perfect way to propagate their Orange ideals.

Figure 3.1 Front pages of two editions of Edith O'Gorman's book (O'Gorman, *Trials and persecutions of Miss Edith O'Gorman*, 1871 & 1913)

The Grand Master of the Grand Lodge of New Zealand (North Island), David Goldie, invited O'Gorman to New Zealand in 1885.[64] In his annual address, he noted her 'good work in England and Scotland in exposing the evils of Convent life'.[65] In New Zealand, O'Gorman was warmly received by her audiences. She gave general lectures as well as a 'ladies only' session.[66] Her lecture to a large crowd of women was described as an 'eloquent address, in which pathos and humour were blended, lasting nearly two hours, and the fair auditory wept, laughed, and applauded by turns'.[67] O'Gorman's lecture series throughout New Zealand was mostly uneventful apart from a rather theatrical debate in Dunedin.[68] This was in stark contrast to the heckling and abuse and physical threats of violence which had occurred in England.[69] The Grand Orange Lodge of New South Wales also invited O'Gorman to speak after her New Zealand visit, where her tour was similar to her English experience.[70] O'Gorman was boycotted, and halls often rejected her lectures. There was a riot at Lismore.[71] Despite the troubles with the Australian tour, however, they only reinforced the view of the Catholic Church trying to shut down any voice of dissent. A possible explanation for the lack of physical violence and open disruptions in New Zealand was a decision by the Catholic hierarchy to simply ignore her. This is best summed up by a correspondent from the *New Zealand Tablet*, who stated that O'Gorman had been in Auckland for a number of weeks.

she [O'Gorman] had been pouring out all the filth in her capacious vocabulary on popes, bishop, priests, and nuns in general, and on Irish 'papists' in particular, and moved all the powers of earth and hell for that purpose. But her thundering has vanished into thin air, and the only mementoes left to record her visit are the empty purses of her credulous deluded patrons.[72]

The lectures of former religious clergy like O'Gorman gave the Orange diaspora a platform to promote their views. These views drew on a large body of anti-Catholic literature that was common in Protestantism, and therefore the Orange Order endeavoured to attract other like-minded Protestants to their fraternity. The mixture of violence and vitriol by both Catholic and Protestant crowds at these events reinforced already entrenched views. These visits did bolster membership, but it was never sustainable. Eventually, the Orange Order had to look for other means of promoting their views.

Print

One of the most common ways that the Orange Order tried to disseminate their views on a range of topics important to them was through the print media. This, however, created its own problems as some newspapers were hostile to the Orange Order and there are plenty of instances of editorial comment that was scathing of their ideals. Grand Lodges in various countries had to deal with this in a number of ways. Either they had to identify a newspaper sympathetic to them or they had to create their own newspapers. This latter option was fraught with difficulty due to publishing costs and the need to maintain a solid subscription base.

In the case of the north of Ireland in the early days, Orange members supported a sympathetic newspaper. This was a companion to the *Belfast News Letter* (or the *News Letter*) called the *Belfast Weekly News*. Published weekly from 1855, it provided members locally and overseas with news about Orange meetings and other Orange related activities. The *Belfast Weekly News* has been identified as a useful historical source to demonstrate the maintenance of transnational networks by Orange members.[73] The paper served members well until 1973 when the Grand Orange Lodge of Ireland decided to establish their own newspaper, the *Orange Standard*, in response to what they felt was the 'one-sided propaganda which was emanating from republican circles about Northern Ireland in the early 1970s'.[74] The purpose of the newspaper was not only to put 'across the Protestant and Unionist perspective', but to also reach a wider audience beyond their membership base.

While the Orange Order in Ireland and later Northern Ireland relied
for many years on sympathetic newspapers, the situation was mixed in
the Orange diaspora. The desire by the Orange diaspora to have their
own newspapers to propagate their message was strong but they sometimes struggled to be financially viable. New Zealand provides a good
case study of the struggle to create this 'voice' in disseminating Orange
rhetoric to the local population. The *Nation* newspaper was founded
in 1906 and that same year was made the official organ of the Grand
Orange Lodge of New Zealand (North Island). The paper had a standard format with sensationalist news about a set range of topics, notably
the Roman Catholic Church, events in Ireland, and the Bible in Schools
debate in New Zealand. There were also reports from various Orange
lodges around New Zealand as well as lists of lodges and contact details.
Most advertising came from regalia and emblems sellers, and businesses
run by members. The paper also promoted various texts, mostly focusing on the Catholic Church and its violent history and the writings of
former nuns and priests.

Within two years, however, it was already running at a loss.[75] There
was a push by the Grand Executive to promote the paper, and at every
Grand Lodge session there was an appeal to members to support it.
Irish-born Grand Master John Middleton (1860–1937) noted in his
annual report in 1909 that the Australian lodges had success through
The Sentinel and *Watchman* newspapers. He therefore urged members
to support the *Nation* and 'by doing so, we will soon have a real good
paper in which to ventilate our cause'.[76] However, not until 1911 did it
become the official organ for the amalgamated Grand Orange Lodges.[77]
By 1916 there were still problems, with Grand Master Alexander
Donald noting that only 20 per cent of 'active Orangemen in New
Zealand' were subscribers.[78] The *Nation* was given a boost with the
rise of the Protestant Political Association, whose stories dominated the
paper. However, this only attracted criticism in 1918 by Grand Master
J. A. Hay, who claimed that 'during the past year it has been published
more perhaps in the interests of the Protestant Political Association
than the LOI'.[79] In 1970, only a few years before its demise, there were
further signs of decay at the annual sessions of the GOLNZ. A short
report outlined the difficulties of the *Nation*, along with the startling
revelation that the majority of subscribers were members of the public
and not members of the Orange Order.[80] By the end of 1971 the paper
had ceased to exist.

The lack of support from Orange members was evident throughout the
paper's existence, yet the closure of the *Nation* left a gap in the reporting

of Orange activities in New Zealand. The Order's Public Questions Committee in 1972 lamented this lack of a platform and immediately started to claim they needed a newspaper or journal that could reach members who rarely attended meetings to 'publicise our ideals and activities to the public as well'.[81] By 1975, the Grand Executive initiated a replacement called *Orange News*, which was lauded as 'stimulating added interest in the Lodges'.[82] This paper continues to be the main source of reporting on lodge activities and other issues relevant to the Orange Order in New Zealand.

The troubled history of the *Nation* highlights the ongoing problems that the Orange Order, particularly in the Orange diaspora, has faced, that is, how to disseminate its message both to members and to the wider community. Having one's own newspaper or magazine does provide a level of control over the content, but cost and resources are always an issue. This was a problem that many of the Grand Lodges around the world have encountered and continue to encounter. The solution to some of these problems has come in the form of new technology.

DIGITAL MEDIA

Throughout the world the Orange Order still uses print media, public meetings and lectures to promote its ideas. However, changes in the use of technology in wider society have prompted various Grand Orange Lodges to enter the digital age. What worked in the nineteenth and twentieth centuries no longer reaches a broad audience. Early adopters in creating basic websites were the Irish, Canadian, English and Scottish Grand Lodges. Also, one of the early influencers in reaching out to Orange members across the globe was the website OrangeNet. Based at an address in Newtownards, County Down, Northern Ireland, the aims of OrangeNet were to

> [p]romote the global nature of the Orange Order and to provide comprehensive coverage of its historical, cultural and religious aspects; [t]o provide a central resource for Orange Order web sites and help improve wider access to individual lodge sites; and to [b]ring a better standard of design, presentation and professionalism to existing web pages.[83]

OrangeNet began in 1999, and the lofty ideals of promoting global Orangeism created the opportunity to spread the Orange message to existing and potential members. OrangeNet created a platform for many lodges across the world to have an online presence at a time when the internet was a new medium for people in general. For example, in the initial stages, there were only two Canadian, one American and one Scottish district lodge on the site. Eventually, as more lodges saw the opportunity, they created websites.[84]

Initially, all seemed to be going well, and the Orange Order had a global presence that was more easily accessible than previous print media or public meetings that required a physical presence.[85] In 2003 and 2006 the activities of OrangeNet eventually came to the attention of the Imperial Orange Council. There was a problem occurring in Australia surrounding the use of the platform to 'spread malicious rumours and gossip about certain respected members' as well as communicating confidential lodge business. Some members were therefore undermining the Orange Order in Australia through OrangeNet. There was a further claim of the site being used to promote the Independent Orange Order in Australia. In a later session of the Imperial Orange Council, there was a discussion about this report from Australia. There were comments that the internet is a 'dangerous tool', and that some members on OrangeNet had a 'vendetta' against the Orange Order in Australia. What eventually transpired was that all of these comments were happening on the 'O lists' or chat-rooms. One voice of reason suggested that OrangeNet was fine, but it was just the chat-rooms that were troublesome.[86] The OrangeNet example demonstrates that the move to a digital world with people having a platform to express contrary opinions is not easy to control. In the past, the Orange Order could expel members for this kind of behaviour, but it was now much harder in an online environment to control members. OrangeNet ceased to operate around 2012.

The Grand Lodges continue to spend much time updating and adding value to their websites. A perusal of these sites shows that they have adapted to the modern age in providing a wealth of content. For instance, the front pages of the websites of the Grand Orange Lodges of Ireland and Scotland have a modern appearance, with colourful pictures and stories that could attract the reader to click to see more.[87] Just like many modern businesses, the Orange Order also has Twitter, Facebook, YouTube and Flickr accounts. Paper-based newspapers still exist, such as the *Orange Standard* for Northern Ireland and the *Orange Torch* for Scotland. In the case of the *Orange Standard*, it has undergone an overhaul with a move to full colour since 2010. Apart from other sales, over 5,000 copies are printed for lodges and individuals. In 2017, it moved to a digital format.[88]

In a similar vein, the Scottish Grand Lodge has the *Orange Torch*, in full colour since 2006. Reporting on this at the Imperial Orange

Council, the Grand Secretary of the GOLS noted that their relationship with the media had been cultivated and now had 'more fair and objective coverage than formerly'. For instance, the Grand Master had interviews with Catholic newspapers like the *Scottish Catholic Observer*.[89] The Orange Order in Scotland, as with Northern Ireland, has also digitised its paper. The *Orange Torch* is also hosted by the Canadian Orange Order on their website. This reflects the close ties of Canadian members with their Scottish brethren. Having an online presence means they can inform readers of what they do and promote their events, history and viewpoint on a range of news items.

The personalisation of content helps to maintain a bond among members as they strive to maintain their identity in a digital world that has many distractions to compete for people's time. Something that has often been missing from the Orange Order is the documentation of its history. This has been rectified to some extent in recent times, with the Canadian and English websites uploading stories and pictures of their past. In England, the Orange archivist Michael Phelan has produced a wealth of articles using primary Orange sources to document an array of events. Notably, these articles focus on the Orange Order's involvement in World War I, particularly the Orangemen who were in the navy.[90] The Orange Order presence on the internet through these digital platforms means they can tell their stories and promote their beliefs globally.

BENEVOLENCE

Benefit Societies

The early Orange Order was first and foremost a fraternal society with a focus on upholding the Protestant faith and loyalty to the British Crown. In this sense, they did not intend to offer benefits since this was the preserve of friendly societies, which Orange members could and often did join. Yet the Order did offer benefits due to need and opportunity. Sometimes Grand Lodges in different parts of the world set up funds for widows of members. At other times they would administer a government scheme that would financially benefit Orange members.

The Orange Order in Canada was an early adopter of benevolence compared to their brethren in Ireland. At the first meeting of the Grand Orange Lodge in Canada in 1830, there was provision under their 'Objects' to 'afford assistance to distressed members of the order, and otherwise promote such laudable and benevolent purposes, as may tend to the due ordering of Religion, or Christian charity'.[91] In practice, it was left up to individual lodges to assist members. This practice can be identified in the various by-laws of Orange lodges.[92] By 1881 the Grand Orange Lodge set up the Orange Mutual Benefit Fund.[93] This provided national coverage for members. In the present day, it is simply called the Orange Benefit Fund. That it still exists, when so many fraternal friendly societies offering insurance no longer do, demonstrates its adaptability to changes in wider society.

The Scottish Orange Order's early involvement in forming friendly societies demonstrates an expansion of the original intent of simply being a loyalist fraternal society. The Glasgow Orange Union Funeral Society, founded in 1834, included benefits for the husband, wife and children. Other Orange lodges in Scotland soon followed Glasgow but included a provision for members when they were sick.[94] Of particular interest was Patna Loyal Orange Friendly Society. While registered in Edinburgh, it was established in the mining village of Patna. These initiatives benefited working-class Orangemen, especially miners who were banned from other friendly societies. In this instance, the local Orange lodge was supporting disadvantaged members. Eventually, the GOLS set up the Loyal Orange Institution of Scotland Friendly Society in 1899.[95]

In Ireland, in 1912, the Grand Orange Lodge of Ireland (GOLI) established the Orange and Protestant Benefit Society. The context was the introduction of the United Kingdom's National Insurance Act of 1911, which precipitated the decline of friendly societies. The Act granted a basic sickness payment to workers and covered medical and prescription costs. Although limited, as it did not cover hospital care or non-working dependants, the Act did include private agencies in the administration of the state social benefits.[96] The GOLI had three reasons to establish this new benefit society. First, they felt it was their duty to assist those parts of Ireland where there was 'no insurance machinery existing'. Second, there were parts of Ireland where no friendly societies existed for Protestants to join. Finally, 'Roman Catholics had financial associations devoted to the advancement of the interests of Roman Catholics', yet there were no similar organisations for Protestants.[97] The Insurance Act was therefore an opportunity to advance the interests of employed Protestants.

As the Act was a UK-wide initiative, the Grand Orange Lodge of England (GOLE) eventually established a branch of the Orange and Protestant Society in England. Interestingly, the initiative came not from the leadership of the GOLE but from Robert Brownlie, a collier from Durham, who advocated for branches to be established. This lack of leadership did not go unchallenged. There was open criticism of the

GOLE in the Belfast-based Orange and Protestant Benefit Society's annual report: 'hitherto the English Grand Lodge had done nothing.'[98] This blunt criticism was followed up with financial support from the Irish branch of the organisation. They did not want the scheme to fail, and membership reached 8,000 in a short time. Similarly, there were already 10,000 applicants wanting to join the society in Ireland. The early success of the Orange and Protestant Society was due to the existing network of the Orange Order.[99] One researcher claims that the Orange and Protestant Society 'administered the National Insurance system for their members' rather than doing any friendly society business.[100] This was not, however, necessary as the Orange Order had its own lodge framework, so there was no need to provide the extras.

The Orange Order in England, Ireland and Scotland followed similar patterns. This was mostly because of their proximity and the centralised UK government influencing all of these countries. Canada, being autonomous, was able to create its own system of insurance. In the southern hemisphere, Australia and New Zealand had thriving friendly societies that provided welfare for Orange members before the advent of a stable social welfare system in each country. The main Orange influence of these friendly societies was the Protestant Alliance Friendly Society of Australasia (PAFSA), founded in Victoria, Australia, in 1868.[101] It was a benefit society that was founded by Orangemen. The PAFSA first opened a branch in Thames, New Zealand, in 1873. It was not that successful as 'it never broke the 1000 membership mark'.[102] A possible reason may have been that there were other options for Protestants and the PAFSA association with the Orange Order might have deterred potential members. There was still the 'no marrying Catholics' rule, which other Protestant men may not have had a problem with.[103]

Orphans

The financial support given to widows was extended to the orphans of members. The GOLI was an early supporter of such a scheme and, on 7 December 1887, they set up the Lord Enniskillen Memorial Orange Orphan Society. This provided financial assistance to the orphans of deceased members of the Orange Order. The criteria focused on the father of the orphan, who needed to have been a regular and active Orangeman with a membership of at least five years. Only in exceptional cases would discretion be shown.[104] This particular fund to support orphans is still a mainstay of the present-day Orange Order in Northern Ireland.

The English Grand Orange Lodge was in 1919 originally going to set up an orphanage as a 'Memorial to the Orangemen who have made the supreme sacrifice'. However, this changed into setting up an orphan fund, which, according to Grand Secretary Louis Ewart's 1920 resolution, was 'to work on similar lines to the Lord Enniskillen Memorial Orphan Society'.[105] Ewart canvassed for the original orphanage idea. There is no record as to why this plan changed in the meeting, as it was stated as having passed unanimously. Maybe the success of the Irish one made for a more straightforward model to mimic. There was a serious intent on behalf of members for this to succeed as the Grand Master, Deputy Grand Master and Grand Secretary were on the organising committee. It has proved to be a successful charitable arm for deceased members' children as it still operates today. Operationally, there has been little change. Each orphan receives a grant every quarter and also a birthday present each year. Exact numbers are not publicly available as the Society does not give out the number of orphans on its books.[106]

These orphan funds seemed to be fairly straightforward in their focus and are often cited as examples of Orange benevolence. The New Zealand situation provides a good instance of the evolving nature of such funds. Following closely on from the English Orange Orphan Society's establishment, the Grand Orange Lodge of New Zealand had recommended starting an Orphan's Fund in 1922. It was up to the Grand Executive to administer the fund, which was to relieve 'any Orangeman's orphan in need, and [to] car[e] for the deceased Orangeman's children if otherwise unprovided for'.[107] This fund was initially slow to gather contributions from members. However, by 1930 nearly every lodge had donated something to the fund. Much credit for raising the money was given to the ladies' lodges.[108] Eventually, the fund was going to be closed, and a Benevolent Fund set up, but it was kept, so there were then two funds. Support for these two discrete funds was given by the Grand Master G. M. Galbraith, who wanted a fund that could be used at the discretion of either the Grand Master or the Grand Executive.[109] By 1933 this became a reality with some clarity over using the fund for helping members or their dependants in times of distress or hardship.[110] This proved to be a popular fund and the Grand Executive had to make a plea for more funds as members were making full use of it. Both funds continued to provide benefits for members in need for many decades.[111] Finally, they were merged into the Orange Social Welfare Fund after a successful motion was put forward at the annual sessions in 2000. The reasoning was to have one fund for all charitable purposes.[112]

While England, Ireland and New Zealand were focused on the funds to support orphans, in Canada and the United States the building and running of orphanages dominated their benevolence. In the Canadian context, Orangewomen were heavily involved in this area, as were other Protestant women from the mid-nineteenth century through to the early to mid-twentieth century.[113] One instance involved an associate Orange organisation, the Loyal True Blue Association (LTBA). In 1910 in New Westminster, British Columbia, the LTBA began with only one orphan. As they increased numbers, the Ladies' Orange Benevolent Association assisted the LTBA from 1920. By 1925 they became partners in running the home. Its new name, Loyal Protestant True Blue and Orange Home for Children, reflected the funding by the Loyal True Blue Association, the Grand Orange Lodge of British Colombia, and the Ladies' Orange Benevolent Association. This orphan home lasted until 1983 before it finally had to close.[114]

The American Orange lodges, just like their Canadian counterparts, felt the need to build a place for orphans. On the occasion of the opening of the Orange orphanage in Hatboro, Pennsylvania, there was a Labor Day celebration in 1902 that had 3,000 marchers.[115] The home could hold upwards of 300 orphans.[116] This opening picnic and parade was an annual event that highlighted the charitable work carried out for the orphans. By 1948, the home for orphans had been converted into a home for the aged called the Orange Home. The Labor Day rallies continued with fundraisers for building extensions.[117] The Orange Home was sold in 1995, and this money now forms the basis of the Orange Foundation. Reporting to the Imperial Orange Council in 2006, Walter Wilson succinctly noted, 'the mission envisioned by working men and women of the Orange Fraternity at the end of the nineteenth century has been revitalised in a form adapted to the needs of the twenty-first century.'[118] The money was now available to help various charities as well as support children and the elderly.

These orphan homes or orphanages provided an essential social welfare function in the nineteenth and early twentieth centuries. There have been many stories that reveal that these places were regimented and characterised by strict discipline. However, the move to foster care that replaced these institutions has not always been trouble-free either. David Maunders, in his study of Protestant orphan homes in Australia, Canada and the United States, interviewed people who had spent time in these institutions and foster care in the 1950s and 1960s. Some had preferred to go back to an orphan home rather than stay in foster care, where they had experienced more hostility from the foster home's natural children.[119] The involvement by the Orange Order in orphan homes was just as much an outworking of their Christian faith as it was upholding the principles of their organisation as a whole.

Fundraising

The charitable aspect of the Orange Order often took the form of fundraising for various causes either within the jurisdiction of a country or dealing with needs in a transnational sense. The recipients of this fundraising were, and to some extent still are, a combination of members within the Order itself or other charitable organisations. As the birthplace of the Orange Order was in the north of Ireland, there often was a focus on this region during times of conflict or political crisis resulting in monetary needs. As well as providing for orphans of their own members, the Grand Orange Lodge of New Zealand did the same for those in Ireland. In 1921, they made an appeal for members to support the orphaned children of 'the murdered and dispossessed Protestants of Ireland'.[120] The following year's update revealed a disappointing response, which was blamed on the 'slow returns'.[121] While this seems negative, it was a reflection on members being asked to financially contribute despite already contributing to their own churches. Moving forward into the late 1990s, transnational support continued. For example, the Grand Orange Lodges of New South Wales and Victoria in Australia both financially supported the Orange lodges in Togo for many years.[122] Members saw this as a form of Christian mission work, as Africa was also a common destination of Christian missionaries. Other Orange countries also helped the Orange Order in Togo, with the GOLI donating a minibus.[123] Togo offered an opportunity for the Orange Order to help their Orange brethren in need and also to try and assist the growth of Orangeism in West Africa. The Grand Lodge in Togo also solicited assistance from the Grand Lodges in Australia for their evangelism work. In the case of the Grand Orange Lodge of Victoria, they gave $500.[124]

Opportunities to fundraise did not always arise from need as with the Grand Lodge of Togo's requests. The Orange Order in Australia created women's auxiliaries in order to fundraise for charitable purposes. In this instance, Orangewomen took the lead in fundraising as part of their lodge work. The amount of money raised never seemed significant, but given the constraints of low membership and the individuals not being of substantial financial means, it was successful. To illustrate this point, the Grand Lodge Ladies' Auxiliary that began on 29 June 1946 in New

South Wales, Australia, raised $50,000 over fifty years. In the same period, their numbers dropped from seventy-four to seven.[125] They were responsible for paying for half of the Orange hall that was purchased in Annandale, Sydney.[126] In Victoria, the Orange Women's Auxiliary was founded in 1978 by Orangewomen 'to put into action the requirements of the Orange Qualifications to care for the welfare of man'. This group, later renamed the Loyal Orange Women's Auxiliary, raised over $60,000 in just under twenty years. Their money went to hospitals, missions and their own Loyal Orange Homes for the elderly.[127]

This mixed model of fundraising for Orange causes and wider societal charities is particularly apparent across the Orange world. This focus has become more critical in the later twentieth and early twenty-first centuries. In some ways, this is redefining the work of the Orange Order. Now there are set charities that the Order focuses on. In Scotland, the Ladies' Orange Association gave out £25,000 to their Combat Stress and Scottish Orange Home Fund charities.[128] The array of charities that the Association of Loyal Orangewomen of Ireland give to are often displayed in the *Orange Standard*, with one example showing photo after photo of the Grand Mistress, Grand Secretary and Grand Treasurer handing over cheques from as little as £250 to just over £7,500. The 'good causes' ranged from their own Junior Orangewomen's Association of Ireland to Epilepsy Action, Mindwise and the redevelopment of an Orange hall in County Fermanagh.[129] Present-day examples include many of the charities that are so desperate for money. The amounts given are never enormous as members have to fundraise, and sometimes these can be the initiatives of individual lodges. The Ladies' Grand Council in England organise fundraising events and make donations to charities regularly. Most of the charity donations, however, are made by ladies' private lodges and are not recorded officially.[130] The common element in all of this fundraising over the years has been the work of Orangewomen. While men are still involved in the fundraising, it is the women who are first and foremost the leaders in organising these events.

CONCLUSION

The Orange Order's activism has taken many forms, with active political involvement, propagation of their beliefs, or benevolence. The political involvement was an early one often born out of the conviction that it would counter the encroachment of the Catholic Church into the lives of ordinary citizens. The plethora of Protestant associations and the changing input from various Orange lodges around the world has created a mixed response to political issues. These still tended to have an anti-Catholic stance. In terms of promoting themselves, the Orange Order used the platform of public lectures and meetings to their full effect. The nineteenth-century lecture series by Edith O'Gorman exemplified the traditional means to impart the anti-Catholic message, which in turn bolstered Orange membership. The counterproductive nature of this resulted in reinforcement of the negative image of the Orange Order. This was especially so when riots or sectarian violence ensued at these kinds of events.

Print media, such as newspapers, were a primary means of disseminating information about the Orange Order's activities. The problem for many of the Orange jurisdictions was whether to use existing sympathetic newspapers or start their own. In the New Zealand context, the *Nation* showed the problem when even members failed to support it. In Northern Ireland, the *Orange Standard* has been successful and managed to survive the digital shift. The same is true for the *Orange Torch* in Scotland. Both of these are well read beyond their borders and also include content from other parts of the Orange world. The change to digital formats has increased the spread of news about the Orange Order. Websites like OrangeNet, while now defunct, did create a space to promote individual lodges. While there is still a place for these kinds of one-stop websites, having social media like Facebook means individual lodges can promote themselves.

Benevolence provided an opportunity for the Orange Order to display a softer side to the public compared to the negative images of the past. Orangewomen have led benevolence, particularly in the areas of orphans and fundraising. While members, both locally and transnationally, have predominantly been the beneficiaries of this benevolence, it has also provided wider public support.

Nevertheless, the successes in the area of benevolence have been overshadowed by political issues. It is these political issues intertwined with attempts to counter the influence of the Roman Catholic Church that have always been met with charges of bigotry. Orange members have often felt aggrieved that their political involvement is highlighted more than their charitable work. Members point to the children's homes and homes for the aged that have managed to survive, generally free of the types of scandals that have dogged the Catholic Church. However, it is the political activism that still defines the Orange Order in the minds of the public. An aspect of Orangeism that has created solidarity among its members has been the Orange parade. These parades were the public face of the Orange Order, and will be examined in more detail in the following chapter.

NOTES

1. *Report of Proceedings of the 19th Annual Session of the Grand Orange Lodge of New Zealand. Also 5th Annual Session of Ladies' Grand Chapter, Invercargill, April 15th, 16th, and 18th, 1927* (Dunedin: Crown Print Ltd, 1927), p. 5.
2. McFarlane was born in Dalry, Ayrshire, Scotland. He was Grand Master in 1926–27 and was Grand Treasurer in two stints, 1911–25 and 1945–48.
3. A. T. Q. Stewart, *The Ulster Crisis: Resistance to Home Rule, 1912–14* (London: Faber & Faber, 1967, 1979); Paul Bew, *Ideology and the Irish Question: Ulster Unionism and Irish Nationalism, 1912–1916* (Oxford: Clarendon Press, 1994); Philip Currie, 'Toronto Orangeism and the Irish question, 1911–1916', *Ontario History*, 87:4 (1995), pp. 397–409; Robert McLaughlin, *Irish Canadian Conflict and the Struggle for Irish Independence, 1912–1925* (Toronto: University of Toronto Press, 2013).
4. These are just a few notable examples of earlier and later research into Orangeism and unionism: Peter Gibbon, *The Origins of Ulster Unionism: The Formation of Popular Protestant Politics and Ideology in Nineteenth-Century Ireland* (Manchester: Manchester University Press, 1975); David W. Miller, *Queens Rebels: Ulster Loyalism in Historical Perspective* (Dublin: Gill & Macmillan, 1978); Henry Patterson and Eric Kaufmann, *Unionism and Orangeism in Northern Ireland since 1945: The Decline of the Loyal Family* (Manchester: Manchester University Press, 2007); Graham Walker, *A History of the Ulster Unionist Party: Protest, Pragmatism and Pessimism* (Manchester: Manchester University Press, 2004).
5. Pamela McKane, '"No idle sightseers": The Ulster Women's Unionist Council and the Ulster Crisis (1912–1914)', *Studi Irlandesi: A Journal of Irish Studies*, 8:8 (2018), pp. 327–56. Diane Urquhart, 'Unionism, Orangeism and war', *Women's History Review*, 27:3 (2016), pp. 468–84; *Women in Ulster Politics, 1890–1940: A History Not Yet Told* (Dublin: Irish Academic Press, 2000).
6. Patricia Rooke and R. L. Schnell, *Discarding the Asylum* (Lanham, MD: University Press of America, 1983), p. 103.
7. D. A. J. MacPherson and Donald M. MacRaild, 'Sisters of the brotherhood: Female Orangeism on Tyneside in the late nineteenth and early twentieth centuries', *Irish Historical Studies*, 35:137 (2006), pp. 40–60. D. A. J. MacPherson, 'The emergence of women's Orange lodges in Scotland: Gender, ethnicity and women's activism, 1909–1940', *Women's History Review*, 22:1 (2012), pp. 51–74; 'Irish Protestant women and diaspora: Orangewomen in Canada during the twentieth century', in D. A. J. MacPherson and Mary J. Hickman (eds), *Women and Irish Diaspora Identities: Theories, Concepts and New Perspectives* (Manchester: Manchester University Press, 2014), pp. 168–85; *Women*

and the Orange Order: Female Activism, Diaspora and Empire in the British World, 1850–1940 (Manchester: Manchester University Press, 2016).

8. Donald M. MacRaild, *Faith, Fraternity and Fighting: The Orange Order and Irish Migrants in England, c. 1850–1920* (Liverpool: Liverpool University Press, 2005), chapter 6.

9. Ibid. p. 241.

10. Some older postgraduate research in Canada focused on an Orange newspaper. See Andrew Thomson, 'The Sentinel and Orange and Protestant Advocate, 1877–1896: An Orange view of Canada' (MA, Wilfred Laurier University, 1983).

11. Orange Institution of Ireland, *Laws and Ordinances of the Orange Institution of Ireland. Revised and Adopted by the Grand Orange Lodge of Ireland, June 3rd, 1896* (Dublin: Br. James Forrest, 1896), p. 1.

12. Ibid.

13. Edward Vallance, 'Loyal or rebellious? Protestant associations in England, 1584–1696', *The Seventeenth Century*, 17:1 (2002), pp. 1–24; Eugene Charlton Black, 'The tumultuous petitioners: The Protestant Association in Scotland, 1778–1780', *The Review of Politics*, 25:2 (1963), pp. 183–211.

14. Gilbert A. Cahill, 'Some nineteenth-century roots of the Ulster problem, 1829–1848', *Irish University Review*, 1:2 (1971), pp. 229–30.

15. They represented a range of Protestant denominations such as Congregationalist, Baptist, Episcopal, German Reformed, Methodist and Presbyterian.

16. American Protestant Association, *Address of the Board of Managers of the American Protestant Association, with the Constitution and Organization of the Association* (Philadelphia: American Protestant Association, 1843), p. 7.

17. American Protestant Association, *Minute of Proceedings of the Worthy Grand Lodge of the American Protestant Association of the State of Pennsylvania* (Philadelphia: Jared Craig, 1873), pp. 5–15.

18. Cecil J. Houston and William J. Smyth, 'Transferred loyalties: Orangeism in the United States and Ontario', *American Review of Canadian Studies*, 14:2 (1984), p. 206.

19. Humphrey Joseph Desmond, *The APA Movement: A Sketch* (Washington, DC: New Century Press, 1912), pp. 45–6.

20. *New York Times*, 19 June 1894. He was also the Vice President of the Imperial Grand Orange Council of the World.

21. This was the ethnic group that helped to swell the ranks of the Orange Order in the United States. He was previously Supreme Grand Master of the American Orange Order (1891–92).

22. *Report of Proceedings of the Sixth Annual Session of the Grand Orange Lodge of Michigan Held in West Bay City, Michigan May 1, 2 and 3, 1894* (Saginaw: Jones & McCall Co., 1894), pp. 15–17.

23. Ibid. p. 19.
24. Ibid. p. 40.
25. For a full account of the American Protective Association's activities, see Donald Louis Kinzer, *An Episode in Anti-Catholicism: The American Protective Association* (Seattle: University of Washington Press, 1964).
26. Mark Paul Richard, *Not a Catholic Nation: The Ku Klux Klan Confronts New England in the 1920s* (Amherst: University of Massachusetts Press, 2015), p. 4.
27. See Tyler Cline, '"A dragon, bog-spawned, is now stretched o'er this land": The Ku Klux Klan's patriotic-Protestantism in the northeastern borderlands during the 1920s and 1930s', *Histoire sociale/Social History*, 52:106 (2019), pp. 305–29; '"A clarion call to real patriots the world over": The curious case of the Ku Klux Klan of Kanada in New Brunswick during the 1920s and 1930s', *Acadiensis*, 48:1 (2019), pp. 88–100; '"Orangeism, a great Protestant crusade": The nativist legacy of the Orange Order in the northeastern borderlands', *American Review of Canadian Studies*, 48:2 (2018), pp. 125–37.
28. Gordon Pentland, 'The indignant nation: Australian responses to the attempted assassination of the Duke of Edinburgh in 1868', *The English Historical Review*, 130:542 (2015), pp. 57–88.
29. New South Wales Protestant Political Association, Manifesto, *Rules and By-Laws of the New South Wales Protestant Political Association* (Sydney: Samuel E. Lees, 1872), pp. 4–5.
30. *Sydney Morning Herald*, 22 June 1901.
31. Australian Protestant Defence Association, *Constitution and By-Laws for the Use of Branches* (Sydney: W. M. Madgwick & Sons, 1904), p. 3.
32. Protestant Defence Association of New Zealand, *Constitution and By-Laws* (Dunedin: Otago Daily Times, 1903), p. 4. They decided not to simply be a branch of the Australian organisation, but an organisation in its own right.
33. *Press*, 17 April 1903. Dill Macky's meeting to found a branch of the APDA in Wyalong, NSW, was attacked and the Riot Act was read. See *Maitland Daily Mercury*, 27 March 1903.
34. *Otago Daily Times*, 17 April 1903.
35. Ibid., 5 May 1903.
36. *Tuapeka Times Post*, 4 September 1907. This was in reference to Dunedin.
37. Patrick J. Coleman, 'Transplanted Irish institutions: Orangeism and Hibernianism in New Zealand 1877–1910' (MA, University of Canterbury, 1993), pp. 110–11.
38. See Harold S. Moores, 'The rise of the Protestant Political Association: Sectarianism in N.Z. during World War I' (MA, University of Auckland, 1966).

39. James W. McAuley and Jonathan Tonge, '"For God and for the Crown": Contemporary political and social attitudes among Orange Order members in Northern Ireland', *Political Psychology*, 28:1 (2007), pp. 33–52.
40. *Irish Times*, 12 March 2005.
41. *Orange Standard*, June 2005.
42. Thomas Hennessey, Máire Braniff, James W. McAuley, Jonathan Tonge and Sophie Whiting, *The Ulster Unionist Party: Country before Party?* (Oxford: Oxford University Press, 2019), p. 179.
43. This magazine provides members with information about lodge activities, historical events and the latest political events affecting Scotland.
44. *Orange Torch*, February 2014, p. 1.
45. Ibid., March 2014, p. 3.
46. Ibid., April 2014, p. 3. In addition to their own political material, the front page of the *Orange Torch* has since 2013 displayed the British Together logo and website.
47. *The Guardian*, 13 September 2014.
48. *Daily Mail*, 15 September 2014.
49. Ibid.
50. *Orange Torch*, November 2014, p. 9.
51. David Bryce, Orange archivist, Scotland, email to author, 23 July 2016.
52. *Orange Torch*, November 2014, p. 9.
53. Ibid. pp. 8–9.
54. Some of these aspects of secularisation and sectarianism are explored in chapter 3 of Graham Walker's *The Labour Party in Scotland: Religion, the Union, and the Irish Dimension* (London: Palgrave Macmillan, 2016).
55. Orange Institution of Ireland, *Laws and Ordinances*, p. 1.
56. Imperial Grand Orange Council of the World, *Thirty Second Triennial Conference. House of Orange, Belfast, Northern Ireland, 15th and 16th July, 1976* (Belfast: LOI, 1976).
57. Ibid.
58. *Belfast News Letter*, 3 March 1893; *Daily Telegraph*, 2 May 1893.
59. Coleman, 'Transplanted Irish institutions', chapter 5.
60. Edith O'Gorman, *Trials and Persecutions of Miss Edith O'Gorman: Otherwise Sister Teresa de Chantal, of St. Joseph's Convent, Hudson City, N.J.* (Hartford: Connecticut Publishing Co., 1871).
61. Rene Kollar, 'An American "escaped nun" on tour in England: Edith O'Gorman's critique of convent life', *Feminist Theology*, 14:2 (2006), pp. 208–10; Neil J. Byrne, 'Edith O'Gorman, religious controversialist: The Australian lecture tour of 1886–1887', *Women Church*, 27 (2000), pp. 21–7.
62. *Derby Mercury*, 7 December 1881; *Preston Guardian*, 24 November 1883. O'Gorman and her handlers were 'roughly handled' on the train trip between Preston and Liverpool.
63. *Birmingham Daily Post*, 6 May 1885.

64. David Goldie (1842–1926) was later Mayor of Auckland and also became a Member of Parliament.

65. Grand Orange Lodge of New Zealand, *Report of Proceedings for the Year Ending January 1884, Auckland, New Zealand* (Auckland: John Brame at the Free Press Office, 1884), p. 14.

66. The lecture was called 'Secret Mysteries of the Confessional; the Inner Life of Convents'.

67. *New Zealand Herald*, 13 October 1885, 14 October 1885.

68. *'Is the "escaped nun" a fraud?' Being a full report of the public discussion between Mr Fred Fulton and Miss O'Gorman (Mrs Auffray) at the Garrison Hall, Dunedin, 2 March 1886* (Dunedin: J. Powers, Smith & Co., 1886), p. 1.

69. The previous references from the English newspapers are full of the local Irish communities actively challenging O'Gorman on her lecture tour throughout England.

70. *New Zealand Herald*, 10 October 1885.

71. *Sydney Morning Herald*, 29 October 1886.

72. *New Zealand Tablet*, 25 December 1885.

73. For an explanation of this newspaper's importance by historians see Donald M. MacRaild, 'Networks, communication and the Irish Protestant diaspora in northern England, c. 1860–1914', *Immigrants & Minorities*, 23:2–3 (2005), pp. 311–37.

74. Grand Orange Lodge of Ireland, 'The Orange Standard Newspaper', <https://www.goli.org.uk/orangestandard> (accessed 25 October 2023).

75. Grand Orange Lodge of New Zealand, North Island, *Forty-Second Annual Report 1908* (Wellington: W. J. Lankshear, 1908), p. 9.

76. *Report of the Second Annual Session of the Grand Orange Lodge of New Zealand. Held in Dunedin, April 10, 12, 13, 1909* (Dunedin: Wallace's Crown Print, 1909), p. 7.

77. Loyal Orange Institution of New Zealand, *Fourth Annual Session of the Grand Orange Lodge of New Zealand. Held in Christchurch, April 15, 17, & 18, 1911* (Dunedin: Wallace's Crown Print, 1911), p. 25.

78. *Report of Proceedings of the Eighth Annual Session of the Grand Orange Lodge of New Zealand. Held in Wellington, April 22, 24 and 26, 1916* (Christchurch: Frasers Limited, 1916), p. 9.

79. *Report of Proceedings of the Eleventh Annual Session of the Grand Orange Lodge of New Zealand. Held in Ashburton, April 19, 21 and 22, 1919* (Wellington: Wright & Carman, 1919), p. 13.

80. *Report of Proceedings of the Forty-Ninth Session of the Grand Orange Lodge of New Zealand and the 34th Session of Ladies' Conference. Held in Invercargill, 27th to 30th March, 1970* (Wellington: Digest Print Ltd, 1970), p. 30.

81. Loyal Orange Institution of New Zealand, *Reports for 1972–1973 Period* (Wellington: LOI, 1973), pp. 35–6.

82. Loyal Orange Institution of New Zealand, *Reports for 1975 Period* (Wellington: LOI, 1975).

83. 'OrangeNet', <https://web.archive.org/web/19990831053937/http://www.orangenet.org/about.htm> (accessed 19 May 2023).

84. The lodge sites were: Centennial LOL No. 3272, Port Perry, Hackett LOL 805, London, both Ontario, Canada; Ulster-Scots LOL 1690, California, and Bishop Burnett Memorial District LOL 48, Kilwinning, Scotland.

85. *Report of the Forty-First Meeting of the Imperial Orange Council, 1867–2003. Held at the Swallow Hotel, Glasgow, Scotland, 20th–25th July, 2003* (Glasgow: LOI, 2003), p. 34; Imperial Grand Council of the World, *Report of the Forty-Second Meeting of the Imperial Orange Council 1867–2006. Held at the Marriott Airport Hotel, Toronto, Canada, 17th–22nd July 2006* (Toronto: LOI, 2006), p. 31.

86. Ibid. p. 58.

87. Grand Orange Lodge of Scotland, <https://orangeorderscotland.com> (accessed 23 August 2023); Grand Orange Lodge of Ireland, <https://www.goli.org.uk> (accessed 10 April 2023).

88. GOLI, 'The Orange Standard Newspaper'.

89. Imperial Grand Council of the World, *Report of the Forty-Second Meeting of the Imperial Orange Council*, p. 50.

90. 'Orange History', <https://www.orangehistory.net/articles> (accessed 23 February 2024).

91. *Rules and Regulations of the Orange Institution of British North America: Adopted by the Grand Lodge at its first meeting. Held in the Court House, Brockville, Upper Canada 1st of January 1830* (Brockville: Thomas Tomkins, 1830), p. 5.

92. Loyal Orange Association of British America, *By-Laws of Strathroy Lodge, L.O.A., No. 537* (Strathroy: Dispatch Book and Job Office, 1867).

93. Cecil J. Houston and William J. Smyth, *The Sash Canada Wore: A Historical Geography of the Orange Order in Canada* (Toronto: University of Toronto Press, 1980), pp. 132–4.

94. Elaine McFarland, *Protestants First: Orangeism in Nineteenth-Century Scotland* (Edinburgh: Edinburgh University Press, 1990), p. 50.

95. David Bryce, *A History of Scotland's Orange Friendly Societies* (Glasgow: GOLS, 2004).

96. Michael Heller, 'The National Insurance Acts 1911–1947, the approved societies and the Prudential Assurance Company', *Twentieth Century British History*, 19:1 (2008), pp. 1–2.

97. Orange and Protestant Friendly Society, *Executive Committee's Report: to be submitted to Annual Meeting on October 4th, 1912* (Belfast: Thos. Brough & Cox, 1912), p. 3.

98. Ibid. pp. 6–7.

99. *Irish Times*, 12 April 1912.

100. Anthony D. Buckley, '"On the club": Friendly societies in Ireland', *Irish Economic and Social History*, 14 (1987), p. 56.

101. Brian Stevenson, *'Stand Fast Together': A History of the Protestant Alliance Friendly Society of Victoria* (Brisbane: Boolarong Press, 1996).

102. Jenny Carlyon, 'New Zealand friendly societies, 1842–1941' (PhD, University of Auckland, 2001), p. 40.

103. *Laws of the Protestant Alliance Friendly Society of Australasia: Adopted by the Grand Council of Representatives, at Thames, in the Colony of New Zealand* (Thames, NZ: The Society, 1882).

104. Loyal Orange Institution, *Enniskillen Memorial Orphan Scheme, Rules and Constitution* (Dublin: James Forrest, 1888), p. 5.

105. *Report of Proceedings of the Annual Meeting of the Grand Orange Lodge of England. Held in the City of Birmingham, 7th and 8th July 1920* (Birmingham: GOLE, 1920), p. 16.

106. Billy Owens, Chairman of the Loyal Orange Orphan Society, email to author, 24 January 2016.

107. *Report of Proceedings of the Fourteenth Annual Session of the Grand Orange Lodge of New Zealand. Held in Auckland, April 15, 17 and 18, 1922* (Wellington: Wright & Carman, 1922), p. 19.

108. *Report of Proceedings of the 22nd Annual Session of the Grand Orange Lodge of New Zealand. Also 8th Annual Session of Ladies' Grand Chapter. Held in Wellington, April 18, 19, 21, 1930* (Dunedin: Crown Print, 1930), pp. 5, 21.

109. *Report of Proceedings of the 25th Annual Session of the Grand Orange Lodge of New Zealand. Also 10th Annual Session of Ladies' Grand Chapter. Held in Wellington, March 25, 26, 28, 1932* (Dunedin: Crown Print, 1932), p. 18.

110. *Report of Proceedings of the 26th Annual Session of the Grand Orange Lodge of New Zealand. Also 11th Annual Session of Ladies' Grand Chapter. Held in Christchurch, April 14, 15, 17, 1933* (Dunedin: Crown Print, 1933), pp. 27–8.

111. *Report of Proceedings of the 38th Annual Session of the Grand Orange Lodge of New Zealand Incorporated. 23rd Session of Ladies' Conference and Centenary Celebrations 1843–1943. Held in Auckland, March 25, 26, 27, 29, 1948* (Dunedin: Stanton Bros, 1948), p. 15.

112. *Report of Proceedings Wellington Easter 2000 Grand Orange Lodge 64th Sessions* (Wellington: LOI, 2000).

113. Patricia Rooke and R. L. Schnell, 'The rise and decline of British North American Protestant orphans' homes as woman's domain, 1850–1930', *Atlantis*, 7:2 (1982), pp. 21–35.

114. Historic Places Canada, 'Royal City Christian Centre', <http://www.historicplaces.ca/en/rep-reg/place-lieu.aspx?id=16786> (accessed 23 August 2023).

115. This represented twenty lodges from New York, Chicago, Camden, Buffalo, Wilmington, Canada and Pittsburgh as well as thirty lodges from the local region.

116. *Philadelphia Inquirer*, 2 September 1902.

117. Samuel Ernest Long, *A Brief History of the Loyal Orange Institution in the United States of America* (Dromara, County Down: Samuel Ernest Long, 1979), p. 29.

118. Imperial Grand Council of the World, *Report of the Forty-Second Meeting of the Imperial Orange Council*, p. 56.

119. David Maunders, 'Awakening from the dream: The experience of childhood in Protestant orphan homes in Australia, Canada, and the United States', *Child & Youth Care Forum*, 23:6 (1994), pp. 393–4.

120. *Report of Proceedings of the Fifteenth Annual Session of the Grand Orange Lodge of New Zealand. Held in Dunedin, March 31, April 2 and 3, 1923* (Palmerston North: Watson & Eyre, 1923), p. 19.

121. *Report of Proceedings of the Sixteenth Annual Session of the Grand Orange Lodge of New Zealand. Held in Wellington, April 19, 21, and 22, 1924* (Dunedin: Crown Print, 1924), p. 13.

122. Loyal Orange Institution of New South Wales, *Annual Report 1995* (Sydney: LOINSW, 1995), pp. 17–18; *The Banner*, Issue 1, 1997, p. 5.

123. *The Banner*, Issue 1, 1997, p. 5.

124. Loyal Orange Institution of Victoria, *Annual Report 1994* (Melbourne: LOIV, 1994), p. 14.

125. Loyal Orange Institution of New South Wales, *Annual Report 1997* (Sydney: LOINSW, 1997), p. 3.

126. Loyal Orange Institution of NSW, *Sesqui-Centenary of the Grand Orange Lodge of New South Wales 1995* (Chipping Norton, NSW: Gowans & Son Pty, Ltd, 1995), p. 35.

127. *The Banner*, Issue 2, 1997, p. 10.

128. *Orange Torch*, November 2013, p. 8.

129. *Orange Standard*, March 2013.

130. Gillian Rimmer, Grand Mistress 2015–present, Ladies' Loyal Orange Institution in England, email to author, 31 December 2015.

4

Orange Cultural Performance:
Band and Parades

On 12 July 1690 at the Battle of the Boyne, William III, Prince of Orange, defeated the Catholic King James II of England. The battle became the defining moment in the Orange Order's history and has come to be commemorated worldwide by an annual parade.[1] The Orange Order's first attempt at public processions was across Ulster on 12 July 1796. Colonel Robert Wallace (1860–1929), 'a prominent Orange member', described the day as "'twas on a Tuesday morning, the sun rose bright and clear'.[2] This innocuous description of the first Orange parades belied the simmering tensions across Ireland that culminated in the 1798 uprising. Most of the parades in 1796 were numerically small with the exception of County Armagh, Ireland.[3] They managed to pass off reasonably peacefully, though members were all carrying rifles in case they were attacked by the local Catholic population.[4] This signalled the genesis of what would be the Orange parading tradition.

Research on Orange parades has generally emphasised three often overlapping themes of riots, peaceful parades and bands. Research on the first of these, the Orange riot, has mostly focused on the nineteenth century and identifies Orange parades as the catalyst for riots and conflict during this century especially. In the twentieth and twenty-first centuries, the riots that occurred at Drumcree, Northern Ireland, are the notable exceptions to this nineteenth-century-dominated research focus.[5] Since the early twentieth century, however, parades have largely become more peaceful throughout most of the diaspora, though less so in Northern Ireland.[6] This approach to the research moved beyond the idea of merely looking at riots to include peaceful demonstrations. These were used to assert the dominance of a particular group, in this instance the Orange Order. In the Northern Irish situation it was the field of anthropology that saw a shift from a focus on riots to including peaceful parades.[7] Despite some exceptions, however, such as the exploration of peaceful parades, the dominant literature focuses on parades as flashpoints for riots and conflicts and generally takes a microhistory focus or Northern Ireland emphasis.

Meanwhile, research into the bands that play at these marches has tended to concentrate on their role in aggravating the conflict and, again, focuses mostly on Northern Ireland. Notable examples are the 'Blood and Thunder' bands, which have been identified as a source of conflict during the marches.[8] Exceptions to this emphasis on conflict have been investigations into youth culture, links to sectarian paramilitaries by the bands, and gender.[9] Outside of the Northern Irish context, a few articles focus on Scotland, but even there we see a Northern Irish flute band taking part in a Scottish parade.[10]

This chapter examines the role of the bands in the resurgence of the Orange Order across the world. A key question is how did the Orange Order attempt to counteract the negative connotations of parades? This in turn leads to an additional question of how did the parades lead to either a decline or a resurgence around the Orange world? A noticeable lack of comparative research has meant the existing focus on riots has been region specific and does not draw on events in other countries which also had Orange riots. This chapter, therefore, addresses this deficit in the literature by drawing attention to the increased legislation across several countries where the Orange Order has flourished. An important point here is that the Orange Order has played a key role in the way governments have sought to control public displays. The flow-on effect has been to limit other groups from marching, not just the Orange Order, whose marches and associated conflict created the initial legislative response. This chapter emphasises the changing membership reflected at the parades, particularly in modern-day England, Northern Ireland and Scotland. A central argument here is that the Orange leadership has failed to maintain respectability at these parades. There is clear evidence of progress, but they have not won over a hostile public. The negative image of Orange parades remains.

The overarching issue of the failed attempts to overcome negative public perceptions underpins this chapter, which is divided into two main sections. The first section begins with a brief explanation of the meaning and regulations that underpin Orange parades. Uniformity in practice tended to be the intention of these regulations. The next important aspect of this section is how the Orange Order had to respond to the negativity around their parades. These responses were quite different depending on the country. The second section focuses on the decline in the parading traditions in terms of low participation, and the factors that led to this. A declining membership, influenced by changes in the wider societies throughout the Orange jurisdictions, either reduced or completely halted Orange parades. Important factors discussed include the secularisation of society, the lessening of anti-Catholicism generally, and the demographic changes brought by immigration. The chapter closes with the resurgence of the parades mostly associated with the bands. Again, the comparative model helps to distinguish between situations in the various Orange jurisdictions. Some notable examples of attempts to maintain the parades are in the United States, with their alignment with the Ku Klux Klan through joint parades, and the revitalisation of the parading tradition in South Australia, fuelled by Northern Irish immigrants. The section closes with the role of women in slowing the decline as they helped both to bolster numbers and also to maintain the parading tradition.

SECTARIAN VIOLENCE VERSUS PEACEFUL CELEBRATIONS

Meaning and Regulations

To understand the significance of Orange parades, an explanation of their meaning is vital. This is particularly crucial when trying to understand the precursors to conflict resulting from the parades since the Orange ritual parade is at the forefront of any public displays by Orange members globally. Originating in Ireland, the Orange parades inevitably have an Irish influence. This Irish dimension permeates the literature about parades including the interdisciplinary approaches to analysing the meaning of these parades. Before considering these varied meanings, it is essential to scrutinise the various rules and regulations of the Orange Order as these outline the focus and the intent of the demonstrations. Early regulations in 1799 stated:

> That we are to meet every first day of July (old style) in full body, to commemorate the signal victory gained by King William, Prince of Orange, at the Boyne, who bravely supported our Rights, and established the Protestant Religion: that on this day we are to walk wherever may be agreed on, always behaving with propriety and decorum.[11]

These early regulations are quite explicit in their intent. The signalling of Protestant King William's victory over the Catholic King James II as a first reason to parade, followed by the idea of 'our Rights' and 'Protestant Religion', encapsulates the ongoing issues over these parades. The reference to the 'walk' and the way members are supposed to behave seems quite innocuous. Yet these points are essential, as the idea of a right to march to remember past victories formed the basis of arguments when legislation was enacted to prevent marches.[12] Indeed, this was a leading argument against any attempts to restrict or criticise the marches. One historian used the concept of creating new memories to understand the parading culture. This idea was used in the Northern Irish context when parades were contested. Not all of the parades had an old history, but they were sometimes linked to particular places or political events.[13] Therefore, having a 'right to march' regardless of whether a particular marching route or parade had a long history was laden with symbolic significance.

Surprisingly, subsequent regulations from Ireland do not refer to any 'walk' or even 'procession'. This does seem anomalous in light of the right to march. A possible rewording may have been in response to various marching bans in Ireland and throughout the world:

> They shall in the same manner commemorate the Anniversary of the Boyne on the 12th day of July yearly; carefully abstaining from anything in word or behaviour which might unnecessarily give offence; and in all cases strictly obeying the law of the land, on pain of expulsion or suspension for any disobedience.[14]

The addition of 'strictly obeying the law of the land' and the threats of expulsion are surely in reaction to the various riots and disturbances which were the result of the early marches. This careful wording was used for many years, and not just in the Irish context but also by the Orange diaspora.[15] The rules and regulations for Orange members in Ireland and the Orange diaspora do not provide any more guidance on the marches. Instead, the best guide to early practice was newspaper reports. These form the basis for most descriptions of parades except for published eyewitness accounts.

To further understand an Orange parade, a brief description of what constitutes a typical parade is needed. Whether in Ireland or across the world, a typical march begins at an Orange hall, where members are marshalled in their respective lodges. At the front, the main officers of the lodge carry items such as an open Bible, a crown on a cushion, and banners.[16] Depending on the size of the parade, there may be a band either attached to a lodge or hired for the occasion. Sociologists Jennifer Edwards and J. David Knottnerus have noted that the hierarchical nature of the Orange Order is evident in parades, with the top officers marching at the front.[17] These ritualised parades can visibly reinforce the organisational structure. The destination of the march was generally a local Protestant church, although on some occasions it may have been another hall large enough to accommodate the marchers and other sympathisers. There they attended a church service, with the minister providing a suitable sermon for the occasion. After that, they marched back to their hall. This was the standard march or walk. Variations included having picnics or sports days, again depending on the location and the climate. The relative uniformity of these parades was a way of linking the past to the present. On the surface, this all seems quite benign, and yet riots and conflict are commonly associated with these marches. How did this dichotomous situation occur?

Conflict, Legislation and Party Tunes

A key to understanding the violent past of these seemingly highly structured and ritualised parades begins in Ireland. The Irish parading tradition was established against a backdrop of political and social tension. Following the peaceful processions of 1796, there was the brutal aftermath of the 1798 Rebellion that firmly crushed any notions of Irish Catholic resistance to the Protestant Ascendancy. There followed a period of relative calm, and the July processions were not particularly significant. It was from 1820 until 1829 that the rise of Catholic Emancipation and Daniel O'Connell saw increased conflict and unrest at Orange processions. This whole period has been well documented, with faction fights occurring at fairs, meetings and Orange processions.[18]

Early pressure on the very existence of the Orange Order came via the proliferation of legislation in response to these parades. Of particular importance were the Unlawful Societies Act 1825 and the Party Processions Act 1832. These precipitated the voluntary discontinuation of the Orange Order in 1835.[19] Neil Maddox remarked that this last Act 'represented the most extreme legislative response to contentious parading ever witnessed on the island of Ireland'.[20] He was referring to the total ban on parades. No legislation since that time has been so extreme in its scope. The immediate effect was a reduction in parades. The ban was lifted in 1845 and marches increased. However, this was short-lived as on 12 July 1849 the infamous 'Battle' of Dolly's Brae took place. The clash occurred in a rural area in County Down when a group of Orangemen marched through a Catholic area. About thirty Catholics and members of the agrarian secret society called Ribbonmen were killed, with no Orange casualties. There were also Catholic houses wrecked and burned by some of the Orange marchers. None were arrested for their actions.[21] The event has been celebrated in song, and the following verse captures the sentiment from an Orange perspective:

And when we came to Dolly's Brae they were lined on every side,
Praying for the Virgin Mary to be their holy guide;
We loosened our guns upon them and we gave them no time to pray,
And the tune we played was *The Protestant Boys* right over Dolly's Brae.[22]

The result of this clash led to the Party Processions Act of 1850.[23] Despite the ban, in practice some processions continued, as it was up to the local magistrates to enforce it. Sympathetic magistrates turned a blind eye or parcelled out token punishments for infringements. Eventually, the ban was overturned with the repeal of the Party Processions Act in 1872.[24] These physical and legislative conflicts in nineteenth-century Ireland in some ways defined the Orange Order. The ongoing justification for their existence continued to play out in the public forum through parades.

In contrast to the situation in Ireland, the Orange diaspora had a mixed response to their early parades. England had a peaceful introduction to the first documented Orange processions, as Ireland had done. The Orangemen in England had a problem-free march in Oldham in 1803. However, unlike the Orangemen in Ireland, this gentle introduction to marching did not last long. England saw riots in Manchester in 1807 fuelled by rising levels of anti-Catholicism. This culminated in a period of regular riots and clashes between Orange members and the Irish Catholic community. This conflict switched from Manchester to Liverpool, mostly because of the larger Orange and Irish Catholic communities there.[25]

Patterns in other parts of the Orange diaspora were quite varied compared to Ireland and England. Scotland did not have its first Orange public march until 1821 in Glasgow. A possible reason was the low number of members, as only three lodges took part in the march. This was due in part to Scotland not having the same kind of revolts and potential revolutions as were occurring in Ireland from 1798 until the 1820s. During their first Orange march, members were roughed up by some Irish Catholic onlookers but generally it did not resemble the confrontations taking place in Ireland. This pattern was repeated the following year, though this time seven lodges and 127 marchers took part.[26] In 1823, the parades were abandoned in Glasgow until 1842.[27] Once these parades resumed, there was a shift towards parades from Glasgow to other Scottish towns and cities with large Irish populations. These parades mimicked England and Ireland's cycle of incessant conflict. Similar to these countries, Scotland seemed to have a correlation between large pockets of Irish Catholic settlements and conflict with the Orange Order, particularly on 12 July. These Scottish Orange marches were a way of Protestants asserting their dominance over Catholics by 'seeking to impose a familiar sense of "order" on their new surroundings'. This provoked a response from the Irish Catholic population resident in Scotland, who did not want to be dominated.[28] In a sense both groups had transported what was originally an Irish conflict into a new setting. This continued to be the case as the Orange Order spread across the world and the observation of importing troubles was common in editorial comments.

Orange Order parades in North America had contrasting patterns but conflict still ensued. The United States Orange Order had similarities with their brethren in Scotland in that their first recorded Orange parade in 1824 in Greenwich Village, New York, involved conflict. However, rather than heated words and scuffles, it was characterised by significant violence. Around 200 marchers were attacked by around 100 Irish Catholic weavers from a local carpet factory that the march passed.[29] In the following years, any attempts at marches ended in riots, most notably in the 1870s. Orange marches were then discontinued until 1890, when parades recommenced.[30] In contrast to their American brethren, the Orangemen in Canada marched uncontested in York, Ontario, in 1818. Canada took longer to descend into the kind of riots and faction fighting that was prevalent in Ireland and England. The catalyst there for ongoing tensions on the Twelfth was the influx of migrants from famine-stricken Ireland, which significantly changed the demographic make-up of Toronto.[31] Further migration from Ireland after the Famine only served to increase the numbers of Irish Catholics and Irish Protestants within the city. In Toronto, one historian claimed that in a period between 1870 and 1889 the parades were the spark for two-thirds of the clashes between Orange and Green factions.[32] The Canadian census of 1871 produced the statistic that 40 per cent of those living in Toronto considered themselves Irish.[33] These examples suggest that Catholics were the main instigators of disturbances associated with Orange parades. However, Orange Order supporters also behaved in ways that created ructions. This sometimes extended to Orange supporters creating disturbances at Catholic displays of identity or nationalism.[34]

One salient feature that resulted from the early riots and conflict in the diaspora, as in Ireland, was the proliferation of legislation concerning parades. Party Processions Acts were used across the British world to regulate not just Orange parades but any parades. The Orange Order was often the stimulus and target of this type of legislation. The period of the 1840s, when Ireland was undergoing political and social turmoil, saw countries that had large numbers of Irish immigration facing similar issues. Canada, in 1843, introduced their Party Processions Act. Its aim was to restrict the Orange Order.[35] This was not a deterrent, however, as they marched regardless. In 1850 in Brantford, Ontario, despite clear evidence of a march including a King Billy on horseback, the jury refused to convict the local Orangemen. Grand Master George Benjamin (1799–1864) put forward a petition for the Act's repeal in 1851.[36] In the lead-up to the repeal, many of the Toronto lodges continued to march in defiance of the Act, despite pleas by Benjamin not to march.[37] Again, as in Ireland, Orangemen in Canada refused to adhere to laws or even their own leader. This was because juries were sympathetic to the marchers and refused to convict them despite clear evidence of breaches.[38] This paved the way for the Act to be repealed.

In the southern hemisphere, the first official Orange march by New Zealand Orangemen occurred in Christchurch and Timaru in 1879. It resulted in the so-called 'Boxing Day Riots'.[39] The characteristic feature of this conflict was the presence of large numbers of Irish Catholics and the physical presence of Orange parades in their vicinity. The march the following year was heavily policed and the local Catholic priest, Father Ginaty, also weighed in to preserve the peace. Future parades passed off without any incident, due to a large police presence and the strong influence of the Catholic Church, whose priests, with the local bishop's backing, kept the peace.[40] While these riots have attracted some attention, subsequent marches through to the twentieth century continued without any major incidents. From this point on, the marching tradition in New Zealand had only the weather and the ability to muster the numbers on the ground as its notable opponents.

Across the Tasman Sea, the Australian Orange Order experienced quite a different situation. Melbourne in 1845 saw the local Orangemen advertising their intent to parade. In response, some Irish Catholics advertised for a hurling match at Batman's Hill.[41] This was a veiled threat against the Orangemen, who decided not to march but to hold a banquet dinner instead.[42] The following year, the Orangemen only had a dinner. However, the banners and flags outside their venue attracted hundreds of Irish Catholics, which ended in a riot. The government response was to pass a Party Processions Act similar to the Irish one. Besides banning processions that might create 'religious and political animosities', the Act also noted banners, flags and even music in the legislation.[43] From an

Orange perspective this was harsh, given they never marched. To further restrict their right to march, this Act was extended in 1849, 1855 and 1859.[44] Further legislation in 1865 made it permanent.[45]

Further north in Brisbane in 1890 their first Orange procession was heavily regulated by the Party Processions Act. Despite having about 600 marchers, they were only allowed one banner and no party tunes. Mounted police oversaw the whole parade.[46] It was a 'no banners or music' march the following year. The Australian example demonstrates that the colonial governments were not prepared to take any risks, and would have had the benefit of seeing the Irish situation. Over time more legislation and repeals enabled the resumption of marches in the nineteenth century for both Melbourne and Brisbane.[47]

While the marches in New Zealand were watched by the public, there was less impact from sectarian feeling than had been seen with the northern hemisphere parades. The fact that New Zealand was predominantly Protestant, and that marches did not traverse Catholic neighbourhoods, were other factors. This was a point of difference compared to Australia, which had a larger Irish Catholic population, but even in Australia the conflict over Orange parades dissipated over time. However, it was a different story in the northern hemisphere. Cities like Liverpool and Toronto saw almost ritualistic clashes into the early twentieth century. As a result, they earned the sobriquets 'the Belfast of England' and 'the Belfast of Canada', though this sent a mixed message, acknowledging both the violence and the strong monarchist values and influence within civic life of the Protestant majority in both cities.[48] However, it was the Orange Order's notoriety that was cemented in the public consciousness with these highly publicised sectarian clashes. Despite this, violence ceased in these countries, but continued in what is now Northern Ireland.

Indeed, the negative image of nineteenth-century-style Orange parades and protests in Northern Ireland remains in the public consciousness. The most notorious example of this was the annual July march to Drumcree Church, Portadown, County Armagh. This historic route goes back to 1807, and passed through an area that with demographic shifts is now mostly Catholic. Previously it had seen some violence throughout its history; however, from the mid-1990s until 2000 it drew international coverage. Images splashed across newspapers and television showed Orangemen and loyalist supporters involved in clashes with police, security forces and local Catholic residents.[49] All that was negative about historic Orange parades was magnified. The Parades Commission was established in response and oversees the parades, both

Orange and other, throughout present-day Northern Ireland. It has seen a gradual reduction in the overall number of parades; the Commission's own figures show that the increased numbers of loyalist parades steadily rose from 1,897 in 1985 to reach a peak of 2,851 in 2015, but then dropped to 2,435 in 2017.[50]

The ongoing issue of Orange parades in Northern Ireland continuing to generate conflict is complex. While there are still contentious parade routes, not all parades result in conflict. Even at the height of the Troubles, in the mid-1990s, the Chief Constable noted that the vast majority of more than 3,000 parades and demonstrations each year passed off with little or no trouble. However, they still require a substantial deployment of police resources.[51] This view is supported by the Parades Commission, which noted the thousands of parades that took place with very few restrictions.[52] An example of this was the 2006–7 season that saw less than 7 per cent of parades attract closer scrutiny. Although conflict at these parades was not widespread, this does not mean that it did not occur. The riots in 2005 were seen as an anomaly in light of the falling costs around policing and conflict since the 1990s.[53] There was an acknowledgement that all parties, whether loyalist or nationalist, had to work together.[54] Subsequent reports made similar comments.[55] The Parades Commission itself has been credited by some as being a factor in the reduction of conflict in response to contentious parades. The 2005 example was the result of a number of changes to routes through predominantly Catholic areas.[56]

There has been considerable focus on the resulting conflict at parades with 'triumphal marches' through neighbourhoods or within sight of Irish Catholics. The catalyst for the conflict has often been the bands and the music they play. The use of bands within the Orange Order goes back to the beginning of the Order itself. They followed traditions of the Volunteer movement that was prominent in Ireland in the 1780s, which employed fife and drum bands. This musical tradition was integral to the Orange parades in the 1790s.[57] Many of the Orangemen were employed in the army or other militias and therefore had a clear model to follow. The move from military-style fife and drum bands to flute bands, including the controversial Lambeg drum, has been well documented.[58] Also, this militaristic aspect of Orange bands forms part of the negative image of these parades. From a Catholic perspective, having bands and people in military-style uniforms march through their territory in remembrance of past victories against Catholics is surely a recipe for conflict.

The music or 'party tunes' used in these Orange parades provoked strong feelings within Irish Catholic communities. This was because these songs had lyrics that expressed a triumphalism over the historic defeats of Catholics. Examples of the controversial party tunes include 'The Boyne Water' and 'Croppies Lie Down'. In Scotland, these were often the catalyst for conflict when they were played near Catholic churches.[59] There are numerous instances of the use of 'The Boyne Water' causing dissension. The obvious cases are in Northern Ireland, which have been well documented. However, strong feelings about this music occurred elsewhere too.

The provocative nature of using 'party tunes' in Orange parades is best illustrated in the case of Mossend, a town in North Lanarkshire, Scotland, in 1897. Thirteen members of the Bellshill Conservative Flute Band had been fined by local magistrates for playing party tunes including 'The Boyne Water'. This case was questioned in parliament by William Johnston, MP of South Belfast. He asked whether 'playing Protestant tunes in the streets is contrary to the laws of Scotland'. In reply, Andrew Graham Murray, the Lord Advocate, noted this band had marched through a predominantly Catholic area playing party tunes. Two bandsmen had been attacked. The bandsmen were charged with 'parading the streets playing those tunes with the premeditated purpose of provoking and exasperating, whereby a breach of the peace was committed'. Murray saw no reason to question the decision.[60]

This example has all of the elements of Orange parades, both past and present. The first issue was whether the music they played could be deemed musical or inflammatory. The second was the choice of location where they marched. In this case, it was a Catholic area. These precursors to violent conflict, so prevalent in Ireland, also saw parallels in the Orange diaspora. The difference is that Ireland has managed to epitomise all that is negative about the Orange Order, and has maintained this notoriety into the present.

Towards Peaceful Parades

There is no denying the negative aspects of the Orange parades and the various riots and sectarian violence that have emanated from them. Northern Ireland had its own problems with constant conflict before and after Partition. In contrast, it is worth noting how things changed in the Orange diaspora, particularly for the parading culture.

The 1920s were a pivotal decade for many cities and countries. In England, Liverpool saw mass slum clearances in the interwar years which changed its demographic make-up.[61] The problematic places around the city that previously had simmering tensions no longer existed. Further slum clearances in the 1960s also contributed to changing demographic patterns. Ultimately, the Orange areas that had existed en bloc were no more. An immediate impact was that the parades were able to continue without constant opposition. In the USA, the Orange Order transitioned from nineteenth-century problematic parades to relatively peaceful ones. This was due to the decreasing numbers of marchers and the American Orange Order not having a clear public profile. Bystanders could enjoy the spectacle of the parade, but have absolutely no idea about its meaning.[62] In New Zealand, there was relatively little conflict compared to other Orange jurisdictions, and Orangemen marched well into the twentieth century, with parades largely incident-free.[63] A possible explanation was that the marches did not traverse Catholic neighbourhoods. A further factor was that the Orange Order was not numerically strong.

In the twenty-first century, while much of the Orange diaspora has had relatively conflict-free marches, there were issues elsewhere. Ron Bather, Grand Master of the Grand Orange Lodge of England (GOLE), speaking in 2004, claimed that they celebrate 'the Twelfth' because it is 'our heritage'. He then made a telling comment that 'it's a carnival day and the Liverpool parade is very different from the ones that take place in Northern Ireland and Scotland'.[64] This view of Orange parades in England, deemed to be carnival-like, highlights the difference in emphasis between England, Ireland and Scotland. The GOLE, over the years, has also had stricter controls over the parades. For example, any bands invited to parade must provide a 'valid band/contract/clearance form from their own District/County Lodge'.[65] There is an approved list of bands, and this means the problems likely to arise are minimised as band members would have to be members of the Orange Order. This is a factor in helping to maintain relatively peaceful parades.

This point of difference emphasised by the English Order is something that the hierarchies of the Orange Order in Ireland and Scotland have attempted to change, with both the Irish and the Scottish Orders seeking greater control over their bands. The challenge for the Irish was that while there had been 'contractual agreements' between bands and lodges, there was no uniformity in usage. This changed in 1986, with the Conditions of Engagement. These eleven clauses included band members obeying parade marshalls, an alcohol ban, and church parades having hymns and 'sacred marching arrangements'.[66] While some bands have been suspended, there has not been strict enforcement of these rules.[67] The GOLS followed suit, though they stipulated it was only Orange church parades that had alcohol bans and only 'recognisable Hymn tunes' should be played. An additional condition was that bands taking part in Orange church parades in Scotland had to attend the church service.[68] These controls were only applicable to church parades and therefore many parades that did not fit this category were essentially exempt. Ultimately, these were all attempts to control 'undesirable' loyalist sympathisers at the parades.[69]

Dealing with potentially unruly bands was one problem, but the other was the general violent and drunken behaviour at Orange parades. Again, the Irish and Scottish Orange Orders have tried to rebrand the parades as family-friendly events. The Grand Orange Lodge of Ireland (GOLI) tried this in 1987 by having barbecues and music concerts.[70] However, this was simply not enough. Eventually, the GOLI moved to the 'Orangefest' concept. This originally came through the Grand Lodge Education Committee and was then adopted by County Tyrone to brand their community development and outreach programme and annual Twelfth celebrations, before it was implemented by Belfast in 2009.[71] The GOLS mimicked the Irish model and launched their Orangefest on 6 June 2015. The idea was to showcase Orange culture and provide not just the usual parade and bands, and it also included educational displays and short lectures.[72] Despite these attempts at creating peaceful parades in Scotland, *The Herald* reported on Orangefest being 'staged amid much social media protest and condemnation from some quarters', including an online petition signed by about 30,000 people.[73] The negative image persists, and this is linked to the ongoing anti-social behaviour at the parades.

Governmental responses have been at the forefront of ongoing problems in communities around parades. The landmark Orr Report, commissioned by the Scottish Parliament in June 2004, focused on all parades.[74] Key recommendations included the involvement of communities, and holding organisers liable for the behaviour of those participating in parades.[75] Over the following decades, there were more governmental reports and legislation that attempted to both limit and understand these parades. Notable issues identified were the public and businesses attributing unruly behaviour of non-members to the Orange Order, and other non-Orange parades.[76] This was also a theme of the Orr Report.[77] A government-commissioned independent report in 2016 confirmed the findings of Orr's report. It found the Glasgow Boyne parade was now so well run that police resources were reduced by 55 per cent; however, there were still, like in Ireland, negative public perceptions about parades.[78]

At the core of public opposition to parades was the persistent drunkenness associated with the Twelfth. In response, the GOLI launched a campaign in 2016 with the slogan 'It's about the Battle, not the Bottle'. County Grand Master George Chittick implored those taking part in the celebrations that 'at the Twelfth of July we celebrate victory at the Boyne. It's not about getting drunk.'[79] A commissioned report noted a definite reduction in alcohol consumed. There was a major marketing drive with up to 20,000 leaflets and water bottles distributed, promoting the responsible drinking message. The report also noted that retailers claimed they witnessed only 46 per cent street drinking, as opposed to 66 per cent the previous year.[80] The mixture of governmental and commissioned reports have all stemmed from the problems associated with the parades. The empirical evidence has shown some improvement, but the negative image persists.

THE DECLINE AND RESURGENCE OF THE PARADING TRADITION

Decline

The decline of the Orange parading tradition is as varied as the countries in which they occurred. Common elements were the falling membership and the period in which this ensued. Outside of Northern Ireland, England and Scotland stand out as the main Orange jurisdictions that have managed to maintain reasonable turnouts for their parades. However, this is only a shadow of their physical dominance in times past. Scotland, like Northern Ireland, has many parades, but the ones in Glasgow generally dominate. In 1951 there were 100,000 in attendance but these figures steadily fell in the 1960s and 1970s to around 4–8,000 in the 2010s. The advent of the Covid-19 pandemic saw parades cease but they resumed with figures in the 4,000s by 2023.[81] The Orange parades remain a regular feature of the Scottish landscape. Further south in England, the trend for high turnouts for parades in the Merseyside area has been on the decline since the 1980s. There were consistently 10–20,000 turning out for these marches from the 1930s up until the 1980s.[82] However, even now their numbers are boosted by lodges from other regions. For example, in a 2017 parade there were 125 lodges from Birmingham, Liverpool, London, Manchester, Sunderland, Scotland and other parts of the UK.[83] They too had disruptions due to the Covid-19 pandemic but have resumed parades.

The fall-off in attendance at parades in England and Scotland in the 1950s and 1960s seems to coincide with secularisation. In particular, the fall in church attendance has been mapped as a symptom of the lessening influence of Christianity in these countries.[84] The Orange Order had an expectation of churchgoing members coupled with their Reformation Protestantism. These prerequisites, alongside a decline in churchgoing, meant they had a diminishing base of potential members. This was further exacerbated by the immigration of other cultures, but also other religions, so the Catholic-Protestant divide was lessened.[85] An interesting shift has been that anti-Catholic rhetoric is no longer the preserve of Protestantism. A secular movement has sprung up opposed to the Pope and various beliefs of the Catholic Church and its influence in society. This same movement is also opposed to the influence of evangelical Christianity.[86]

Canada was probably the only part of the Orange diaspora in the past that could rival Ireland in terms of parades and numbers on the ground, with Toronto at the heart of Canadian Orangeism. The changes in the demographic make-up of Toronto, however, contributed to the fall in numbers attending parades. Unlike in England and Scotland, the heyday of Canadian Orangeism occurred much earlier, in the 1920s and 1930s, when 10–12,000 regularly marched.[87] Despite numbers falling to only the hundreds, the parade continues each year, and on the 200th anniversary of the parade in 2020 there were estimated to be about 400 people in attendance. Many came from the UK and other parts of Canada to celebrate.[88] Areas like Brampton, a city in the Greater Toronto Area, used to have large Orange parades. Now, however, the symbolism of orange flags represents the beginning of the Sikh Khalsa Day celebrations rather than Battle of the Boyne marches. Almost half of the city are recent immigrants, with about one-third originating from South Asia.[89] This changing demographic is largely the case for many parts of Canada. The change in ethnic make-up means the Orange Order is no longer as relevant as it once was.

Further south in the United States, the Orange Order never had parades the size of Canada's. Their major parades were, however, larger in New York and Philadelphia since the close proximity of these cities helped them support each other's parades and in turn boost parade numbers. The major difference between Canada and the United States was the lower membership of the American Orange lodges. This was exacerbated by the very nature of the American Orange Order, as not only were they a loyalist organisation in a republic, but there were already other 'native' American fraternal organisations to compete with.[90] Other factors contributing to the decline in parading were internal problems. There was a split in 1914 in the American Orange Order over the leadership of the organisation.[91] Dividing into two groups meant that the 12 July marches had separate parades. For example, in July 1916 1,500 marchers, representing the 'drys' or total abstinence side of the Orange Order, marched. The 'wets', who allowed alcohol, had 15,000 marchers with twenty-five bands.[92] These kinds of disputes, coupled with a lack of ability to expand their base numbers, diminished the power of the American parades.

The furthest outpost of the Orange Order, New Zealand, saw parades decline faster than elsewhere. The number of marchers in the main centres in New Zealand tended not to move much above 200–300 people.[93] The noticeable exceptions were increases of up to 700 marching in Auckland in the interwar years, which was probably due to the offshoot of the Orange Order, the Protestant Political Association.[94] Reported numbers at parades beyond the 1930s are difficult to ascertain as newspapers no longer gave figures and internal Orange sources did not report numbers either. The last recorded Orange parade was in Christchurch in 1967.[95] The following period coincided with the Troubles in Northern Ireland and local churches were hostile to Orange members having their services there. A bomb threat in 1967 also meant the parades ceased and finding churches willing to hold services was problematic.[96] Currently, New Zealand has a reputation in the Orange world that they do not march.[97] A salient factor in this has been a falling membership directly influenced by older members dying and not being replaced.[98]

Australia is an anomaly compared to the other Orange jurisdictions. As noted earlier, its parading history was affected by constant parading legislation. While Ireland had similar constraints, there was more defiance by members who paraded regardless. The Canadian Orange Order had a similar attitude to Ireland. The Australian Orange Order, despite its reputation, was more law-abiding than the others. In the face of the legal constraints on parades, they tended to have indoor demonstrations. Sydney managed to have huge turnouts of between 5,000 and 8,000 people in the late nineteenth century.[99] Brisbane followed a similar pattern to Sydney, with indoor processions.[100] They too began marching, bolstered by other fraternal organisations, with figures in the 1890s as high as Sydney's.[101] The 1890s were important for the Sydney lodges as they managed to have outdoor parades and continued to do so well into the 1980s. While there were turnouts of around 4,000 in 1950, the lodges were in decline by the 1960s and 1970s, with marches only attracting members in the low hundreds.[102] The patchy history of parading certainly affected the Australian Orange Order as they struggled to deal with legislation and then falling numbers. The demise of the Orange parades in New South Wales occurred when the Grand Orange

Lodge of New South Wales decided to stop having parades in 1987.[103] Brisbane fell from having highs of 2–3,000 in the 1930s to only seventy by 1970.[104]

Both Australia and New Zealand also experienced wider societal changes, particularly the increase in secularisation and the immigration of other religious groups. The extremes of other European societies and the Americas were not as pronounced in New Zealand, while there was never a state church, and there were two premiers in the nineteenth century, John Ballance and Robert Stout, who were Freethinkers.[105] Despite the heated religious tensions already mentioned in the interwar period, as the twentieth century progressed the brand of Christianity in New Zealand was less combative. Under these conditions, the Orange Order struggled to attract significant members. This, in turn, had an impact on parade attendance.

Australia saw a slightly different situation. New South Wales effectively had a state church in the Church of England. This changed with the passing of the Church Act of 1836. Once this was in place, Catholics and Protestants had equality in religious practice.[106] From this time, once the other Australian states were established, there was a continuance of the separation of church and state in regard to setting policy. These conditions were very similar for both Australia and New Zealand, which resulted in societies that were keen not to import Old World animosities into their respective countries. Falling membership for both Australian and New Zealand Orange lodges occurred as each country became more secular in focus and liberal in practice. Marching in July, celebrating victories over Catholics, no longer drew members nor crowds. Being winter in the southern hemisphere also meant the weather was colder and wetter than at the summer parades of the northern hemisphere.

Attempts at Resurgence

The decline of the Orange parading tradition is evident in the dwindling numbers of marchers on parade and in the number of parades across the Orange world. As already noted, New Zealand no longer has parades at all, and places like Canada no longer have sizeable parades involving thousands of marchers. Does that mean the Orange parading tradition is dying out? The answer to this is a little more nuanced.

The best place to find a possible answer is in Ireland, where the signs of a vibrant marching tradition seem to lie with the bands. While Northern Ireland has a long history of marching bands, it was the 1970s that saw the sheer number of parades exponentially increase. Some of this can be attributed to the increase in band parades.[107] Some researchers found that the motivation to join bands was not necessarily sectarian but socio-economic. There were many unemployed young Protestant males who were given a positive leisure activity by joining a band. It was also an alternative to joining paramilitary organisations.[108] Another crucial element in this change since the 1970s has been the shift from bands being connected to an Orange lodge to bands that often have no connection to the lodge. The working-class Protestant males who make up the demographic of many bands use them to express their Protestant identity rather than as members of Orange lodges. Often, these young men see being Protestant as a cultural and political expression of their identity rather than as a religious one.[109]

Currently, there are over 600 marching bands within the Protestant community of Northern Ireland and the border counties of the Republic of Ireland.[110] This correlates with the increased number of parades in the region. There are typically five types of bands in Northern Ireland. The least common are the silver and brass bands. The only real difference between these bands is that silver bands are brass bands with their instruments silver plated. The instruments are expensive so this, combined with a fall in the traditional sponsors, factories, has led to their decline. The next type is the 'kilty', pipe or bagpipe bands, found mostly in County Tyrone. A fourth type is the accordion bands, which originally had a rebellious reputation. However, this has now been offset by the involvement of more female band members.[111]

By far the largest band type is the flute band, prevalent in Counties Antrim, Down and Londonderry. Subsets of flute bands are blood and thunder, melody flute and part-music bands. A 2006 survey showed that although the total number of flute bands was high at 327, of these 231 are the 'blood and thunder' or 'fuck the pope' flute bands.[112] 'Kick the pope' bands is used as a euphemism by reporters to lessen the impact of the offensive language of the other phrase.[113] The blood aspect comes from drummers banging their drums so hard that they bleed. Although these were essentially flute bands, they attracted a different demographic, particularly in terms of age, gender and socio-economic status. Melody flute bands are mostly drawn from working- and middle-class males. Their uniforms are more British military band-style rather than based on regiments. They play mostly British military tunes with some Orange tunes and hymns.[114] Part-music flute bands are mixed gender and more middle class. They are generally involved in competitions, with only a few taking part in Orange parades. Musically they range widely, from jazz and pop to Orange tunes and hymns.[115] Blood and thunder flute

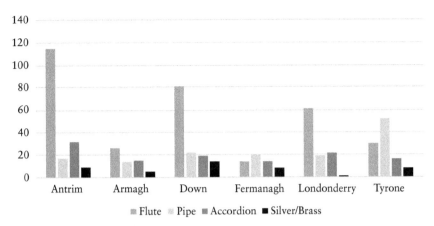

Figure 4.1 Protestant bands, Northern Ireland, 2006 (Witherow, 'Band development in Northern Ireland', p. 48)

bands generally attract working-class males with a strong loyalist stance and sometimes feature paramilitary symbols. Since the peace process, this has changed, as their own communities have criticised them, so they have toned down the more aggressive behaviour. They play party tunes but have expanded to pop tunes and even football and movie tunes.[116] As already noted, these were an outlet for working-class Protestant youth who had poor job prospects. Although originating in Scotland, these types of bands have a reputation in Ireland for their boisterous displays.[117]

In a bid to justify the existence of their parading culture, the GOLI commissioned a report in 2013 on the socio-economic impact of parades in Northern Ireland. At this time there were 660 bands with approximately 25,740 members, based on an average membership of thirty-nine in each band. The report estimated that the total economic impact of all 660 bands was £8,866,869 each year.[118] This was an impressive amount and helped provide the GOLI with an economic argument for the continuance of the parades and the bands that performed in them.

Scotland has around 111 flute bands and only nine accordion bands.[119] Scotland also had similar unemployment problems to Northern Ireland, and band membership served as an important social outlet for younger members.[120] On a lesser scale, the bands in England played a role in the revitalisation of lodges. This impact can be quite significant even with the formation of one band. In 1973 King William III LOL 11 in Portsmouth decided to form a band. The members chose the accordion and modelled it on the Ulster part-music accordion bands. The GOLE saw the band's success as encouraging the southern England lodges to hold regular parades.[121] The cost of equipment for bands is a factor noted in Grand Lodge sessions. Even as early as 1898, one lodge in Toxteth Park, Liverpool, voted a show of thanks to local MP Robert Houston for gifting a bass drum to their local band.[122] At the present time, the GOLE's approved list has ten accordion and concertina bands out of a total of twenty.[123] Certainly cost and the family nature of the English parades have been factors affecting the dominance of a less intimating band type and style.

The entire Orange world was influenced by a falling membership with correlating drops in parade attendance. In contrast, the presence of bands at parades has sometimes been cited as a sign of growth for the Orange Order. This certainly was a way for younger members to participate. This may have been true of Northern Ireland, but what about the Orange diaspora? Canada, which has had a strong marching tradition, especially in Toronto, had large numbers taking part as band members. The number of Toronto Orange bands has shrunk considerably since their peak in the 1920s with parades having as many as sixty bands. In the late 1980s, as marchers and bands declined, there were imports from other countries like the Glasgow Rangers Accordion Band from Scotland.[124] Canadian bands reflect the Irish and Scottish ones, with flute, pipe and accordion bands predominating throughout their parading history.[125] The marchers in the parades are generally representatives of the various lodges. The falling numbers at parades have also meant there is no longer the need to have as many bands.

The American case was a peculiar one that had to juggle the loyalist origins of the Orange Order with the patriotism of the American republic. When it came to parades, what did they stand for? The 1920s were the heyday of American Orangeism and, in some ways, this defined what was positive and negative about them. For instance, in 1920, Philadelphia had 8,000 men and 2,000 women march in July, led by twenty-five bands, while New York managed 6,000.[126] These were significant numbers as the USA was not seen as a particularly strong part of the Orange Order. It was a great turnout for the base of the American Orange Order, but the challenge for them was in the other regions of the USA. This often meant trying to bolster numbers and influence by partnering with other patriotic organisations. The conduit for this was the parade.

The peak of the American Orange Order occurred in the 1920s, and this coincided with the second iteration of the Ku Klux Klan (1915–44). One documented and photographed instance of these two 'patriotic' organisations joining for parading purposes was in Maine. On this occasion, the State Grand Lodge of Maine on 9 June 1924 had voted that the local Ku Klux Klan 'be given an invitation to unite with us July 12th at Island Falls'.[127] The reason for the invitation is not noted, but it may well have been an effort to widen the Orange Order's membership base. The profile of both organisations was similar in the American context. Although in other Orange jurisdictions a colour bar for membership was not evident, this was 1920s America, and the Protestant base for members shared similar ideals and a colour bar.[128] Both were wary of the Catholic Church and other immigrants diluting their Protestant base. The local newspapers noted this was the largest Orange march they had ever witnessed in a parade in their town.[129]

More joint processions occurred in Indiana.[130] In Linton, thousands of Ku Klux Klan and Orange members paraded. The evening speaker was English-born Rev. Frederick B. Griffice (1856–1926) from Indianapolis, who used to be a speaker for the influential Ku Klux Klan magazine the *Fiery Cross*.[131] He spoke of the origins and principles of the Orange Order and then proclaimed:

> Brother Klansmen . . . As Orangemen we love you for the cause you represent. Let us stand together. We have a strong and growing Orange order in this country, to which we extend a hearty welcome to such persons as can show a good, clean record.[132]

Griffice's appeal to the Ku Klux Klan members was an apparent attempt to garner extra members. The Ku Klux Klan, like the Orange Order, promoted itself as a fraternal organisation, which in turn created an air of respectability for potential members and supporters.[133] Despite this push for membership through joint parades, it was short-lived, as the Ku Klux Klan had their scandals that resulted in a dramatic drop in membership.[134] The American Orange Order survived, but its numerical strength was never the same. There continued to be parades for many years, even in New York into the 1950s.[135] However, as membership dwindled, so did the parades. The large parades of the 1920s no longer occur; now they are just small parades by a few of the remaining lodges.

New Zealand had a shorter band tradition. Unlike their northern hemisphere counterparts, the number of marches was limited; this was reflected in the band tradition as well. Christchurch, which had the longest-running Orange parades in New Zealand, relied upon brass and pipe bands for their events. These bands also played at other events such as agricultural and pastoral shows and community events.[136] The small scale reflected the fact that only three major pipe bands were established in twentieth-century Christchurch.[137] The advent of pipe bands did mean

Figure 4.2 Orange Order and Ku Klux Klan march, Island Falls, Maine
(Collections of Cary Library, © www.VintageMaineImages.com)

a change in Orange parade bands. The band of choice from the early 1880s to 1908 was the brass band;[138] after this, it was predominantly pipe bands up until the last Orange parade in 1967.[139] New Zealand did not have the numbers in their Orange lodges to sustain Orange bands, and the reliance on bands for hire meant younger members did not see this as an extension of their identity in the way their Irish counterparts did. The scale was never there, so dwindling membership essentially killed off the parades.

Australia, like New Zealand, never had significant numbers of bands, with most parades only having one or two bands to lead it. Once Sydney stopped marching in 1987, there were no Orange parades for many years across Australia; then in Adelaide in 2008, a parade was held with only one Orangeman walking. The resurrection of parades in South Australia has primarily been due to the presence of the Charlie Armstrong Memorial Flute Band. An influx of new members, mostly from Northern Ireland, also helped to re-establish the marching tradition.[140] The choice of a flute band reflects the Irish experience rather than the music scene in Australia. As with what happened in Portsmouth, this band helped reinvigorate the local lodges.

While partnering with other organisations did not really do much to increase membership of the Orange Order, the most obvious partnership was one that occurred within the families of Orangemen. Orange parades are often seen as an all-male affair, and therefore the expected sight is of 'Orangemen' who march on the Twelfth of July rather than 'Orangewomen'. This image in the public consciousness is also an Irish one as again the Orange Order has been portrayed as an Irish organisation. Yet the Orange Order, from its inception, has had female involvement in parades.

There are early examples of parades in Ireland where women marched. An early instance was Englishman Thomas Reid's 1822 description of a march, where he was quite scathing of both the march and the involvement of women. However, the women were there in an unofficial capacity.[141] Over the years, Orangewomen's involvement in Irish parades has been by invitation. In other cases they have been the organisers of the catering and supporters on the sidelines while the men march.[142] Despite all this involvement, the GOLI did not officially allow women the right to walk during marching season until 1990.[143] Any prior instances of women marching were not officially sanctioned. Linda Racioppi and Katherine O'Sullivan See explored this gendered role with an example in Belfast in 1999. They found that out of 250 Orange lodges marching on the Twelfth, only three were ladies' lodges.[144] Their conclusions reinforced perceptions of the gendered role of women as helpers rather than as partners in Orange parades.

Unlike the often strictly gendered parades of the Irish, England has had a reasonably long history of women being directly involved in parades, which helped to increase the number of participants. A notable feature of English parades has been their gender-inclusive parading and family atmosphere. This gender inclusiveness goes back to 1852 when the Grand Protestant Association of Loyal Orangemen (GPALO) also had female lodges. One notable example was where both male and female lodges marched in Lancashire.[145] Over time the English lodges extended the marches, most notably in Liverpool, to become family-friendly. A commonly photographed feature was children dressing up as William and Mary. This goes back to at least 1923.[146] The shift to Southport being the main Orange parade, with Liverpool one of the feeder parades, occurred in the 1940s. Part of the appeal for the GOLE is the presence of tourists and the family-friendly carnival feel of the parades which helps to negate criticism of the Orange Order.

All other parts of the Orange Order, with the notable exception of Ireland, have a history of including women in their marches, and then later children as the various junior or juvenile lodges were formed.[147]

Figure 4.3 Junior parade, Scotland, c. 1963–4 (© David Bryce)

Their inclusion may well have contributed to the lessening of conflict as the presence of women and children made any violence less likely. It may also explain why the conflict in Ireland has continued. The inclusion of women has also led to differences in the look of the parades across the Orange diaspora. The traditional spectacle of men in bowler hats with Orange sashes certainly does not apply outside of Ireland. This certainly helped to keep the parades going longer in the Orange diaspora.

In terms of the visual aesthetic, there was a commonality between the American and Canadian Orangewomen, as both wore distinctive white dresses. In the American case, their regulations stipulate 'short white dresses and orange sashes for parade purposes'.[148] This was definitely a point of difference for the Americas as the other jurisdictions did not have a set colour apart from their regalia. However, that did not rule out certain dress codes. Scotland was notable for its 'trouser' rule. One study of Orangewomen in Scotland documented the struggle for Orangewomen to wear regalia and then not have to wear dresses. The only concession was in 1993 with 'tailored culottes'.[149] The Orange Order is a conservative loyalist organisation, so they followed the conservative norms that were sometimes at odds with the society in which they were situated. This conservatism would not have attracted younger women to the organisation. It definitely would have affected numbers, as a lessening of these constraints might have led to the retention of younger members as they moved through the organisation.

CONCLUSION

Much of the research regarding Orange parades has focused on Northern Ireland, and the key themes of maintaining the Protestant hegemony and unionism have dominated the Orange parade literature. Countries like Australia and New Zealand, while having a history of parades, never had displays to rival their counterparts in Ireland. Meanwhile, Orangemen in the USA, a republic, can only show displays of Protestantism coupled with American patriotism. Their brief dalliance with the Ku Klux Klan only underscored their desperation to do anything to attract members. Canada is the only country where parades could match those in Ireland. Orange members in England and Scotland, while geographically closer to Ireland, have not been able to sustain continuous parades with a large attendance. Probably the most significant differences between Ireland and the Orange diaspora have been the decrease in sectarian tensions and the increase in mixed-gender parades. These differences are due in part to changes in the wider society in terms of migration and increasing secularisation. This has led to decreasing membership, which in turn has led to falling parade numbers, or none at all in New Zealand's case. Conversely, migration and the forming of bands have led to a mini-revival in South Australia. In some ways, the bands may well outlast the Orange Order itself.

Northern Ireland and Scotland have been at the centre of most of the parading controversies throughout the history of the Orange Order. Despite a myriad of legislation, government reports and corporate-type publicity campaigns to deal with the vexed issues around parades, public perceptions are still quite negative. Probably the primary reason for this is the history of conflict with Irish Catholic communities, which in turn led to well-documented riots. Just like the Orange Order's attempt to use parades to celebrate past events, this same concept of memory is also used by the general public to remember the worst aspects of these parades and forget the peaceful ones.

NOTES

1. The original date for the battle was the 1st under the old Julian calendar, but with the advent of the Gregorian calendar it became the 12th. For a good summary of the development of the Twelfth celebrations, see chapter 3 of Dominic Bryan, *Orange Parades: The Politics of Ritual, Tradition and Control* (London: Pluto Press, 2000).
2. Cecil Kilpatrick (ed.), *The Formation of the Orange Order 1795–1798* (Belfast: GOLI, 1999), p. 71.
3. Ibid. p. 72.
4. *Belfast News Letter*, 15 July 1796.
5. Sean Farrell, *Rituals and Riots: Sectarian Violence and Political Culture in Ulster, 1784–1886* (Lexington: University Press of Kentucky, 2000); Michael A. Gordon, *The Orange Riots: Irish Political Violence in New York City, 1870 and 1871* (Ithaca and London: Cornell University Press, 1993); Scott W. See, *Riots in New Brunswick: Orange Nativism and Social Violence in the 1840s* (Toronto: University of Toronto Press, 1993); Christopher D. McGimpsey, 'Internal ethnic friction: Orange and green in nineteenth-century New York, 1868–1872', *Immigrants & Minorities*, 1:1 (1982), pp. 39–59; Seán Brosnahan, 'The "Battle of the Borough" and the "Saige O Timaru": Sectarian riot in colonial Canterbury', *New Zealand Journal of History*, 28:1 (1994), pp. 41–59; Eric Kaufmann, *The Orange Order: A Contemporary Northern Irish History* (Oxford: Oxford University Press, 2007); Dominic Bryan, 'Drumcree and "the right to march": Orangeism, ritual and politics in Northern Ireland', in T. G. Fraser (ed.), *The Irish Parading Tradition: Following the Drum* (Basingstoke: Palgrave Macmillan, 2000), pp. 191–207.

6. P. G. Goheen, 'The ritual of the streets in mid-19th-century Toronto', *Environment and Planning D: Society and Space*, 11 (1993), pp. 127–45; 'Parading: A lively tradition in early Victorian Toronto', in A. R. H. Baker and G. Biger (eds), *Ideology and Landscape in Historical Perspective* (Cambridge: Cambridge University Press, 1992), pp. 330–51; Donald M. MacRaild, '"The bunkum of Ulsteria": The Orange marching tradition in late Victorian Cumbria', in T. G. Fraser (ed.), *The Irish Parading Tradition: Following the Drum* (Basingstoke: Macmillan, 2000), pp. 44–59; Elaine McFarland, 'Marching from the margins: Twelfth July parades in Scotland, 1820–1914', in T. G. Fraser (ed.), *The Irish Parading Tradition: Following the Drum* (Basingstoke: Macmillan, 2000), pp. 60–77.

7. Dominic Bryan, 'The right to march: Parading a loyal Protestant identity in Northern Ireland', *International Journal on Minority and Group Rights*, 4 (1997), pp. 373–96; Bryan, *Orange Parades*; 'Parades, flags, carnivals and riots: Public space, contestation and transformation in Northern Ireland', *Peace and Conflict: Journal of Peace Psychology*, 21:4 (2015), pp. 565–73.

8. Darach MacDonald, *Blood and Thunder: Inside an Ulster Protestant Band* (Cork: Mercier Press, 2010); Neil Jarman, 'For God and Ulster: Blood and thunder bands and loyalist political culture', in T. G. Fraser (ed.), *The Irish Parading Tradition* (Basingstoke: Palgrave Macmillan, 2000), pp. 158–72.

9. Desmond Bell, *Acts of Union: Youth Culture and Sectarianism in Northern Ireland* (London: Macmillan, 1990); Katy Radford, 'Drum rolls and gender roles in Protestant marching bands in Belfast', *British Journal of Ethnomusicology*, 10:2 (2001), pp. 37–59; 'Red, white, blue and orange: An exploration of historically bound allegiances through loyalist song', *The World of Music*, 46:1 (2004), pp. 71–89.

10. Gordon Ramsey, 'Playing away: Liminality, flow and *communitas* in an Ulster flute band's visit to a Scottish Orange parade', in Suzel Ana Reily and Katherine Brucher (eds), *Brass Bands of the World: Militarism, Colonial Legacies, and Local Music Making* (Burlington, VT: Ashgate, 2013), p. 198; Stephen R. Millar, 'Musically consonant, socially dissonant: Orange walks and Catholic interpretation in West-Central Scotland', *Music and Politics*, 9:1 (2015), pp. 1–23.

11. S. Cupples, *The Principles of the Orange Association* (Dublin: W. McKenzie, 1799), p. 17.

12. Neil P. Maddox, '"A melancholy record": The story of the nineteenth-century Irish Party Processions Acts', *Irish Jurist*, 39 (2004), pp. 243–74.

13. Sara McQuaid, 'Parading memory and re-member-ing conflict: Collective memory in transition in Northern Ireland', *International Journal of Politics, Culture, and Society*, 30:1 (2017), pp. 23–41.

14. *Laws and Ordinances of the Orange Institution of Ireland: Revised and*

adopted by the Grand Orange Lodge of Ireland, June 3rd, 1896 (Dublin: GOLI, 1896), p. 9.

15. *Constitution and Laws of the Loyal Orange Institution of the United States of America* (Philadelphia: Protestant Standard Print, 1889); *Laws and Ordinances of the Orange Institution of New Zealand* (Auckland: Free Press, 1883); *Rules and Regulations of the Loyal Orange Institution of New South Wales, Adopted 25th August 1928* (Sydney: The Institution, 1928); *Laws and Constitutions of the Loyal Orange Institution of Scotland* (Glasgow: GOLS, 1986).

16. The open Bible symbolises free access to the Bible, and the crown the importance of the monarchy.

17. Jennifer Edwards and J. David Knottnerus, 'The Orange Order: Strategic ritualization and its organizational antecedents', *International Journal of Contemporary Sociology*, 44:2 (2007), pp. 185–6.

18. Farrell, *Rituals and Riots*, chapters 2 to 4, competently outlines the complexity of the period. Also see Maddox, '"A melancholy record"', pp. 243–74.

19. Unlawful Societies (Ireland) Act 1825 (6 Geo. IV c. 4); Party Processions (Ireland) Act 1832 (2 & 3 Will. 4 c. 118).

20. Maddox, '"A melancholy record"', p. 244.

21. Farrell, *Rituals and Riots*, pp. 1–4.

22. Georges Dennis Zimmerman, *Songs of Irish Rebellion: Irish Political Street Ballads and Rebel Songs, 1780–1900* (Dublin: Four Courts Press, 1966, 2002), p. 312.

23. Party Processions (Ireland) Act 1850 (13 & 14 Vict. c. 2).

24. Farrell, *Rituals and Riots*, chapter 6 outlines the process Orange leader William Johnston and his followers took. Party Processions Act (Ireland) Repeal Act 1872 (35 & 36 Vict. c. 22).

25. Frank Neal, *Sectarian Violence: The Liverpool Experience, 1819–1914* (Manchester: Manchester University Press, 1988; revised 2003), pp. 21, 31.

26. *Glasgow Herald*, 12 July 1822.

27. *Glasgow Courier*, 14 July 1842.

28. McFarland, 'Marching from the margins', pp. 62–4.

29. *New York Times*, 12 July 1871.

30. Samuel Ernest Long, *A Brief History of the Loyal Orange Institution in the United States of America* (Dromara, County Down: Samuel Ernest Long, 1979), p. 13.

31. Cecil J. Houston and William J. Smyth, *The Sash Canada Wore: A Historical Geography of the Orange Order in Canada* (Toronto: University of Toronto Press, 1980), p. 18.

32. Brian Clarke, 'Religious riot as pastime: Orange Young Britons, parades and public life in Victorian Toronto', in David A. Wilson (ed.), *The Orange Order in Canada* (Dublin: Four Courts Press, 2007), p. 114.

33. William J. Smyth, *Toronto, the Belfast of Canada: The Orange Order and*

the Shaping of Municipal Culture (Toronto: University of Toronto Press, 2015), p. 43.

34. Ian Radforth, 'Collective rights, liberal discourse, and public order: The clash over Catholic processions in mid-Victorian Toronto', *The Canadian Historical Review*, 95:4 (2014), pp. 511–44; Gregory S. Kealey, *Toronto Workers Respond to Industrial Capitalism 1867–1892* (Toronto: University of Toronto Press, 1980). See chapter 7 on Orange riots.

35. An Act to restrain Party Procession in certain cases 1843 (7 Vict. c. VI).

36. Gregory S. Kealey, 'Orangemen and the corporation: The politics of class during the Union of the Canadas', in Victor Loring Russell (ed.), *Forging a Consensus: Historical Essays on Toronto* (Toronto: University of Toronto Press, 1984), pp. 60–1.

37. A. H. Birmingham, County Master of Toronto, 1934, *How Orangeism Began in Canada*, <https://web.archive.org/web/20140624032544/http://canadianorangehistoricalsite.com/index-152.php> (accessed 10 July 2023).

38. Kealey, 'Orangemen and the corporation', p. 61.

39. Brosnahan, 'The "Battle of the Borough"', pp. 41–59.

40. *Press*, 13 July 1880.

41. Hurling was code for gathering members to stop Orange processions.

42. *Melbourne Courier*, 14 July 1845.

43. 10 Vict. No. 1, An Act to prevent for a limited time Party Processions and certain other public Exhibitions in the Colony of New South Wales.

44. 14 Vict. No. 49, 19 Vict. No. 1, 22 Vict. No. 68.

45. The Unlawful Assemblies and Party Processions Statute 1865.

46. *The Week*, 19 July 1890.

47. Party Processions Prevention Act 1846 10 Vic No. 1 (repealed 1899 63 Vic No. 9 s 3 sch 3); Party Processions Prevention Act Amendment Act 1857 20 Vic No. 6 (repealed 1899 63 Vic No. 9 s 3 sch 3).

48. *Liverpool Mail*, 24 July 1869; Smyth, *Toronto, the Belfast of Canada*.

49. Bryan, *Orange Parades*. Chapters 1 and 11 focus on Drumcree.

50. RUC Chief Constable's Reports 1986–1998; Parades Commission NI, Annual Reports 2004–2018.

51. The Royal Ulster Constabulary, *The Chief Constable's Annual Report 1995* (Belfast: RUC, 1996). The Chief Constable commands all police in Northern Ireland.

52. The Parades Commission was established in 1997 but only had a non-statutory basis. Its formalised role came into effect with the Public Processions (Northern Ireland) Act 1998. For further information about the Parades Commission and legislation see Mary Baber, *Public Processions in Northern Ireland*, House of Commons Research Paper 98/11 (London: House of Commons, 1998).

53. Michael Hamilton and Dominic Bryan, 'Deepening democracy? Dispute

system design and the mediation of contested parades in Northern Ireland', *Ohio State Journal on Dispute Resolution*, 22:1 (2006), pp. 133–87.

54. Parades Commission, *Parading in a Peaceful Northern Ireland: Forward View and Review of Procedures ...*, 2006–2007 (Belfast: Parades Commission, 2006), p. 3.

55. Access Parades Commission Reports at <https://www.paradescommis sion.org/Publications.aspx> (accessed 1 December 2023).

56. Ciarán O'Kelly and Dominic Bryan, 'The regulation of public space in Northern Ireland', *Irish Political Studies*, 22:4 (2007), pp. 565–84.

57. Gary Hastings, *With Fife and Drum: Music, Memories and Customs of an Irish Tradition* (Belfast: Blackstaff Press, 2003), p. 44.

58. Hastings, *With Fife and Drum*, and Gordon Ramsey, *Music, Emotion and Identity in Ulster Marching Bands: Flutes, Drums and Loyal Sons* (Oxford: Peter Lang, 2011).

59. McFarland, 'Marching from the margins', p. 63.

60. Hansard HC Deb, 4 March 1897, vol. 46 cc 1580–1.

61. Gareth Jenkins, 'Nationalism and sectarian violence in Liverpool and Belfast, 1880s–1920s', *International Labor and Working-Class History*, 78:1 (2010), p. 172. Also see Colin G. Pooley, 'Housing for the poorest poor: Slum clearance and rehousing in Liverpool, 1890–1918', *Journal of Historical Geography*, 11:1 (1985), pp. 70–88.

62. *Philadelphia Inquirer*, 10 September 1987. This parade in 1987 saw people watching who did not even know what an Orangeman was.

63. Patrick Coleman, 'Orange parading traditions in New Zealand 1880–1914', *Australasian Journal of Irish Studies*, 10 (2010), pp. 81–104.

64. *Liverpool Echo*, 10 July 2004.

65. Loyal Orange Institution of England, *Laws and Constitution Enacted by the Grand Lodge of England at Corby 15 September 1995* (London: GOLE, amended 2015), p. 14.

66. Bryan, *Orange Parades*, pp. 124–5.

67. Kaufmann, *The Orange Order*, p. 157.

68. *Laws and Constitutions of the Loyal Orange Institution of Scotland*, pp. 65–6.

69. Joseph Webster, *The Religion of Orange Politics: Protestantism and Fraternity in Contemporary Scotland* (Manchester: Manchester University Press, 2020). Webster notes the differences between the 'rough' or grass-roots Orange members and the 'respectable' members or Orange hierarchy.

70. *Orange Standard*, August 1987.

71. Jonathan Mattison, email to author, 27 March 2018.

72. *Orange Torch*, July/August 2015, pp. 1–5.

73. *The Herald*, 4 July 2015; *Daily Record*, 6 June 2015.

74. John Orr, *Review of Marches and Parades in Scotland: A Report* (Edinburgh: Scottish Executive, 2005).

75. *The Herald*, 23 February 2018.

76. *Justice 2 Committee Official Report 14 November 2005: Police, Public Order and Criminal Justice (Scotland) Bill: Stage 1*, <http://www.par liament.scot/parliamentarybusiness/report.aspx?r=2325> (accessed 1 December 2023).

77. Orr, *Review of Marches and Parades in Scotland*, p. 103.

78. Michael Rosie, *Independent Report on Marches, Parades and Static Demonstrations in Scotland* (Edinburgh: Scottish Government, 2016), pp. 16–17.

79. *Belfast Telegraph*, 5 July 2016.

80. *News Letter*, 1 June 2017; Sarah-Anne Attwood, *Orangefest 2017 Business Feedback & Event Report* (Belfast: Belfast City Centre Management, 2017).

81. *Glasgow Herald*, 1951–2023.

82. *Liverpool Chronicle, Liverpool Echo, The Herald, Liverpool Mail, Mercury, Southport Visiter*, 1930–2018.

83. *Southport Visiter*, 12 July 2017.

84. Callum G. Brown, *Religion and the Demographic Revolution: Women and Secularisation in Canada, Ireland, UK and USA since the 1960s* (Woodbridge and Rochester, NY: Boydell & Brewer, 2012).

85. Ian R. G. Spencer, *British Immigration Policy since 1939: The Making of Multi-Racial Britain* (London: Routledge, 1997).

86. John Wolffe, 'Conclusion: Beyond Protestant-Catholic conflict?', in John Wolffe (ed.), *Protestant-Catholic Conflict from the Reformation to the Twenty-First Century* (London: Palgrave Macmillan, 2013), pp. 263–4.

87. *Toronto Star, Globe and Mail*, 1925–38.

88. *The Sentinel*, 148:2 (Summer 2022), p. 3.

89. *Globe and Mail*, 15 April 2011.

90. Cecil J. Houston and William J. Smyth, 'Transferred loyalties: Orangeism in the United States and Ontario', *American Review of Canadian Studies*, 14:2 (1984), pp. 193–211.

91. See Long, *A Brief History*, for a simple overview of the split. Also, the American Orange Order paper, the *Orange and Purple Courier*, in the 1920s had numerous articles and documents about this issue.

92. *Evening Public Ledger*, 12 July 1916.

93. *Lyttleton Times, Press, Auckland Star, New Zealand Herald*, 1880–1934.

94. See Harold S. Moores, 'The rise of the Protestant Political Association: Sectarianism in N.Z. during World War I' (MA, University of Auckland, 1966).

95. *LOL No. 5 District Lodge, Christchurch, Minutes, August 1957– February 1983* (Orange Hall, Christchurch, New Zealand), 9 July 1967. Christchurch had the most regular parades.

96. Beverley Buist, interview by Patrick Coleman, 11 January 2005.

97. Patrick Coleman, 'The Orange tartan: Scottish influences on the New Zealand Orange Order', *History Scotland*, 18:1 (2018), p. 29.

98. Grand Proceedings from the 1950s and beyond decried the dwindling membership.
99. *Sydney Morning Herald*, 13 July 1886.
100. *Brisbane Courier*, 13 July 1886.
101. The context was the push on state aid to private schools and other Protestant organisations marched in solidarity of the Orange stance against this government aid.
102. *Sydney Morning Herald, Watchman, The Protestant Standard*, 1890–1975.
103. Loyal Orange Institution of NSW, *Sesqui-Centenary of the Grand Orange Lodge of New South Wales. Supplement to Souvenir Book 1995* (Chipping Norton, NSW: Gowans & Son Pty, Ltd, 1995), p. 11.
104. *Brisbane Courier, Queensland Times, The Courier Mail*, 1890–1970.
105. Peter J. Lineham, 'Freethinkers in nineteenth-century New Zealand', *New Zealand Journal of History*, 19:1 (1985), pp. 61–81.
106. Stephen A. Chavura and Ian Tregenza, 'A political history of the secular in Australia, 1788–1945', in Timothy Stanley (ed.), *Religion after Secularization in Australia* (New York: Palgrave Macmillan, 2015), pp. 7–8.
107. Bryan, 'The right to march', pp. 379–83.
108. Ramsey, *Music, Emotion and Identity*, pp. 90–1.
109. Jarman, 'For God and Ulster', p. 165.
110. Jonathan Mattison, email to author, 27 March 2018.
111. Bryan, *Orange Parades*, p. 126.
112. Jacqueline Witherow, 'Parading Protestantisms and the flute bands of postconflict Northern Ireland', in Jonathan Dueck and Suzel Ana Reily (eds), *The Oxford Handbook of Music and World Christianities* (Oxford: Oxford University Press, 2016), pp. 384–402.
113. Rosanne Cecil, 'The marching season in Northern Ireland: An expression of politico-religious identity', in Sharon Macdonald (ed.), *Inside European Identities: Ethnography in Western Europe* (London and New York: Routledge, 1993), p. 158.
114. Witherow, 'Parading Protestantisms', pp. 393–4.
115. Ibid. p. 396.
116. Ibid. pp. 390–2.
117. Bryan, *Orange Parades*, p. 71.
118. R. S. M. McClure Watters, *A Report on the Socio-Economic Impact of the Traditional Protestant Parading Sector in Northern Ireland* (Belfast: GOLI, 2013), pp. 2–3.
119. Based on information from band Facebook sites and the GOLS.
120. *The Scotsman*, 9 July 2017.
121. Grand Orange Lodge of England, *Grand Lodge Sessions Portsmouth 12–13 September 1997* (Portsmouth: GOLE, 1997), pp. 11–12. While the Portsmouth Accordion Band is an independent band, the members are all Orange members.

122. *The Everett LOL 108, Toxteth Park Liverpool, Minute Book 30 March 1882–5 July 1898* (Central Liverpool Library).
123. Grand Orange Lodge of England, 'Marching bands', <https://web.archive.org/web/20220529024048/https://www.gole.org.uk/bands> (accessed 20 July 2023).
124. *Toronto Star, Globe and Mail*, 1920–2004.
125. An example is the Ulster Accordion Band, founded in 1954 by Northern Irish immigrants. See Ian Adamson, *The Ulster Accordion Band*, <http://www.ianadamson.net/2011/06/04/the-ulster-accordian-band/> (accessed 1 December 2023).
126. *Orange and Purple Courier*, July–August 1920.
127. *28th Annual Session of State Grand Lodge of Maine No. 7, 9 June 1924, State Grand Lodge of Maine, Annual Session Minutes, 1923–1968*, Collection D0462, 1993–103 (Historical Society of Pennsylvania, Philadelphia, USA).
128. Originally you had to be white to be a member of the American Orange Order. See Loyal Orange Institution, Supreme Grand Lodge (U.S.), *Constitution–General Laws, Regulations and Rules: Supreme Grand Lodge of the Loyal Orange Institution of the United States of America, Inc. Adopted at 48th Session of the Supreme Grand Lodge August 1940* (Philadelphia: LOI, revised 1964), p. 35.
129. *Houlton Times*, 16 July 1924.
130. *Orange and Purple Courier*, July–August 1924.
131. The *Fiery Cross* was based in Indianapolis, Indiana.
132. *Fiery Cross*, 29 August 1924.
133. Ku Klux Klan, *Letter from Ku Klux Klan to E. C. Mickey, August 23, 1920*. W. E. B. Du Bois Papers (MS 312), University of Massachusetts Amherst Libraries.
134. Mark Paul Richard, '"This is not a Catholic nation": The Ku Klux Klan confronts Franco-Americans in Maine', *The New England Quarterly*, 82:2 (2009), p. 285.
135. *New York Times*, 9 July 1950.
136. Many bands used Orange halls for non-Orange events like local fundraisers or concerts.
137. *Press*, 27 January 1902.
138. *Press*, July 1883–1908.
139. *LOL No. 5, Christchurch, Minutes*. The City of Christchurch Highland Pipe Band led the marchers for their final parade.
140. Ray Nolan, email to author, 10 May 2014.
141. Thomas Reid, *Travels in Ireland, in the Year 1822* (London: Longman, Hurst, Rees, Orme, & Brown, 1823), pp. 187–9.
142. This is demonstrated in the various minute books across the world that document invitations to marches, but also note the domestic duties of the female lodge members.
143. Christi McCallum, 'Orangewomen show their colors: Gender, family, and

Orangeism in Ulster, 1795–present' (PhD, Southern Illinois University Carbondale, 2011), p. 48.

144. Linda Racioppi and Katherine O'Sullivan See, 'Ulstermen and loyalist ladies on parade: Gendering unionism in Northern Ireland', *International Feminist Journal of Politics*, 2:1 (2000), p. 13.

145. *Preston Guardian*, 17 April 1852.

146. *Liverpool Echo*, 23 July 1923; Peter Day, 'Pride before a fall? Orangeism in Liverpool since 1945', in M. Busteed, F. Neal and J. Tonge (eds), *Irish Protestant Identities* (Manchester and New York: Manchester University Press, 2008), p. 277.

147. Patrick Coleman, '"In harmony": A comparative view of female Orangeism 1887–2000', in Angela McCarthy (ed.), *Ireland in the World: Comparative, Transnational, and Personal Perspectives* (London and New York: Routledge, 2015), pp. 110–36.

148. Loyal Orange Ladies' Institution, Supreme Grand Lodge (U.S.), *Constitution and By-Laws of the Supreme Grand Lodge of the Loyal Orange Ladies' Institution, Inc. Also Constitution for Subordinate Lodges with Rules of Order, 1996* (Philadelphia: LOLI, 1996), p. 6.

149. Deborah Butcher, 'Ladies of the lodge: A history of Scottish Orangewomen, c. 1909–2013' (PhD, London Metropolitan University, 2014), pp. 125–8.

5

More than Banners and Sashes: The Material Culture of Orangeism

Orangeism has often been defined by the public spectacle of men marching (they would say 'walking') along the main streets of cities and towns throughout the 'Orange world'. The main way onlookers would recognise them is through the orange colour of their sashes (later collarettes) and the banners they often carry with a picture of King William III astride a white horse, with the lodge name emblazoned across the top and bottom of the banner. Studies of Orange parades have mainly focused on the conflict, and in some cases full-scale riots, that these parades have sparked.

This chapter seeks to move beyond the world of parades and into the inner world of Orange material culture. In its most straightforward form, material culture can be conceptualised as the study of inanimate objects and the way they interact with people and the environment in which they are used.[1] In this context, these objects, which are symbolic expressions of Orange beliefs, are evident in parades, particularly various emblems, banners and regalia.

Studies of such Orange objects are sparse, and all have concentrated on Northern Ireland. Neil Jarman, for instance, writes about the banners, murals and the 'Orange arch' with a focus on their symbolism as a way of expressing Orange identity within a Northern Irish context.[2] He also deploys a material culture approach to analyse banners, linking them to the textile industry in the north of Ireland. It was the rise of this industry that enabled the provision of locally made uniforms, banners and sashes to the Orange Order and other fraternal organisations.[3] Anthony Buckley, meanwhile, explains the biblical symbolism on the regalia of the associate Orange organisation called the Royal Black Institution.[4] David Cairns assesses the material culture of loyalism by analysing four marching seasons in the 1990s.[5] In particular, he emphasises the links between flags/football strips and sectarianism. His point is that limiting sectarianism to its violent and intimidating elements misses an opportunity to show that the everyday aspects of material culture and associated rituals are sectarian as well but done in a 'socially acceptable manner'.[6]

Cairns identifies the narrow focus of previous studies of sectarianism and conflict, which elide consideration of individual attitudes being formed by the public and private display of objects. Cairns and Jim Smyth, while making some references to various Orange banners, regalia and badges, emphasise the overall role of Orangeism in carrying 'the symbols of Protestantism in Ireland'.[7] Their main conclusions focus on the ritual parade being an 'expression of communal solidarity' that is crucial to Protestant identity.[8] However, in the context of attempts to halt these marches, especially at Drumcree, County Armagh, Northern Ireland, also in the 1990s, the parades were 'seen by many Orangemen as a last stand to protect their identity, culture and country'.[9] All these studies had the same location, Northern Ireland, and generally restricted their focus to banners and regalia, mostly in the context of the parading culture of Orangeism. No study has analysed other types of Orange material culture in Northern Ireland or other parts of the Orange world.

Orange material culture is, however, more than the banners and sashes, and this chapter seeks to link these other material objects to Orange practices. This is important as the material objects used by Orange members across the world are also regulated in the various rules or laws of the Orange Order. Linking these 'rules' to their practices reveals the underlying reason why members act and dress in the way they do. They form a kind of Orange diasporic function.[10] This means that the use of these objects helps to build a sense of solidarity in the Orange communities across the world. Orange members have a shared past and present, and the material objects not only identify members in the public sphere but also are used with a sense of common purpose. This chapter will demonstrate that these objects are a vital link in the transnational nature of the Orange Order. The objects used in the Orange Irish context have been transported to distant countries and have generally had the same use. This, in essence, has helped to build the overall sense of a global community with a shared understanding of the function and purpose of these material objects.

This chapter examines the meaning, importance and changes over time of Orange material culture around the Orange world. Diverse forms of material culture will be analysed in conjunction with other sources to uncover not only the historical context of these items but also how these artefacts gave and still give members a sense of identity and solidarity. The analysis proceeds in six sections. The first section focuses on the built culture of the Orange halls and buildings. These buildings are the core of Orange Order activities, and changes in their use and function are explored. The warrants and certificates are the paper-based material objects that, while fragile, are highlighted as evidence of the right of members to form lodges and to be members. Although a small object, the ballot box is explained as a device used to decide which members can join. The process of this is outlined. Minute books are then explored to show how members document their activities and record the membership of individual lodges. Then, the variety and changes in the use of banners are outlined across the Orange world. The sashes and badges members wear are explained for their symbolism and function. Lastly, the use of crowns in public and private ritual is explored. The overarching premise of this chapter is to demonstrate that the majority of Orange material culture has emanated from Ireland, but some variations generally result from local conditions or as a means of pragmatic adjustment over time.

BUILDINGS/HALLS

Buildings have life cycles. Date stones celebrate beginnings while commemorative plaques mark past achievements. Like their makers, buildings change over time. Their parts and materials wear out, break, rot, rust, or decay. Structures are refurbished or reconfigured to meet new demands or the latest fashions and are often recycled to serve entirely new functions.[11]

This rather bleak but realistic view of the life cycle of buildings in general, as described by architectural historian Carl R. Lounsbury, is also an accurate picture of the Orange hall. All the elements of a building's life cycle can be found across the countries that have Orange lodges. The halls that survive are a physical reminder of the impact of the Orange Order on the architectural landscape. The following discussion will outline the function and purpose of Orange halls around the world.

The early Orangemen in Ireland first met in Dan Winter's cottage following the Battle of the Diamond in 1795 in County Armagh. This humble cottage, which is now a tourist attraction, is regarded as the birthplace of the Orange Order.[12] In these formative years, lodge meetings were held in private homes before numbers began to rise. The building of Orange halls was more a practical step than a reflection of any grandiose plan. The members needed a place to meet and conduct their Orange rituals. The expansion of any organisation often means a change of focus and purpose. Besides having lodge meetings, there developed a need to have a multi-functional building.

As the Orange Order spread across the British Empire, the need to find places to meet was paramount. Temporary meeting places were the norm until the lodges formed into large organised bodies. The push to have these dedicated halls meant an extension of the Orange Order's global reach. By virtue of the Orange Order being loyal to the Crown, it was also an extension of empire. However, to keep some perspective, unlike the Freemasons, who had more pretentious aspirations with their often classical-style buildings, the Orange Order was generally more broad-based and therefore functionality was paramount.[13]

The importance of these Orange halls is reflected in the ceremonies for the dedication of a new hall. In one example from Sydney, Australia, in 1928 the Orange Order, in Old Testament style, made three circuits of the inside of the building sprinkling corn, wine and salt on the floor. This symbolic practice was based on the Children of Israel and the priestly offerings to God and was in keeping with their Protestant principles of seeing the activities of the Orange Order as God's work.[14] Therefore, the buildings that they used were also meant to be places where this work was celebrated.

Differences in the style of Orange halls reflected the geographical situation, the wealth of members, and the building materials available. Orange halls in Ulster tended to be made of either brick or wood and often had tin roofs. The construction of these halls was funded 'mostly through jumble sales and sales of work and other unremitting labour by the ladies'.[15] More importantly, these halls were community halls and were generally very plain. They contained basic furnishings including wooden chairs and trestle tables, a picture of the Queen, King Billy in a painting, and the lodge banner on display for important occasions. The community nature of these halls meant they could be used by other people or organisations, not just the Orange Order.

There were restrictions on the use of these halls by Orange members. This is evident from Orange laws or rules. In 1872 the Orange Institution of Ireland stated: 'No Publican shall hold office in any Lodge, nor shall any Lodge be held in the house of a Publican, unless first submitted to and approved both by the District and County Grand Lodges.'[16] This condition was expanded by other Orange jurisdictions like New Zealand, where it was decreed that the 'Grand Lodge forbids the introduction and use of all spirits and alcoholic liquors in any building used for Lodge purposes by any person on the night of the meeting, and the use of any intoxicating liquors at any Lodge functions'.[17] Orange

Canadian regulations were similarly worded.[18] This prohibition of alcohol at Orange halls reflected the temperance movement that was prevalent in the nineteenth and early part of the twentieth century in Protestant churches.[19]

However, the temperance focus was a later influence. In England a number of lodges met in pubs.[20] Across in Canada, while rural lodges built their own halls, in Toronto land values made this process prohibitive. There were plenty of rent options, so in 1856 ten out of the twenty-one lodges in the city of Toronto met in hotels or inns. This had changed by 1860, as the shift to temperance and mutual aid became a feature of these lodges; even the single lodge that still met in an inn had to move out to remain respectable in the community.[21]

Some other countries in the Orange world had a mixture of cooperative communal help and strategic placement in their building of Orange halls. The community nature of these halls followed the Irish example. In the Canadian context, the Orange hall was a physical presence that demonstrated that the Orange Order was part of the local community.[22] In order to build these halls, the cooperation of the community was required. The Canadian Orange halls were commonly made of wood, sometimes simply logs. These halls were not ostentatious like the Masonic temples, or resemblant of other fraternal societies such as the Oddfellows. These halls were more like community halls and 'reflected a broad social spectrum and the generally humble condition of rural and small-town Canada'.[23] The strategic location of these halls meant they were close to schools and churches, all important buildings within a community in the nineteenth and twentieth centuries.

The English Orange lodges also built Orange halls that were shared with or used by other organisations. However, some lodges could not afford to have the whole building dedicated to Orange activities, or even to own their halls. This situation led to purpose-built buildings to accommodate lodge meetings from other organisations. In Figure 5.1 the James Gibson Memorial Orange Hall in Hebburn-on-Tyne is shown. Although it is owned by the Orange Order, they let the ground floor to the Hebburn Protestant Conservative Club.[24] The need to meet was more important than the location, since the Protestant tradition placed greater importance on the people than the building. This was especially true of the nonconformist tradition of Baptist, Methodist and Presbyterian churches.

In stark contrast to the austere Orange halls in Ireland were some of the Orange halls in the Orange diaspora. One example is the Protestant Hall in Beaufort Street, Perth, Western Australia, which was built in Federation Free Style. In the report to determine whether this building

Figure 5.1 James Gibson Orange Memorial Hall, Hebburn-on-Tyne (© Michael Phelan)

met heritage standards, there was the following comment: 'the relief of William of Orange is an unusual feature in the façade of a Western Australian building.'[25] This 'unusual feature' is shown in Figure 5.2, which represents a resplendent King William in his bright red coat, astride his white horse. An important date in the Orange calendar is represented on either side: 1690. This was the year of the Battle of the Boyne. The Protestant Hall in Perth was purpose-built in 1901 for the Protestant Alliance Friendly Society (PAFS).[26] Not long after the building was opened, Twelfth of July celebrations with the local Orangemen occurred. At these celebrations, around 420 Orangemen marched in a procession from the Protestant Hall to Queen's Hall, where the annual service was held. Also included in the parade were members of the PAFS.[27] The Protestant Hall provides evidence of the expansion and the intensive building programme that occurred in the city of Perth as a result of the Western Australian 1890s gold boom. This was an instance where the ability to build something that was multi-purpose and imposing was the result of members having the financial capacity to do so.

Just as the Orange halls heralded the vibrancy of the spread of Orangeism throughout the Orange world, so its decline was mirrored in these buildings. Reflecting on the Canadian Orange Order, historical geographers Cecil Houston and William Smyth maintained that the landscape was impacted by the closures of Orange lodges. This was

Figure 5.2 The Protestant Hall, Perth, Western Australia (© Calistemon, 2 July 2023, CC by 4.0)

particularly evident in rural areas, where dilapidated halls with broken windows and faded flagpoles made a 'somewhat poignant statement about the state of the Order'.[28]

Images of decay, abandonment and conversion provide an insight into the current state of Orangeism in Canada. As membership numbers have fallen and the members age, the halls themselves reflect the gradual decline of the once proud Canadian Orange Order. These same images are reflected across the Orange world which has seen this decline in numbers, as Orange halls are either demolished or repurposed. While they cannot 'talk' in the sense a text may record events, the halls provide visual documentation of this decline. The decaying nature of the buildings reflects the life cycle of both the building and the Orange Order. Eventually, the Protestant Hall in Perth was vacated by the PAFS in 1981. Finally, the Orange Order in Western Australia sold the building in 1982. From the late 1980s and into the early 1990s, the place operated as 'Qazar', an entertainment venue where customers played simulated laser-tag war games throughout the building. A similar situation can be seen with churches and other fraternal organisations that peak in membership and then, as numbers fall, see their buildings being sold.

WARRANTS AND CERTIFICATES

Warrants

The warrant was probably one of the most important paper documents in the Orange Order. Needed in order to form a lodge, they were issued by the Grand Lodge of the country members came from. This whole process was borrowed from the Freemasons and adapted for the Orange Order's situation.[29] The warrant was evidence of an Orange lodge's right to operate. Without one, the members were seen as illegal and needed to get the proper authorisation. This is reflected in the rules:

> No Lodge shall be held without the authority of a Warrant from the Grand Lodge, signed by the Grand Master, the Grand Secretary, and the Grand Treasurer, countersigned by the like Officers of the County, and sealed with the seals of the Grand Lodge and of the County Grand Lodge.[30]

An example of this occurred when Orangemen in New Zealand wanted to establish lodges. To do this, the members needed a warrant from the Grand Orange Lodge of Ireland. While they also could have chosen to contact the Grand Orange Lodge of England, Ireland was chosen as these members were predominantly Irish and therefore had a close connection with Ireland.[31] A notable instance of this was when the first Orange lodge in the Middle Island (South Island) of New Zealand was formed in 1864 in Lyttelton. The original warrant No. 1886 was issued to County Armagh-born Francis Redpath (1821–1904).[32] Redpath had applied for the warrant, which was issued on 24 June 1865.[33] One of the signatories on the warrant was Henry C. Lanauze, later Grand Secretary. In 1869 he wrote to the Grand Orange Lodge in Ireland asking for their status to be upgraded to Grand Lodge in New Zealand.[34] The original warrant has all of these changes written over it. In this sense it was a living document that could be written on.

The warrant in Figure 5.3 is dated 1908. This was a pivotal year as this was when the Grand Lodge of the Middle Island of New Zealand and the Grand Lodge of the North Island amalgamated to form one Grand Lodge. Even the lodge number, 32A, reflects this change, as there were two no. 32s, the North Island lodges having lodge numbers paralleling the southern ones. The signature is that of County Cavan-born John Middleton, who was the first Grand Master of the amalgamated Grand Lodges. The design on the warrant has a mixture of Orange history and New Zealand history. The coat of arms of the UK is on the left, but as New Zealand only achieved dominion status in 1907 the design for a coat of arms was

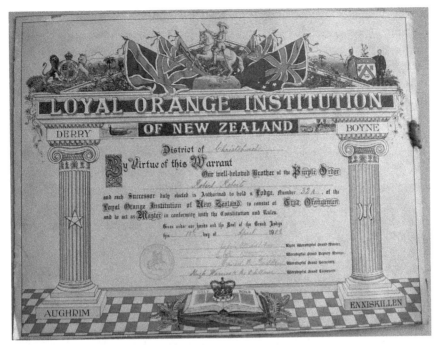

Figure 5.3 Warrant for LOL No. 32A, Christchurch, New Zealand, 1908
(© Patrick Coleman)

not available. On this warrant there is an alternative crest with a Māori warrior and a missionary, with some iconic symbols like the kiwi also present. The Union Jack and the New Zealand flag are evident on either side of a stylised King William III on horseback, with the key date of 1690 underneath. The pillars are labelled with the names of the famous battles at Derry, Aughrim, Boyne and Enniskillen. The open Bible with the crown on top is in the foreground. All of these symbols are important to the Orange Order's history and beliefs. The added touches on this warrant demonstrate the diasporic connection within an Orange context.

Throughout the Orange world, warrants were mandatory for setting up lodges in any country or region. The *Laws and Ordinances*, which were the rules governing the lodges, were used to provide clear guidance for operational matters from Grand Lodge to private lodges. They were written as a legal document and in the case of the Orange Institution of Ireland stated, 'No Lodge shall be held without the authority of a Warrant from the Grand Lodge, signed by the Grand Master, the Grand Secretary'.[35] This requirement was stated in other *Laws and Ordinances* as the other Orange jurisdictions followed a similar template in their general rules. Warrants had to be paid for and also renewed and were instrumental in the process of the spread of the Orange Order. These warrants gave the user the right to form a lodge, and their use was common among Orange members in the military.[36] Countries such as Australia and New Zealand have attributed the origins of the Orange Order in their countries to the use of these warrants.[37] Without having in their possession a physical warrant, these lodges would be operating illegally.

An interesting aside to this are the incidences of members taking warrants that were issued in one part of the world to use in others. As noted in Chapter 1, both Australia and New Zealand had stories of early members taking warrants with them and using them to set up lodges. Ultimately, they all had to ask permission when they formalised their lodges but this demonstrated not only the transnational linkages that occurred but also the initially loose way in which members operated once they were in a new country.

Over time, some aspects of the design of the warrants may have changed, but fundamental information about dates and who was given the initial authority to form a lodge remained the same. For historians, these documents form a chain in the Orange network that showed the local, national and international aspects of lodges as they were established around the world.

Certificates

Individuals who took part in Orange activities were issued certificates and this was evidence that the member belonged to a particular lodge. A certificate was issued to the member when they first joined and also as they moved to the Purple degree.[38] This degree was the final ritual degree they were initiated into. These certificates show a range of information from the member's name and the date of initiation through to the signature and names of the Master or Mistress of the lodge and the secretary. The other kind of certificate was the transfer certificate, which came into effect when members moved from one Orange jurisdiction to another:

> Any Member who shall satisfy his Lodge that he is about to emigrate, or to be admitted into a different Lodge, shall be granted a certificate of membership, signed by the Master or Officer presiding, under the seal of the Lodge, and countersigned by the Secretary; for which he shall pay not less than One Shilling.[39]

A certificate effectively became an unofficial passport of Orange membership that could be recognised when members emigrated. This system was used across the Orange diaspora.[40] While it gave some proof of membership, it was not kept by the member, but by the private lodge. This was a checking system to ensure the member was who they said they were. In this sense, it was proof of identity. Collections of these certificates provide some material evidence of the movement of Orange members. A lodge in Christchurch, New Zealand, for instance, could have certificates from the various states in Australia, Ireland and Scotland.[41] Figure 5.4 shows this for John McLoughlin from Royal Oak No. 374, Sandy Row, Belfast, who had his transfer certificate signed on 17 July 1925. He was transferring to LOL No. 2A, Christchurch. After noting he had received the Orange and Purple degrees and vouching for his character, the certificate (as a part of the common wording) states: 'We, therefore, request that all the Orange Institutions in the Universe do recognize him as such.'[42] McLoughlin needed this certificate to gain entry to his new lodge. However, a closer inspection shows that not all parts of the Orange universe were in agreement. On the back of this certificate is a warning that 'NO applications from the United States of America for Transfer Certificates are to be entertained other than those received through the Office of the Grand Secretary of Ireland'.[43] This particular warning about the United States was in reference to the split that had occurred in the American Orange Order. In this case, there were two Supreme Grand Lodges in the United States, each organisation claiming they were the rightful representatives of American Orangeism. While this dispute was being resolved, the certificate reflected the uncertainty.[44]

A sampling of forty-four certificates over the period 1845–1928 that are held in this Christchurch lodge reveal that thirty-five came from Ireland. Of that number, thirty-three came from the province of Ulster (inclusive of Cavan and Monaghan, now in the Irish Republic).[45] The remainder are six from Australia and three from Scotland. While this is clearly a tiny sample, it shows the heavy reliance on membership from Ireland. While those that did make the transition from other countries to New Zealand tended to stay, some were already here. One of the certificates was of Henry James Ranger (1863–1946). He was born in Christchurch but went to Melbourne to train as a bicycle repairer.[46] While there he joined the Orange lodge and then returned to Christchurch to open his own bicycle shop and later become Grand Master of the Middle Island.[47] This example shows the mobility of some members who end up joining the Orange Order in another country and maintaining membership on return to their birth country. The situation could be true in reverse with members deciding not to join when migrating for a variety of reasons, including the lack of lodges.

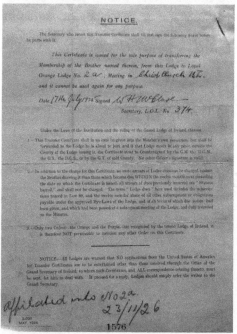

Figure 5.4 Transfer certificate for John McLoughlin, Belfast, 1925
(© Patrick Coleman)

BALLOT BOXES

If one walks into an Orange hall, there is plenty of competition for the senses with banners, cabinets with Orange-branded crockery, photographs of past members and certificates adorning the walls. The ballot box must seem the most innocuous and overlooked object within an Orange hall. Yet the humble ballot box probably has a more powerful role than any of the other Orange items. When new members want to join the Orange Order, they must be subject to the vote of existing members, generally done by ballot. The most common balloting method, particularly in the nineteenth and early twentieth centuries, was having one black bean in seven preventing any chance of a new candidate joining. This rule applied to both male and female private lodges regardless of country.[48] The exceptions were the Orange Order in Canada and the United States. The Canadian Orangemen still balloted members, but they allowed for three ballots cast against them before the member was rejected.[49] In the case of the American Orangemen, they appointed a committee to investigate a candidate according to their character. This committee then decided whether to accept or reject the candidate.[50]

In the most common process of using a ballot box, the beans were put into a slot, then later taken out and counted. If successful, this was the beginning of a member's life in the Orange lodge. The only place the result is recorded is in the minute books of lodges. One example of the voting process comes from the same lodge rooms as the ballot box seen in Figure 5.5 below. The process was very formal as it occurred during a regular lodge meeting, and the business of the lodge was suspended while the candidate was elected. The minutes read: 'a Ballot was taken for the admission of Mr H. Brown into the Orange Order (carried). Mr H. Brown was duly initiated into the Orange Order.'[51] This rather bland entry does not explain the whole process of voting and the initiation ceremony that took place after Brown's election. Given that the minutes were written for members who knew the finer detail, and not for outsiders, the lack of detail is not surprising.

The ballot box in Figure 5.5 testifies to the functional nature of the box itself. Passing the voting phase then allowed the new member to start the process of other rituals. The box is plain and has no apparent markings that suggest it belongs to the lodge. This anonymity ties in with the anonymous nature of the voting. The Worshipful Master presides over the ballot, inspects it and declares the results.[52] In Brown's case, he was now a member and could enjoy the friendship and fraternal activities

Figure 5.5 Orange lodge ballot box, Christchurch, New Zealand
(© Patrick Coleman)

that went with membership. While members could potentially blackball an initiate, this was unlikely as members only put forward those whose backgrounds they knew. This democratic process started the life of the candidate as they sought to change their identity and become part of a worldwide movement. The counting of white beans was the beginning of this process to become an Orangeman or Orangewoman.

MINUTE BOOKS

The most visible aspects of Orange material culture have always been the banners and the regalia that are both colourful and in the public eye whenever there is a parade or demonstration involving members. Less conspicuous, but more important to the Orange Order and indeed historians, are the minute books. On the surface, they are perceived as mundane and ordinary as they seem to be simply summaries of meetings. Outsiders and sometimes critics of the Orange Order have looked at the public image of riots and violence and assume that is the purpose of the organisation. Yet parades are only a small fraction of the life of the lodges. The minute books therefore reveal the richness of Orange Order culture and are important material culture objects that document the ongoing life of Orange lodges throughout the centuries.

The culture of lodge meetings forms a significant basis of activities, whether at the local private lodge level or the Grand Lodge level. These meetings were mandatory and were held monthly. The Master or Mistress of the lodge was responsible for holding these meetings and they could be suspended if they were not held.[53] Members were also required to attend. Just like any organisation, the Orange lodges kept minutes of meetings, which recorded incoming correspondence, issues of importance, changes to rules, decisions made and much more. The minute books were not just used to record the meetings, as shown in Figure 5.6, but members also pasted in extra information about themselves from newspapers. This was their way of recording history. Minute books form a part of the written record for the existence of lodge activities. Members were not known for writing their own histories, so the minute books are what remains of the regular and routine life of Orange members.

The importance of minute books is shown in the way many historians use them in order to uncover names of members or a lodge's responses to various political or social issues of the time. What has been overlooked is that these physical minute books are sometimes the sole surviving evidence of lodge activities outside of newspapers. The newspapers only

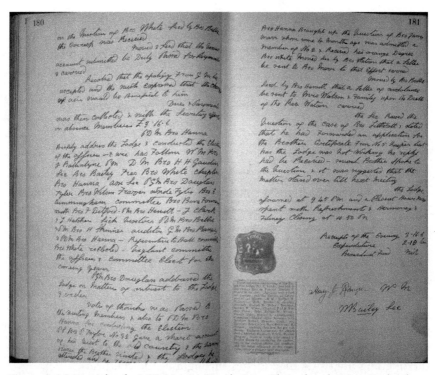

Figure 5.6 Minute book, LOL No. 2A Purple Star, Christchurch, New Zealand
(© Patrick Coleman)

recorded major events and certainly did not note all the members. Yet within minute books, sometimes the names and addresses of members were given. The minute books recorded initiations:

> Mr Henry Parry was next introduced by Bro. J McLean and Bro G Hawkes to WM who ably instructed him into the first degree of Orangeism and in the signs and passes. Bro Hawkes and WM next went through the lecture.[54]

The above example was taken from a minute book in Liverpool in 1898. It documents the process of a new candidate on their first day at a lodge meeting. Other information recorded included the organising of social events or donations to various causes. The minute books sometimes also recorded not just who was initiated as members but challenges to this. In one instance in Sydney in 1870, a Bro. Berry (often only surnames were used) was rejoining but it was thought prudent to 'put him to the test'. He was taken outside and questioned. On return a Bro. Mitchell noted while believing that Berry had received the Arch Purple degree he 'had forgotten almost all about it'.[55] Consequently, they just admitted him as an Orangeman and he paid his subscription. This process was one that was a part of the Orange Order's method when administering their rituals. It also demonstrates uniformity in practice, as members used this process no matter where in the Orange world they were.

Those interested in the history at the upper end of the Orange Order structure use the annual proceedings, which record the decisions made by members at a national level. This 'history from below' enables historians to see the normality of lodge meetings. These meetings were the norm, whereas the public parades and even the annual meetings were the exceptions.

The minute books also reflected the changing importance of the lodge over time. For example, the first minute book of LOL No. 1A Maiden City at Lyttelton, Christchurch, New Zealand, had a very cheap soft cover for the early years September 1875 to December 1881.[56] After this, the minute books were sturdy hardcover ledgers. As membership increased, so did the money coming into the lodge and therefore there was now a reason to purchase the higher-quality ledgers. This has also gone the other way with more recent lodges using inexpensive school exercise books instead of the traditional ledger. The variation in writing also reflects differences in education. Sometimes the minute keeper had beautiful copperplate handwriting and wrote in ink (usually black or blue but even red was used in rare instances). Other times, minute keepers wrote in pencil with almost illegible handwriting. This might reveal the vagaries of who agreed to do the job, but it also reflects the relative importance of this job. These minute books also had a certain amount of self-censoring. While they recorded members being initiated, they did not record the ceremony itself. This was a secret ritual and therefore recording details was unnecessary. For the other actions that occurred during the meeting, it depended on the skills of the notetaker. This could end up as barebones recordings or ones with extensive notes. Again, this process was idiosyncratic and is reflected in the surviving minute books across the world.

The mundane aspect of the minute books has also led to their own lack of importance. Many minute books have survived but many have been destroyed by fire, water and the deliberate acts of disaffected members. In the end, this administrative act of minute book keeping played its part in documenting the activities and decision making of members and therefore shows evidence of their solidarity (and sometimes not). All of these variations and ways of record-keeping (and destruction) were common in Ireland and in the Orange diaspora.

BANNERS

Throughout the whole history of Orangeism the Orange parade has been the major event for members to celebrate and demonstrate visually the link between the past and the present. It is through the Orange parade that members walk around a specified territory displaying their identity symbolised in banners. These banners are one of the main visual pieces of material culture that are on display. In the context of Northern Ireland, 'these parades are not simply about mobilizing numbers or affirming territorial rights, they are the principal opportunity and medium for displaying and elaborating the nuances of collective identity'.[57] This identity, displayed through banners, bannerettes and flags, is all about the 'ideological and political nature of the Ulster Protestant identity'.[58] This analysis may well be true of Northern Ireland, but is it applicable for the Orange diaspora? Given the overwhelming number of banners and various designs, the following analysis will consider their meaning, their importance and the degree of difference between Orange banners in Ireland and the diaspora.

In terms of what can be represented on the banners, there are a few constraints. Most countries in the Orange diaspora did not have any regulations around the subject material for banners. However, the Grand Orange Lodge of Scotland was quite prescriptive: 'The portrait or painting of any living person shall not be placed on any banner in connection with the Loyal Orange Institution of Scotland. A portrait of King William III must appear on one side of any banner.'[59]

The Scottish Orange regulation of having an image depicting King William III on horseback crossing the Boyne in Ireland has dominated most banners across the Orange diaspora. This is not surprising as he is at the centre of the Orange Order and it is his colours they have adopted. The ideals of 'civil and religious liberty' and the upholding of the Protestant tradition are at the core of any Orange members' beliefs. William's 1690 defeat of King James II at the Boyne is a pivotal event commemorated in the Orange calendar. William's importance cannot be underestimated; his image on a banner makes the past present and is a crucial reminder of the Orange Order's beliefs and identity. This identity forms a diasporic function, as wherever there are Orange lodges, there is the dominant image of King William III.

The particular image of King William ('Billy') III on horseback crossing the Boyne is based on the famous contemporary painting by Jan Wyck (1652–1702). It is important to note it is not historically accurate but is instead a stylised image of the events. It was part of the Williamite propaganda campaign to legitimatise William as he was ousting the current King James II. The image of William III as a powerful leader and soldier in battle was essential to consolidate his acceptance by the British people.[60] The original horse was chestnut, but the white horse is a symbol of the House of Orange. The coat William wears in the early Wyck paintings is green but was replaced by the traditional red, which is now very common. Again, this symbolism emphases his right as the British monarch, despite being Dutch and essentially a usurper of the reigning monarch.

There are numerous examples of banners with this image that could be chosen as an exemplar of the iconic William on horseback. The banner pictured in Figure 5.7, which is on display in the Orange hall in Christchurch, is a rarity not for its image, but because it is one of the few old banners left in New Zealand. It was made for the Ladies' Loyal Orange Lodge No. 1 No Surrender, which formed on 26 April 1889 in Christchurch.[61] It depicts the Battle of the Boyne, with William in his familiar pose crossing the Boyne. One unusual feature of this banner is William wearing blue rather than his traditional red. In the original battle, historians believe he was likely to have worn blue or green, so this example is closer to reality. The likely origin of the banner is Belfast, as New Zealand Orangeism usually sourced their banners from overseas.[62] Other documented examples of banners sent to New Zealand include the True Blue Orange Lodge Auckland. This lodge bought their banner from Belfast. They held a celebration in 1878 to celebrate the unfurling of the banner:

> It is emblazoned on a blue ground. On the obverse side is the effigy of King William on horseback, with the mottos, Loyal Orange Lodge, Newmarket True Blues. At the corners were inscribed the names—Derry, Enniskillen, Aughrim, and Boyne. The reverse side bore similar inscriptions, but the centre-piece was occupied by the Crown and Bible, the Sword and Sceptre, and a scroll.[63]

What has been described illustrates not only a similar banner to the ladies' lodges just described but also that New Zealand did not seem to have any distinctive features about their banners and just adopted the ones used from Belfast. This was a banner that was created in the prescribed manner of any Irish Orange banner. There are no signs of an attempt to exhibit a local identity. This demonstrated that the diasporic connections were strong as they affirmed a collective Orange identity regardless of the country in which an Orange lodge was founded.

Historical images form a major part of the depictions on many banners, and these are part of the Orange historical narrative that

Figure 5.7 Banner, LLOL No. 1 No Surrender, Christchurch, New Zealand
(© Patrick Coleman)

helped to preserve and maintain a collective identity. Some aspects of social identity theory provide insight into the overall meaning of these banners. Stating that the banners portray various people or historical events only touches the surface of the deeper meaning. Drawing on the example of Sikhs and Hindus from 1980s India, Baljinder Sahdra and Michael Ross examined how group identity affected historical memory, particularly of past violent events. They asked:

> Why might groups commemorate and preserve memories of tragedies? One answer is that memories of ingroup suffering are also important to people's social identity. Such memories and associated rituals can provide temporal continuity and cultural coherence. Commemorations of past suffering articulate as well as enhance ingroup solidarity.[64]

In this context, the images on banners that the Orange Order use to represent historical events important to them tend to be tragic ones. In this way, while the image of King William has been a dominant feature on Orange banners over the years, this has changed in some countries. The example from a Scottish Orangewoman's banner shown in Figure 5.8 depicts Margaret Wilson, the covenanting martyr, who has been a popular subject for the ladies' lodges' banners in Scotland.[65]

Figure 5.8 Banner, LLOL No. 81 Barrhead, Paisley District 6, Scotland (© David Bryce)

Wilson is a great example of the youthful martyr who, with her older sister Margaret McLaughlin, refused to recant the covenant.[66] Both were condemned to die by being tied to a pillar at low tide and eventually drowning. Interestingly, it is hard to find a banner depicting both women, but the youthful Wilson exemplifies the steadfast heroine who, though young, was unwilling to compromise her beliefs. These types of images convey historical events that are important in maintaining a sense of identity. The use of the Covenanters formed a strong part of the Scottish Orange narrative that symbolised their tragic past, as current members need to be vigilant in order that events like this never occurred again.

Following the focus on history and tragedy there is a banner from Florida-based Heirs of Cromwell LOL 1599. It creates Orange history with a local twist. The banner has an image of Oliver Cromwell, a known upholder of the Protestant tradition, and one who avenged the massacre of 1641 with a ferocity that is still felt in Ireland. There are many examples of Irish banners using Cromwell's image. In this case, the artist has Cromwell holding the Stars and Stripes, which gives the banner a contemporary feel and astutely avoids any royalist symbolism that is at odds with a republic.[67] However, historically, American lodges have tended to brand themselves as being '100% American' and '100% patriotic'. The banner in Figure 5.9 from Philadelphia exemplifies this. The use of the image of Founding Father George Washington on the banner of Washington LOL No. 43 is so iconically American that it maintains the combination of American patriotism with an Orange flavour.

Other changes that have occurred over time and space include adaptations in the way the banners are carried. In Canada members who were in the early days a lot younger and stronger had no trouble carrying banners for long distances on their annual Twelfth of July parades. One lodge, Centennial LOL No. 327, Port Perry, Ontario, at a parade in 2011, however, had members using a special platform with wheels to carry their banners. John Wells, County Secretary of the County Orange Lodge of Toronto, explains that 'the Toronto Orange Parade is approximately 3 miles and for a group of elderly members the task of carrying the banners may have proven to be too arduous, not to mention the temperature of 85–90 F as well'.[68]

The huge banners with their large carrying poles, while spectacular, have proven problematic to members not just in Canada but also in Scotland. David Bryce, Orange archivist in Scotland, has stated that 'these have now disappeared due to their weight and fewer members doing heavy manual work'.[69] He notes that the bannerette is being used by some ladies' lodges as their members are able to carry it. This

Figure 5.9 Banner, Washington LOL No. 43, Philadelphia, USA, 1952
(*Philadelphia Evening Bulletin* © Special Collections Research Center, Temple
University Libraries, Philadelphia, PA)

difference, brought about by a change in membership, and the desire for
ladies' lodges to carry their own banners, has meant the size of banners
needs to be adjusted to accommodate changes in modern society. The
days of burly working-class tradesmen or labourers carrying the coveted
banners are now beginning to be a thing of the past. Finding banner
carriers had become a problem, so the lodges ordered smaller banners

with lighter poles and this now means the women in the Orange lodges could take their turn. These innovations out of necessity were shared by the Orange diaspora, as they saw what others were doing and often had the same issues with an ageing membership or not having people strong enough to carry the traditional banners.

SASHES, BADGES AND CROWNS

Sashes and Badges

In summarising some of the issues around the role played by symbols and 'ethnonational' conflict, Kris Brown and Roger MacGinty outlined ways in which group identity was maintained in the context of Northern Ireland. Of interest is the way a group 'develops a specialized symbolic inventory of colors, flags, or historical references that are appropriated or mobilized to suit particular purposes'.[70] While noting the complexity that may occur in these symbols, they state that they can be condensed 'into a single unifying image, slogan, or movement'.[71] These comments are indicative of the way material culture was and still is used, and are also a way of understanding the uses of other symbols by the Orange Order.

The most identifiable and unifying aspect of Orange material culture is the regalia that members wear. In particular, it is the wearing of a sash and later a collarette with its various badges that publicly identifies a marcher as belonging to the Orange Order. The meaning of the sash and the badges may be apparent to the wearer, but this is not necessarily so for the general public. The wearing of sashes by Orangemen did not occur until the mid-nineteenth century.[72] Leading up to this time, members wore orange ribbons, and orange and purple if they were in the Purple Order.[73] This type of regalia originates from the military history of the Orange Order, as members were part of loyalist militias that fought the various uprisings in Ireland such as those in 1798 and 1848. Like most military groups, they needed uniforms to show who was on which side, and any badges would have denoted rank. The Orange sash signified that they were members of the Orange Order and not any other group. In terms of meaning, this gives the sash a militaristic focus. In this sense, they were an army of God within the Protestant tradition. The meaning of the sash marked out visually who was in the Orange Order to fellow members and also to onlookers if they were on parade.

Mervyn Jess has described the move from sash to collarette. He claims that in the 1920s the lodges in Ireland had sashes, but they changed to the collarette because of the cost of production and the convenience of the smaller size. The sashes were made of silk while the newer collarettes were made from a variety of cheaper materials.[74] Despite this change, the colour was still Orange, and all members wore them both on parade and at lodge meetings. The use at lodge meetings was a part of the ritual and also helped to distinguish various members by their office. In this sense, it was still like the military who had uniforms to distinguish soldiers by rank. This change to collarettes also occurred in other countries as the standardisation of regalia happened alongside that of banners. Fraternal organisations across the world had banners and regalia that were similar in design, but it was the colours and symbols that differentiated the various groups.

The meaning of the sash or collarette differed depending on whether the individual was the wearer or the onlooker. While Orange members were proud of displaying their beliefs and heritage, along with all the other aspects of the Orange Order, others, especially many Irish Catholics, were offended by what they felt the Orange sash represented. This was a source of sectarian tension whenever Orangemen marched as it was the 'Orange' they were wearing that proved they were Orangemen. The Boxing Day Riots in Christchurch and Timaru in New Zealand in 1879 had rioters enraged about the 'colours' of the marchers.[75] This was also true of the riots in New York, where the same symbolism, particularly the colour orange, was a factor in the riots.[76] For the marchers, they believed they were representing the catchcry of King William III of 'civil and religious liberty', whereas for Irish Catholics the colour orange was a symbol of oppression. This was particularly true in the nineteenth and early twentieth centuries. However, except for Northern Ireland, all 'Orange' countries no longer have such violent opposition to both their marches and colours. This is due to either demographic changes, falling numbers or, in some instance, no parades.

The importance of the sash or collar is demonstrated when someone joins the Orange Order as they are 'initiated' into the Orange degree. They are then entitled to wear a plain orange collar. These are usually supplied by the lodge for six months or so before the member is entitled to be 'advanced' to the Purple degree. At that point, the member acquires their collar, which is coloured orange with purple down the sides. The ceremonies marking the transition from the Orange to the Purple degree are fairly simple and are done in the lodge of which the brother or sister is a member. All of this was regulated, and in the Orange lodges in Ireland not wearing your sash at a lodge meeting meant you were 'deemed guilty of disrespect to the Institution'.[77] There were gender differences in the sense that the second degree for ladies' lodges was a different colour, which was blue. The main exception to wearing a variety of colours occurred in Canada. This was because the Canadian Orangemen had more degrees in their order and, therefore, more colours were used. For example, some members could have a base of orange and then blue and purple stripes.[78]

An example of a typical collarette worn by Orange members is shown in Figure 5.10.[79] The newer collarettes had more than the simple colour orange; there were other symbols on them. A common feature was the abbreviations showing which lodge they belonged to: the appliqué 'LOL' or Loyal Orange Lodge followed by a number for their particular lodge. The 'extras' on the sashes or collars were the badges and jewels that those in the Orange Order are entitled to attach.[80]

Immediately below the '844' is a badge with the words 'County Leitrim Grand Orange Lodge'. This has the arms of the province of Connaught. There are still a few lodges in County Leitrim, the only Orange lodges still in existence in the province of Connaught. The family of sash owner Michael Phelan was from Kilkenny in the south of Ireland, and so he felt a duty to support the Orange brethren in

Figure 5.10 Orange sash, John E. Bingham, LOL 844, Sheffield (© Michael Phelan)

the south. Despite the fact that Phelan was from Sheffield, those trans-national links were important enough for him to display this. At the very bottom of the collar, there is a further jewel attached. It is two plumed pens, crossed, denoting the office of Secretary. He received this jewel when he was Provincial Grand Secretary of the Manchester Province around the years 1979–81.[81]

These collarettes, as previously mentioned, were a way to denote not just that one was a member of the Orange Order, but also, through the use of badges, the various offices within it. The degree of the Royal Arch Purple is considered the most complex degree in English Orangeism, and can only be conferred by members who have learned the degree to the extent that they can recite it from start to finish. They are called 'Lecturers'. The degree also entitles Lecturers to wear a different collar, where the orange and purple colours are reversed. While the examples given are about a member of an English lodge, Phelan obtained the two collarettes from the firm of Cookes on the Shankill Road in Belfast.[82] This shows a reliance on Northern Irish manufacturers of regalia and also possibly a way of supporting businesses in Northern Ireland. Again, these transnational connections are apparent and are important to individual members.

The main change over time has been the shift from the sash to the col-larette. This may have in part been pre-empted by the use of collarettes that were worn by the officers of the lodges whereas the rank and file were meant to wear just plain sashes. An example of this appears in early New Zealand rule books where regalia was specified. Members had to wear 'a plain Orange Sash five (5) inches wide . . . over the right shoulder, extending to the knee, fastened at hip'. In contrast, an officer of a private lodge was meant to wear 'Collars of Orange Ribbon, with Purple stripe near each edge'.[83] They also then had various badges denoting their particular office. This format for the wearing of regalia was fairly standard across the Orange world but, as already noted, the Canadian Orange lodges had differences in the types of coloured regalia.

This standardisation occurred because the early Orange lodges had a variety of colours and types of regalia. The move to uniformity is illustrated in the Canadian context. The Grand Orange Lodge of British America (Canada) made a pronouncement on regalia on 2 June 1875. They stated that they wanted to regulate their regalia as 'the grotesque and ridiculous things often worn as Regalia make a laughing stock not only of those who wear them, but of the Association'. They also made a change that distinguished between rank and file members and offic-ers. The private members were to wear sashes, whereas officers were recommended to wear collars 'made of Orange Velvet, trimmed with Gold Lace, or Fringe, or both'.[84] The idea was for the Orange Order to look more respectable, 'with its tens of thousands of members, suitably clad, and presenting an appearance which will reflect credit on them and the influential Society they represent'.[85] This move to respectability and a focus on uniformity in their regalia reflected not just the Canadian situation but feelings across the Orange world as these were attempts to make the Orange Order more acceptable to the wider public. This transnational focus was important as each jurisdiction reflected on the others. While the look of the regalia changed from sashes to collarettes, this did not diminish the fact that the colour orange was still there and was the main identifier of members in the public sphere. The use of badges was a more private matter, as it reflected the offices and rituals that were a part of the private sphere.

Crowns

The crown, which is a prominent symbol and important ritual object used by loyalist organisations, is a common feature in Orange imagery. The symbolism in the Orange Order is of the British Crown or monarchy. This potent symbol is as common as the image of King William III in the Orange Order. The early rules and regulations state: 'We associate, to the utmost of our Power, to support and defend his Majesty, King George the Third, the Constitution and Laws of this country, and the Succession to the Throne in his Majesty's illustrious House, being Protestant.'[86] This statement, noting the allegiance to the British Crown, has kept pretty much the same wording, except for references to different reigning monarchs or use of a neutral term like 'rightful monarch'.[87] Therefore, any use of the symbol of a crown, either as an image or a physical one, is symbolic of this conditional allegiance.

Some regulations even capitalise the term 'BEING PROTESTANT' to leave in no doubt the conditional loyalty of the Orange members.[88] The use of the crown as a symbol had different implications to Catholics, who were also under the monarchy in the various regions of the British Empire and later Commonwealth. They saw it either as simply the symbol for the monarchy they served or, in the case of those who were sympathetic to republican views, as a symbol of oppression. The crown therefore meant different things to different people depending on their religious or political persuasion.

In the Orange context, the physical crown served two functions: it was either used as part of a ritual during a lodge meeting or carried at the front of parades. Michael Phelan, Orange archivist in England, recalls:

> I remember particularly from Scottish parades I've been on, the Chaplain walked at the front carrying a cushion, usually in purple velvet. On it there would be an open Bible and the crown placed on the top of that. If the walk was a long one there would be a chord attached to the cushion to help the Chaplain carry it.[89]

This use of a crown was a centrepiece at the beginning of Orange parades around the world. The use of an open Bible coupled with the crown was symbolic of the Christian gospel being openly declared, which meant freedom of religious expression and maintaining the Protestant British monarchy. These public displays of well-known symbols demonstrated the loyalism of the marchers. This was an instance of public ritual, and the crown on a cushion carried at the front is a staple feature in England, Canada, Ireland and Scotland.[90] The transnational connections were strong as the promotion of this type of Protestantism was important to the Orange Order and therefore they readily used the same symbols.

The ritual use of the crown was in conjunction with the Bible, which was also ordinarily open but in Figure 5.11 is closed.[91] The scene depicted is of the main table at an annual general meeting of the Grand Orange Lodge of Queensland. In this instance, the crown follows the

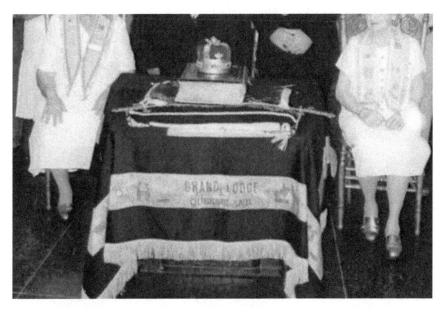

Figure 5.11 Annual general meeting of Grand Orange Lodge of Queensland (© Thomas Leary)

traditional colours of gold bands around and over the crown with red for the rest. These gold and red colours represent the British monarchy, the red being representative of the red rose of England. The Scottish Orange lodges sometimes use their national colour of blue instead. Again, national variations demonstrate there is flexibility in the use of colour, which has different meanings for different countries. Yet these Orange diasporic differences still maintained the central element of the monarchy regardless of the chosen colours based on local conditions.

The crowns themselves were sometimes handmade, as is shown in Figure 5.12.[92] This crown from Scotland, made from wool and felt, is almost homely in appearance. Symbolically, significant elements are still there, with a white cross on top and the beads representing jewels that would normally be encrusted on a crown belonging to a king or queen. A crown such as this was used for in-house lodge ritual rather than for a parade. Lodge meetings were regular events, and so there was an opportunity for members to create their own ritual objects. Public displays were different, and so the manufactured crowns would have taken precedence.

Figure 5.12 Handmade crown for ritual use, Scotland (© David Bryce)

An unusual example of Orange ritual involving the crown fused with a local culture comes from Canada, as is shown in Figure 5.13. The Orange ritual crown was normally used for parades and also in ritual work within the lodges. In this example, the crown is decorated in Haudenosaunee (Iroquois) beading with Orange symbols sewn on to it. The beadwork technique comes from the First Nation people from western Quebec and eastern Ontario, Canada, known as the Haudenosaunee (Iroquois). This particular style of beadwork originated in the late nineteenth century and continued to about 1920. It was the Haudenosaunee women who developed this type of 'raised' beadwork, making items in this style for tourists such as picture frames, bags, moccasins and hats.[93] A unique feature of this style of beadwork is the flowers and leaf-forms on the arches, which help create the crown shape.

The familiar figure of King William of Orange, dressed in a red coat on his white horse with his sword in his right hand, typically features on Orange banners, but not a crown. This example is a one-off as Orange crowns are generally just decorated as a crown. Other commonly used Orange symbols that were embroidered on this crown are the crossed swords, Jacob's ladder, a five-pointed star and the Ark of the Covenant. The pictured crown most likely dates from the late nineteenth century and is probably from one of the Mohawk lodges in Ontario. The Mohawk were one of the Five Nations that made up the Iroquois Confederacy, later six after 1722. Only one of these lodges survived into the twenty-first century, LOL No. 99, which was founded in 1848. With two notable exceptions, all of the members were Mohawk.[94] LOL No. 99 still held meetings on the Tyendinaga Mohawk Territory well into the mid-2010s. The lodge has now closed and an educational facility called the Ohahase Education Centre now runs in the building.[95] This striking and rare adaptation of an Orange crown by an indigenous people demonstrates the appeal of Orangeism beyond the Irish Protestant context that most research has focused on.

CONCLUSION

The material culture of the Orange Order is an essential yet surprisingly neglected area of study. There is no shortage of material objects produced by the Orange Order, as they are in museums and private collections across the world. This chapter has demonstrated that the material objects are diverse and yet integral to the day-to-day activities of Orange members. It was the Orange Order in Ireland that led to the conditions for these objects being created. However, while there were

Figure 5.13 Haudenosaunee beaded crown showing King William, late nineteenth century (© Canadian Museum of History, 75-1365)

simple transferences of some objects, there were also examples of adaptations. The built material culture has had a mixed history as old halls were either demolished or reused for other purposes. Their architectural merits were not always so evident, though Western Australia did give recognition to the Protestant Hall in Perth because of the bas-relief of King William. The various warrants and certificates provide evidence of the existence of lodges and membership and enable researchers to track the movements of members. They also provide evidence of transnational connections, as these warrants allowed members to move around the British world and be recognised in any Orange lodge. Diligence in record-keeping has transmitted useful information about lodge activities for researchers. Unfortunately, it was more from a lack of good archival practices that so much has been lost. The banners, sashes and crowns all provide displays of Orange culture through the use of symbolism and their deployment in public and private rituals. Though sometimes the objects used now are curiosities in museum displays, the example of the Mohawk headdress does indicate a melding of Orange and Mohawk culture. It also reveals the openness of other cultures to join the Orange Order as long as they are not practising Roman Catholics.

The most enduring symbol of Orangeism, and an image on Orange material objects, is the figure of King William on horseback and the 'civil and religious liberty' that he proclaimed still manages to live on. His image is a potent symbol of the transnationalism of the Orange Order. This symbol was recognised by members and even potential members no matter which country it was used in. Orange members do not want to forget the past but live in the present that is linked to this past that King William created. This repetition is also a way of building an identity with William at the centre. His image, as well as the other aspects of Orange material culture, was a way in which members could build not just an identity but also solidarity in the societies that they were a part of. This legacy of the belief in King William III was transmitted from Ireland to the Orange diaspora. These diasporic connections were maintained where other images did not have the same potency. The material culture that was left behind and is still being created has played a role in the Orange Order continuing to exist.

NOTES

1. Ian Woodward, *Understanding Material Culture* (London: Sage Publications, 2007), pp. 3–4.

2. Neil Jarman, *Material Conflicts: Parades and Visual Displays in Northern Ireland* (Oxford: Berg, 1997). Chapter 8 deals with his analysis of the banners and slogans. Also see Neil Jarman, *Displaying Faith: Orange, Green and Trade Union Banners in Northern Ireland* (Belfast: Institute of Irish Studies, Queen's University Belfast, 1999); 'The Orange arch: Creating tradition in Ulster', *Folklore*, 112:1 (2001), pp. 1–21.

3. Neil Jarman, 'Material of culture, fabric of identity', in Daniel Miller (ed.), *Material Cultures: Why Some Things Matter* (Chicago: University of Chicago Press, 1998), pp. 121–45.

4. Anthony D. Buckley, '"The chosen few": Biblical texts in the regalia of an Ulster secret society', *Folklife*, 24 (1985–86), pp. 5–24.

5. David Cairns, 'The object of sectarianism: The material reality of sectarianism in Ulster loyalism', *The Journal of the Royal Anthropological Institute*, 6:3 (2000), pp. 437–52.

6. Ibid. pp. 449–50. The reference to football strips applies especially to Glasgow Rangers, which Cairns identifies as a 'sectarian uniform'.

7. David Cairns and Jim Smyth, 'Up off our bellies and onto our knees: Symbolic effacement and the Orange Order in Northern Ireland', *Social Identities*, 8:1 (2002), p. 144.

8. Ibid. p. 156.

9. Ibid.

10. This term is used by D. A. J. MacPherson, 'Irish Protestant women and diaspora: Orangewomen in Canada during the twentieth century', in D. A. J. MacPherson and Mary J. Hickman (eds), *Women and Irish Diaspora Identities: Theories, Concepts and New Perspectives* (Manchester: Manchester University Press, 2014), pp. 168–85.

11. Carl R. Lounsbury, 'Architectural and cultural history', in Dan Hicks and Mary C. Beaudry (eds), *The Oxford Handbook of Material Culture Studies* (Oxford and New York: Oxford University Press, 2010), p. 485.

12. There are two cottages about 160 metres apart on Derryloughan Road, one owned by Hilda Winter and the other by her nephew Colin Winter. They are descendants of the original Dan Winter, and each claims their cottage is the original one. See Gerry Moriaty, 'Discontented Winters more concerned with local Orange history than elections', *Irish Times*, 20 May 1996.

13. John M. MacKenzie, *The British Empire Through Buildings: Structure, Function and Meaning* (Manchester: Manchester University Press, 2020), pp. 215–19; Cecil J. Houston and William J. Smyth, *The Sash Canada Wore: A Historical Geography of the Orange Order in Canada* (Toronto: University of Toronto Press, 1980), pp. 135–8.

14. *Rules and Regulations of the Loyal Orange Institution of New South Wales, Adopted 25th August 1928* (Sydney: The Institution, 1928), pp. 36–8.

15. Ruth Dudley Edwards, *The Faithful Tribe: An Intimate Portrait of the Loyal Institutions* (London: HarperCollins, 1999), p. 63.

16. Orange Institution of Ireland, *Laws and Ordinances of the Orange Institution of Ireland. Revised and Adopted by the Grand Orange Lodge of Ireland* (Belfast: News Letter, 1872), p. 17.
17. *Rules of the Loyal Orange Institution Incorporated. Adopted by the Grand Orange Lodge of Dominion of New Zealand. April 1908. Revised to June 1916* (Dunedin: Crown Print Co., 1916), p. 13.
18. Loyal Orange Association of British America, *Constitution and Laws of the Loyal Orange Association of British America* (Toronto: The Sentinel Print, 1883), pp. 31–2.
19. Christopher C. H. Cook, *Alcohol, Addiction and Christian Ethics* (Cambridge: Cambridge University Press, 2006), chapter 5.
20. Donald M. MacRaild, *Faith, Fraternity and Fighting: The Orange Order and Irish Migrants in England, c. 1850–1920* (Liverpool: Liverpool University Press, 2005), p. 86.
21. William J. Smyth, *Toronto, the Belfast of Canada: The Orange Order and the Shaping of Municipal Culture* (Toronto: University of Toronto Press, 2015), pp. 109–10.
22. Houston and Smyth, *The Sash Canada Wore*, p. 134.
23. Ibid. pp. 135–8.
24. Michael Phelan, email to author, 8 October 2013.
25. Heritage Council of Western Australia, *Register of Heritage Places-Assessment Documentation Protestant Hall* (Perth: Heritage Council of Western Australia, 2005), p. 15.
26. One of many voluntary associations for mutual aid established across Australia from the nineteenth century that were the key providers of medical services and financial assistance in times of need prior to these matters becoming government-managed social services.
27. *Western Mail*, 19 July 1902.
28. Cecil J. Houston and William J. Smyth, 'The faded sash: The decline of the Orange Order in Canada, 1920–2005', in David A. Wilson (ed.), *The Orange Order in Canada* (Dublin: Four Courts Press, 2007), p. 181.
29. R. E. Parkinson, *History of the Grand Lodge of Free and Accepted Masons of Ireland, Volume 2* (Dublin: Lodge of Research, CC, 1957), pp. 268–9.
30. Orange Institution of Ireland, *Laws and Ordinances*, p. 41.
31. Patrick Coleman, 'Who wants to be a Grand Master? Grand Masters of the Orange Lodge of the Middle Island of New Zealand', in Brad and Kathryn Patterson (eds), *Ireland and the Irish Antipodes: One World or Worlds Apart?* (Sydney: Anchor Books, 2010), pp. 96–107.
32. Redpath was the second Grand Master, 1867–68, of the Grand Lodge of the Middle Island of New Zealand.
33. Orange Lodge of Ireland, *Applications for Warrants 1854 to 1890*, held at Schomberg House, Belfast, Northern Ireland, p. 27.
34. Coleman, 'Who wants to be a Grand Master?', p. 98.

35. *Laws and Ordinances of the Orange Institution of Ireland: Revised and adopted by the Grand Orange Lodge of Ireland, June 3rd, 1896* (Dublin: GOLI, 1896), p. 24.

36. David Fitzpatrick, *Descendancy: Irish Protestant Histories since 1795* (Cambridge: Cambridge University Press, 2014). See chapter 2 on Orangeism and military history.

37. W. A. Stewart (compiler), *Early History of the Loyal Orange Institution N.S.W.* (Sydney: Grand Orange Lodge of New South Wales, 1926), pp. 7–8; Joseph Carnahan, *A Brief History of the Orange Institution in the North Island of New Zealand from 1842 to the Present Time* (Auckland: Star Office, 1886), p. 6.

38. The Canadian lodges had five degrees: Orange, Purple, Blue, Royal Arch Purple and Royal Scarlet. This was later reduced to four with the removal of the Purple, and the Blue was renamed Royal Blue.

39. Orange Institution of Ireland, *Laws and Ordinances*, p. 40.

40. Loyal Orange Association of British America, *Constitution and Laws*, p. 34; Loyal Orange Institution of England, *Laws and Ordinances Enacted by the Grand Lodge of England at Leicester, 5th and 6th July 1893. With Alterations and Additions to 1920* (London: Forbes & Co., 1921), p. 30; *Rules of the Loyal Orange Institution Incorporated. Adopted by the Grand Orange Lodge of Dominion of New Zealand. April 1908. Revised to June 1916* (Dunedin: Crown Print Co., 1916), pp. 11–12.

41. The author accessed a variety of transfer certificates at the Orange hall at Hornby, Christchurch.

42. Transfer certificate for John McLoughlin, Belfast, 1925, Orange Hall, Christchurch, New Zealand.

43. Ibid.

44. *Report of Proceedings of the Seventeenth Triennial Meeting of the Imperial Grand Orange Council of the World. Held in Belfast, Ireland, 15th July 16th, 1920* (Belfast: LOI, 1920), pp. 19–29.

45. Orange Lodge Hornby, Christchurch, New Zealand.

46. *The Cyclopedia of New Zealand [Canterbury Provincial District]*, vol. 3 (Christchurch: The Cyclopedia Company, 1903), p. 315.

47. Coleman, 'Who wants to be a Grand Master?', p. 101.

48. Orange Institution of Ireland, *Laws and Ordinances of the Orange Institution of Ireland. Revised and Adopted by the Grand Orange Lodge of Ireland, June 3rd, 1896* (Dublin: Br. James Forrest, 1896), p. 4; *Rules of the Loyal Orange Institution: Adopted by the Grand Orange Lodge of Dominion of New Zealand, March 1910* (Wellington: Wright & Carman, 1910), p. 4; Loyal Orange Institution of Ireland, *Laws and Ordinances of the Association of Loyal Orangewomen of Ireland* (Dublin: Brother James Forrest, Printers, 1888), p. 3; Loyal Orange Institution of England, *Female Branch. Rules for the Regulation of Lodges of Loyal Orangewomen including opening and closing ceremonies* (London: GOLE, 1922), p. 7.

49. Loyal Orange Association of British America, *Constitution and Laws of the Loyal Orange Association of British America* (Toronto: The Sentinel Print, 1883), p. 34.

50. Loyal Orange Institution, Supreme Grand Lodge (U.S.), *Constitution–General Laws, Regulations and Rules: Supreme Grand Lodge of the Loyal Orange Institution of the United States of America, Inc. Adopted at 48th Session of the Supreme Grand Lodge August 1940* (Philadelphia: LOI, revised 1964), p. 36.

51. *LOL No. 24 Walkers Purple Heroes, Christchurch, New Zealand, Minute Book, 17 June 1901* (Orange Hall, Christchurch, New Zealand).

52. Grand Orange Lodge of New Zealand, *Ritual Book* (Wellington: Wright & Carman Ltd, n.d.).

53. The rules adopted by the various lodges around the world all stipulated the regular nature of these meetings.

54. *The Everett LOL 108, Toxteth Park Liverpool, Minute Book 30 March 1882–5 July 1898* (Central Liverpool Library), 18 February 1898.

55. *Schomberg Loyal Orange Lodge, No. 2, Sydney, N. S. W. Minute Books, 1866–1872*, MLMSS 7494 (Mitchell Library, State Library of New South Wales, Sydney, Australia), 14 March 1870.

56. The author had access to minute books at the Orange hall at Hornby, Christchurch.

57. Neil Jarman, 'Material of culture', p. 121.

58. Ibid.

59. *Laws and Constitutions of the Loyal Orange Institution of Scotland* (Glasgow: GOLS, 1986), p. 64.

60. Kevin Sharpe, *Rebranding Rule: The Restoration and Revolution Monarchy, 1660–1714* (New Haven: Yale University Press, 2013), pp. 345–6.

61. *Press*, 29 April 1889.

62. See examples of banners sourced from Belfast across New Zealand in *Auckland Star*, 14 July 1879; *Globe and Mail*, 22 February 1878; *Otago Daily Times*, 13 July 1880.

63. *New Zealand Herald*, 29 April 1878.

64. Baljinder Sahdra and Michael Ross, 'Group identification and historical memory', *Personality and Social Psychology Bulletin*, 33:3 (2007), pp. 384–95.

65. The image looks to have been inspired by John Everett Millais, the Pre-Raphaelite painter who painted *The Martyr of the Solway* in 1871.

66. The Covenanters were a Scottish Presbyterian movement of the seventeenth century who signed the National Covenant in 1638 to confirm their opposition to the interference by the Stuart kings in the affairs of the Presbyterian Church of Scotland.

67. *The Orangeman: Newsletter of the Loyal Orange Institution USA*, March 2015.

68. 191st Orange Parade County Orange Lodge of Toronto, <http://www.orangelodge.org/> (accessed 20 May 2024). John Wells, email to author, 13 June 2014.
69. David Bryce, email to author, 18 September 2013.
70. Kris Brown and Roger MacGinty, 'Public attitudes toward partisan and neutral symbols in post-agreement Northern Ireland', *Identities: Global Studies in Culture and Power*, 10:1 (2003), p. 86.
71. Ibid.
72. Kevin Haddick-Flynn, *Orangeism: The Making of a Tradition* (Dublin: Wolfhound Press, 1999), p. 423.
73. Orange Institution of Ireland, *Laws and Ordinances of the Orange Institution of Ireland* (Dublin: George P. Bull, 1830), p. 17.
74. Mervyn Jess, *The Orange Order* (Dublin: O'Brien Press, 2007), chapter 5.
75. See Seán Brosnahan, 'The "Battle of the Borough" and the "Saige O Timaru": Sectarian riot in colonial Canterbury', *New Zealand Journal of History*, 28:1 (1994), p. 42; Patrick Coleman, 'Orange parading traditions in New Zealand 1880–1914', *Australasian Journal of Irish Studies*, 10 (2010), p. 88.
76. Michael A. Gordon, *The Orange Riots: Irish Political Violence in New York City, 1870 and 1871* (Ithaca and London: Cornell University Press, 1993). See also Christopher D. McGimpsey, 'Internal ethnic friction: Orange and green in nineteenth-century New York, 1868–1872', *Immigrants & Minorities*, 1:1 (1982), pp. 39–59.
77. Orange Institution of Ireland, *Laws and Ordinances*, pp. 20–1.
78. Loyal Orange Association of British America, *Constitution and Laws*, p. 36.
79. This is a collarette owned by the Orange archivist Michael Phelan, who was given it in 1973 when he joined the Orange Order in England.
80. A jewel looks a bit like a medal.
81. Michael Phelan, email to author, 4 November 2013.
82. Ibid.
83. *Rules of the Loyal Orange Institution: Adopted by the Grand Orange Lodge of Dominion of New Zealand, March 1910*, p. 29.
84. Loyal Orange Association of British America, *Constitution and Laws of the Loyal Orange Association of British America* (Belleville, Ontario: Moore Printer to Grand Lodge, 1875), p. 73.
85. Ibid. p. 74.
86. Grand Orange Lodge of Ireland, *Rules and Regulations for the use of all Orange Societies. Revised and corrected by a Committee of the Grand Orange Lodge of Ireland; and adopted by the Grand Orange Lodge, January 10, 1800* (Dublin: Printed by an Orangeman, 1800).
87. Loyal Orange Institution of Queensland, *Laws and Ordinances of the Loyal Orange Institution of Queensland (incorporated by Letters Patent) Passed As Revised by the Grand Lodge of Queensland, 1935 to 1940* (Brisbane: Rallings & Rallings, 1935), p. 5.

88. Orange Institution of Ireland, *Laws and Ordinances of the Orange Institution of Ireland. Revised and Adopted by the Grand Orange Lodge of Ireland, June 3rd, 1896*, p. 1.
89. Michael Phelan, email to author, 27 October 2013.
90. Any descriptions or images of parades in these countries show Orange members carrying crowns on cushions.
91. This is likely to have been taken at the end of a meeting as any ritual was now completed.
92. David Bryce, email to author, 1 November 2013.
93. Christina Bates, 'A wonderful syncretion: A Haudenosaunee (Iroquois) beaded Orange lodge crown', *Ornamentum* (2011), pp. 13–16.
94. Houston and Smyth, *The Sash Canada Wore*, p. 95.
95. 'Ohahase Education Centre', <https://mbq-tmt.org/ohahase/> (accessed 14 December 2023).

6

Cradle to Lodge:
The Junior Orange Movement

The lodge was opened in the usual manner by singing and ode and the chaplain leading us in a prayer after which the chaplain read a portion of scripture. The minutes of last meeting were read and adopted. The first business was the initiation of Mathew Muldoon age 8 years 41 Underwood Road. Bro Gemmel next said a few words to the new member. As this was all the business the lodge was then closed by hymn and a prayer.[1]

This example of a lodge meeting in 1916 is taken from one of the first Orange juvenile or junior lodges ever established, called Scotland's First Juvenile LOL No. 1, from Paisley, Scotland.[2] This lodge was founded in 1875. The noticeable aspect of this entry is the mundaneness and ordinariness of it. It mimicked the meetings of the adult lodges, which also had a set structure. More important was the clear Christian underpinning of the meeting with its 'rituals or customs of behaviour, economic activity, dress, speech and so on which are collectively promulgated as necessary for Christian identity. The protocols are prescribed or implied in discourses on Christian behaviour.'[3]

In essence, these lodge meetings provided the structure to impart the Orange protocols to the next generation of Orange members, which included the values and traditions that were inherent in the Orange Order as a whole. This process took place in Ireland and across the Orange diaspora. The importance of bringing up the next generation of Orange members lay not only in bolstering the Orange Order numerically, but also in providing a solid base of members to maintain their ideals. No organisation can survive long term if entire generations of members are no longer moving through the organisation. This was the ongoing challenge to the senior leadership of having a vibrant junior movement.

While there have been some recent attempts to redress the lack of focus on women within the Orange Order, the children have received scant research.[4] Their role has been subsumed in the background as passing comments or combined with the adult women in statistical analyses.[5] In his work on the Orange Order in Northern England, for instance, Donald MacRaild devoted just a few pages to the juniors or juveniles. He acknowledged their role in giving the Orange Order a foundation and, through the boys' lodges, a steady supply of musicians for the fife and drum bands.[6] The most notable study, however, is Brian Clarke's work on the Orange Young Britons (OYB), a youth branch of the Orange Order in Canada.[7] Clarke highlighted the generational and behavioural gap between young men with a taste for drink and conflict, and the older teetotal membership of the Canadian Orange Order. Even the Orange Order itself has been remiss in acknowledging its youth, as it too has sidelined the history of its younger members to paragraphs or the odd page in anniversary booklets about the organisation. A notable exception was the locally produced and written booklet on the juniors in Victoria, Australia.[8] This chronological account covering the period 1916–76 documented the origins and activities of the Victorian juniors. It was more nostalgic in focus rather than drawing any conclusions.

This chapter will focus firstly on how and why the junior Orange movement within the Orange Order formed. It will then examine their growth, before assessing reasons for their continuity and then decline. It is important to consider these junior lodges because they helped to maintain the family connections in the Orange Order. The older generation needed the younger generation to pass on their ideals and beliefs. A significant accomplishment of the junior Orange movement was that it provided the adult lodges with leaders and this, in turn, maintained a sense of continuity and stability within the Orange Order.

ORIGINS

The advent of the first junior lodges occurred against the backdrop of the youth movements that were awakening in England, Ireland and Scotland. Probably the most significant youth movements were the temperance societies for children, particularly the Band of Hope, a working-class movement founded in Leeds in 1847.[9] Besides the apparent focus on encouraging children to abstain from alcohol, they provided educational lectures and fun activities to keep the children interested. Band of Hope was a highly successful organisation which grew from only 300 children to three million members by the end of the nineteenth century.[10] Other youth movements like the Boys' Brigade and Boy Scouts formed in the late nineteenth century. These were all Protestant organisations with a focus on maintaining social conformity among the youth, initially in places like England and then further afield in other parts of the British world. It is within this environment of Protestant church-organised outlets for their young people that the junior Orange movement also began. The Orange Order saw the need to retain the young people's membership against competition from these fledgling organisations. Since the Orange Order also drew membership across the various denominations, they were competing for a similar demographic.

Since the Orange Order first formed in 1795, children were there watching the parades or listening to conversations and speeches about the Order. The children would have seen their parents dress up in their Orange regalia and surely would have been inquisitive about the various badges and emblems their parents wore. It was not until the late nineteenth century, however, that the junior or juvenile lodges were first formed. The age range for these kinds of lodges was generally from five to seventeen. In the heart of Orangeism, Ireland, there were Orange lodges for boys in Belfast in the 1870s.[11] However, these were not really part of a formalised movement, but attached to the local male lodge; in the 1880s there were still a few juvenile lodges attached to male lodges. The Rev. Richard Rutledge Kane (1841–98) was the County Grand Master of Belfast at the time. Kane, when promoting the purpose of the juniors, proclaimed, 'when attending their lodges they would be brought under the influence of good and loyal men. They would learn to fear God and honour the Queen.'[12] This demonstrates the dual function being instilled into these young members: Reformation Protestantism and loyalty to the British Crown. Having a strong advocate like Kane for the juvenile lodges was important, as a lack of support from adult Orange members would be a feature of the junior movement in the Orange diaspora.

Although Ireland is seen as the birthplace of the Orange Order, it was Scotland that produced not only one of the earliest juvenile lodges, but also ones that have continued until the present day. Scotland's First Juvenile LOL No. 1 was formed in 1875 in Paisley.[13] This was a boys' only lodge. Further south in England, the first juvenile Orange lodge opened in Plymouth in 1887. The formation of juvenile lodges in England, Ireland and Scotland coincided with the increased numbers of Bands of Hope across the United Kingdom. There were 5,500 of these 'Bands' in 1874, and by 1889 there were 16,000.[14] In this last period, this equated to about two million young people. The move to form juvenile lodges was one born of keeping their youth close and instructing them in the Orange belief system.

Initially, the Orange Order in Canada followed a different trend in their setting-up of junior lodges. Their focus was more on the late teens to the early twenties. In 1853 Ogle Robert Gowan (1803–76), who was Grand Master, proposed the concept of Cadet lodges for their Orange youth.[15] Speaking at the annual sessions in 1856, Gowan painted an idyllic picture of the Cadet lodges as 'a training school, where their minds will be moulded, their energies quickened, and their inclinations encouraged to enter the Orange fold, to feed their youthful minds in Orange pastures, and to watch over, water and cultivate the great Orange Tree'.[16] By 1871, this organisation had become the Orange Young Britons (OYB).

It took many years to establish a junior movement aimed at a younger demographic (five to seventeen years old). At Grand Lodge annual sessions in Winnipeg, Canada, in 1915, there was a desire to establish juvenile Orange lodges 'along the lines of those which are proving so successful in Scotland and Ireland for the education of youth in the principles of pure Protestantism and good citizenship'.[17] The transnational connection was evident as the Canadian Orangemen invoked the example of Ireland and Scotland. This shows they finally realised the benefits of having a younger branch of their organisation. The first juvenile Orange lodge was founded in Manitoba in 1915 and titled the Juvenile Orange Association.

Further south in the United States there was also a gap in time in forming a junior movement. An early attempt in 1883 saw the Grand Orange Lodge of the United States of America receive a petition from young men in New York wanting the Grand Lodge to grant a warrant to institute a junior order to be called Orange Young Americans. It was accepted, and the Grand Lodge wanted to examine their constitution and by-laws.[18] Nothing more came of this request. The proposed name was similar to the Orange Young Britons in Canada, and this was an attempt to set up an organisation for Orange young men like the Canadians. This may well have been a case of transnational influence, with the American Orange Order looking to their Canadian counterparts.

A slightly more successful attempt occurred in 1923 with the formation of the Orange Young American (OYA) lodges in New Jersey and Maine. The New Jersey OYA No. 1 in Atlantic City also formed its own band. This, as noted in earlier chapters, was an incentive for maintaining membership. A description from the time likened the OYA's relationship with Orangeism to the Order of DeMolay's with the Masonic lodges.[19]

This seemingly oblique reference meant that the OYA had a similar age range (thirteen to twenty-one) to the DeMolay. Named after the Knights Templar Grand Master Jacques de Molay, it had been founded in Kansas City, Missouri, in 1919 as a Masonic organisation for adolescent boys.[20] The choice of a figurehead who had been burned at the stake for alleged heresy fitted well within a climate of anti-Catholicism in nineteenth- and early-twentieth-century America.

Despite the early success of the OYA, these lodges were defunct within a few years. A third attempt to set up the OYA on 21 November 1933 met with more success, with Brookline Rising Sons, No. 1 being formed in Brookline, Massachusetts.[21] Just like their Canadian Orange brethren, the American Orange Order was late in setting up lodges focused on the younger members. Following on from the formation of the OYA, there were American junior Orange lodges set up in Philadelphia in the late 1930s.[22]

The integration of youth in the Australian Orange Order took place early in the twentieth century. Walter Hamon Robilliard (1860–1947), writing in the *Watchman*, advocated the establishment of the juvenile lodges.[23] As a father of seven children, he had a clear interest in seeing the Orange Order spread. In the context of good attendance at celebrations and the rise of the Australian Protestant Defence Association in his home state of Victoria, Robilliard advocated youth lodges, noting that 'many arguments were used against the formation of female lodges, but what a useful body we find them'.[24] This reference to the female lodges demonstrates awareness that Orangewomen had had to fight to create their lodges, and Robilliard was using the same logic. These juvenile lodges did finally eventuate, but not initially in his home state.

Across state lines, in 1909 the Grand Lodge of New South Wales approved the idea of Juvenile Loyal Orange Lodges. In doing so, they proclaimed that 'the hope of Australia lies in her remaining a truly Protestant nation'.[25] They followed this proclamation with action by forming No. 1 Juvenile Lodge in Sydney on 1 July 1909. It was named 'Hezekiah Evers', after an Orangeman, now deceased, who was one of the first to advocate starting juvenile lodges.[26] Evers was the right choice given his prominence in the Orange Order, and he was the father of ten children. Tied to this was his primary lodge, No. 17 LOL Volunteer, which was to oversee the newly formed juvenile lodge.[27] Further north in Queensland, the Grand Orange Lodge of Queensland opened a juvenile lodge in Maryborough in 1911 called Derry, No. 1.[28]

While not the oldest in terms of establishing juniors, the Orange Order in Victoria as early as 1894 called for a juvenile Orange lodge.

However, successive Grand Lodges kept deferring the matter. Once the ladies' lodges were formed in 1903, their success and constant lobbying to establish juniors provided some momentum. Although it took some time, this pressure on the Grand Orange Lodge of Victoria was rewarded, with the first juvenile lodge in the state being formed on 14 September 1916. This was a combined effort of female and male lodges in Brunswick, Melbourne.[29]

Tasmania was one of the smaller Australian Orange jurisdictions. Speaking in 1924, their Grand Master, Rev. Fred Barnes, advocated forming juvenile lodges to 'get the boys and girls early under the banner of Orangeism'.[30] A year later, he was bemoaning the decrease in membership and again advocated the formation of juvenile lodges.[31] Barnes's advocacy came to fruition in 1925 with the first Tasmanian juvenile lodge, called Advance No. 1 Juvenile Lodge, which was in Launceston.[32] The impetus for the juveniles came from Barnes, who had previously been the Orange Grand Master in South Australia.[33]

Across the Tasman Sea, there was a desire to form juvenile lodges in the Middle (or South) Island of New Zealand reasonably early on. In 1889, only one year after the formation of the first ladies' lodges, the Grand Lodge sanctioned the formation of juvenile lodges. They even printed rules and regulations for this purpose. These lodges were to be called Apprentice lodges and were aimed at boys aged between fourteen and eighteen.[34] Despite the desire to form these lodges, nothing seems to have been done. At the local lodge level, however, action was taken. By 1893 the No. 3 Canterbury True Blues held a meeting and a Bro. McCall claimed he had the names 'of a large number of youths wishing to form a juvenile Orange Lodge'. The lodge decided that an Apprentice lodge should begin at once and they arranged for a preliminary meeting.[35] There is evidence that this Apprentice lodge system initially created two lodges in the South Island, No. 1 Blenheim and No. 2 Westport.[36] On 23 April 1907, the North Island Orange lodges opened their first juvenile Orange lodge in Palmerston North, called the Manawatu Young Britons Apprentice Boys, No. 3.[37] All these lodges seem to have been defunct by 1914.[38] There is no record of why these lodges failed. A lack of support from members might have been the reason, as most Orange youth movements failed due to only a few adults doing the work and a lack of support from the others.[39]

William Hunter (1866–1937), Grand Master of New Zealand, stated in 1914 that not only was the opening of juvenile lodges a matter of urgency but 'the instilling of Protestant Principles and Protestant History into the minds of our boys and girls is of vast importance'.[40]

Hunter was echoing a common belief among many members that furthering the spread and cause of the Orange Order began in their children. In the past, there had been a lot of rhetoric and little action, but by 1929 the pleas of Hunter came to fruition. In this instance, it was Scottish Sister Jeannie Salmond, a founding member of the newly formed ladies' lodges in Scotland and a recent immigrant from January 1927, who helped form Primrose Girls' Lodge No. 1 in Wellington in May 1929.[41] This was followed later in the same year, on 21 September, with Massey Boys' Lodge No. 1. Jeannie, who was a key initiator, had migrated from Scotland to New Zealand with her Irish-born husband, Christopher Salmond. He had been an Assistant Superintendent of the Scottish Juveniles between 1918 and 1919.[42] Jeannie was born in Belfast in 1873, but her family had immigrated to Scotland.[43] It was there that she joined with other Irish or Irish-born Orangewomen to form the revived ladies' lodges. The Salmonds brought their first-hand experience in leading lodges in Scotland with them to New Zealand. Their experience showed as they played this crucial role in the formation of the New Zealand junior Orange movement.

In Africa, the Orange Order has always been in a precarious position. The survival of the Orange lodges in Ghana and Togo has been dependent on the transnational assistance of the other Orange jurisdictions. The first juvenile lodge formed in Ghana in 1959 was called Hope of Ghana No. 1. The impetus for this came from the same Rev. Fiawoo who visited the English Orange lodges and set up a ladies' lodge in the same year as the juniors.[44]

GROWTH

Once established, many of these junior Orange lodges in Northern Ireland and the Orange diaspora began to grow in numbers. The purpose of this junior movement was not only to instruct the next generation in the Orange ideals but also to serve as an ongoing boost to the adults' lodges once the children became of age.

By 1918 in the north of Ireland, after the initial grouping of boys' lodges attached to men's lodges, the Irish lodges decided to form an association of junior or juvenile lodges. This was further structured into the Junior Orange Association by 1925.[45] In 1927, following this reorganisation of the boys' lodges, the Association of Loyal Orangewomen of Ireland (ALOI) decided to form their own junior organisation to train their under-eighteen-year-old girls. It was called the Junior Orangewomen's Association of Ireland (JOAI).[46] The gendered approach of separate boys' and girls' lodges was in keeping with the adult lodges that also had separate organisations.

For the boys' lodges, there was rapid growth up until World War II. With so many men, including young men, volunteering to fight, many of the lodges that had seen growth ceased operating. After the war the juniors regained ground and during the next few decades they expanded and opened more County Junior Lodges across Northern Ireland.[47] The JOAI also saw an increase in numbers leading up to the Second World War, with a 1938 report claiming 1,247 members. The juniors had a positive effect on the ALOI. On the eve of the war, there were reports of three lodges in Belfast run by former juniors.[48]

There were similar patterns of growth in the Orange diaspora in the lead-up to both world wars. These were times of crisis and also of great patriotism. The Orange Order was able to capitalise on this as they espoused a strong loyalty to their respective countries. The Scottish Orange juvenile lodges increased numbers in the build-up to the First World War, and so did the ladies' lodges which had recently formed in 1909. This was no coincidence as the Orangewomen started to increase their role in the Orange Order. First, during World War I, the office of Superintendent was officially opened up to Orangewomen because of the shortage of men. Mothers often took their children to juvenile meetings.

With the advent of the ladies' lodges, there was a move to provide girls with their own lodges. At the Grand Lodge sessions in Glasgow in 1912 a motion proposed forming female juvenile lodges or mixing them with the boys. The idea of mixing was likened to the Bands of Hope, Juvenile Templars and Sons of Rechab.[49] The motion was defeated. By 1917 the Grand Secretary, James Rice, wrote an impassioned report promoting the work of the juveniles. He proclaimed, 'Remember the ladies can work, and they are willing.'[50] This was about allowing members of the ladies' lodges to be at the forefront of guiding the juvenile lodges. This time the motion was passed for girls to join the boys' lodges.[51] Only a few years later Rice noted that the wisdom of the Grand Lodge in admitting young girls into 'juvenile Lodges, is, as the days go by, becoming more and more apparent'.[52]

The juveniles continued to gain in numbers until after World War II, with 140 lodges by 1950. To retain teenagers in the Orange Order, the Scottish Grand Lodge in 1945 introduced junior lodges. The juvenile age range was five to sixteen years, with the juniors covering ages thirteen to sixteen. Initially, there was one male and one female junior lodge.[53] In some places, they did not form a junior lodge as they preferred the older ones filling the offices, and the young people liked that too.[54] Growth within the Scottish juveniles, and to a lesser degree in the juniors, continued throughout the twentieth century. The substantial growth that occurred in the 1940s continued until 1980, when they reached 146 lodges. The juniors managed modest growth to forty-four lodges in the same period but had fallen to only thirty-six lodges by 2015.[55] Both branches of the Scottish junior movement provided members, and potential future leaders, to the adult lodges.

Further south in England, the growth rates of the English juniors were not as spectacular as their Scottish counterparts. The cause of this slow growth is unclear. Possible reasons may include a lack of support from the adult lodges. It was a slow start, and it was not until 1902 that numbers climbed to twenty-three. As with the Orange Order in Scotland, the First World War proved to be an impetus for increasing membership, and by 1915 there were eighty-seven juvenile lodges. The outpouring of patriotism and the chance to join a strident loyalist organisation would have helped numbers. Over the following decades numbers fell, reaching thirty-three lodges by 2013.[56]

In Canada, the Orange Order only had the Orange Young Britons (OYB) as an outlet for their youth for the latter part of the nineteenth century. By the early 1870s 600 young men were members. An explanation for their rapid growth lay in the fact they were run and organised by young men. While they were a branch of the Orange Order, they were not under the direct control of the Grand Lodge. They peaked in the 1880s and were restructured as they came under the control of the Grand Orange Lodge of British America.[57] Having an active youth branch did bolster the presence of the Orange Order in Canada, although the OYB lodges did cluster near Toronto.[58] Their rebranding as the Loyal Orange Young Briton Association also came with clear rules of conduct, targeting an age of fourteen to twenty-five.[59]

Meanwhile, the junior Orange movement in Canada for those aged eight to sixteen made steady progress from its beginnings in 1915 to open twenty-eight new lodges by 1928.[60] By 1960 there were 178 girls' and mixed youth lodges and twenty-two boys' lodges.[61] A lot of the success resulted from the early decision in 1933 to hand over the girls' lodges to the LOBA, though the male Grand Lodge still had control over issuing warrants and rituals and constitutions.[62] Having the LOBA organise these junior lodges modelled the Scottish example. This impetus to use the Scottish model would have been influenced by the influx of Scottish migrants in the 1920s, many of whom became members of the LOBA.[63] In Scotland, the Orangewomen who were already caring for children made sure their children went to and were active in the junior lodges. This followed the gendered roles of women as carers of children, which was promoted by the founder of the LOBA Mary Cullum.[64] Ultimately, this combined effort of LOBA organisation and Grand Lodge oversight ensured the continued growth of the Canadian juniors into the 1960s.

The Orange Young Americans (OYA) were only moderately successful but had achieved more stability than in previous attempts. This may well be due in part to the timing of the founding of their lodges. Only three years after the first lodge had been formed, they had eighteen operating lodges with a membership of 356.[65] Most of these lodges were in Michigan, New Jersey and New York. A crowning success for the young men involved was the establishment of a Grand Lodge of OYA. In true independent style, the organiser boasted that 'not one cent of Supreme Grand Lodge funds' had been spent on promoting the OYA.[66] In the meantime, the Junior Orange Order had made a start, though they had merely six lodges by 1940.[67] During a world war was not the best time to begin a youth organisation, but there was a need to do something about membership, so the lodges were instituted.

The growth in the junior Orange movement in Australia was complicated by a number of factors. First, as each state had its own Grand Lodge, the impetus to begin was localised and therefore did not have the centralised support of a national Grand Lodge. Second, the Orange Order in the various Australian states was demographically driven, and therefore New South Wales had a greater population from which to draw members than sparsely populated Western Australia.

Despite these constraints, the various Grand Lodges reported positively on the increases in juvenile lodges in the post-World War I period. This coincided with the already mentioned formation of these lodges from 1909 to 1925. For example, the Grand Orange Lodge of Queensland reported 'a large increase in membership' in 1929.[68] Earlier, in 1927, in Tasmania at the Grand Lodge annual sessions, even the presence of a juvenile lodge was cause for celebration. The Grand Secretary, A. E. Lee, reported that the Launceston Juvenile Lodge was doing well and another at Hobart was progressing. Lee urged that juvenile branches should be established at every centre possible, as the future of the institution, to a considerable extent, rested on the rising generation.[69] The reality was that Tasmania only managed to establish a handful of lodges, while Queensland issued forty-one warrants to form juvenile lodges.[70]

In New Zealand, despite the initial successes in growing numbers, there was competition from other youth organisations. This made progress slow. Many of the friendly societies had juvenile lodges, such as the Ancient Order of Foresters, the Independent Order of Odd Fellows and the Independent Order of Good Templars. Many pre-dated the Orange Order's ones, and there were also the growing clubs and sports organisations catering for youths. As with other parts of the Orange diaspora, the junior Orange lodges increased membership leading into the Second World War, but like the others, they struggled to maintain numbers post-war. By 1905 there were twenty-nine lodges, and this number dipped to sixteen in 1955 before reaching twenty-six in 1960.[71]

In Ghana, the Orange Order was always fairly modest in size for the adults, so it took some time for the junior lodges to flourish following the first at Keta in 1959. The 1980s and early 1990s saw a rise in the number of junior lodges. This coincided with twenty to thirty adult lodges being formed. It was the peak growth of the Ghanaian Orange Order. The Grand Secretary was happy to announce at the Imperial Orange Council in Auckland, New Zealand, in 1994 that since the last meeting junior numbers had risen from fifty to 170 mixed lodges.[72]

CONTINUITY

Younger members were desperately needed to sustain the vitality of the Orange Order but maintaining the growth of the junior Orange movement was a challenge for the Orange Order in Ireland and the Orange diaspora. A report in 1955 from the Grand Secretary of the Scottish Orange Order emphasised the importance of the junior movement. Two points are worthy of comment. One was the claim that while the Roman Catholic Church liked to have children from the age of five, the Orange Order had them from birth and held on to them. The other was that senior members mostly came from the junior movement.[73] With both these points, there is evidence of the intergenerational move from junior to adult lodges resulting in leadership positions.

An example from New Zealand captures both of these positive aspects of the juniors. In 1935 the *Nation* newspaper, the official organ of the Orange Order in New Zealand, published a photo of the Sims family: Thomas Herbert Sims (1884–1978), his wife Ethel Jackson Sims (1886–1961, born Scott) and their seven children. They were presented as a 'rare' achievement of all family members not just being in the Order but also occupying positions of responsibility in their various adult and youth lodges.[74] This situation was and still is a problematic one for the Orange Order.

The Sims family are an example of the ideal Orange family, with everyone an active participant in the life of their lodge. However, since

Figure 6.1 The Sims family, New Zealand, 1935. *Nation*, 10 August 1935

this was not the norm, it demonstrates that even in the 1930s, when New Zealanders were a lot more patriotic than they are now, it was challenging to get all family members involved. It was also not the norm in the other jurisdictions.

The Imperial Orange Council has proven to be the platform for championing the activities of the Orange Order. The Grand Secretary from Ghana, speaking in 2006, proclaimed that their first junior lodge, founded in 1959, had for decades provided the adult lodges not only with members but also with significant leaders.[75] This is only one example of many instances of leaders in the Orange Order coming from the junior movement.

In order to maintain their youth wing, the Orange Order had to provide some focus for these younger members. The junior Orange movement, regardless of the country, had a commonality in the way they organised their youth. All had lodge meetings, ritual work and activities. The difference lay in the detail of these. The first step in maintaining a base membership was to attract new candidates. As previously noted, all the Orange jurisdictions set up their lodges in the nineteenth or early twentieth centuries. Therefore, the rules around membership were a reflection of the late-eighteenth-century-founded Orange Order. Over time these rules and regulations needed to be updated and adapted to a changing society. The first step was the eligibility test. This focused on religion, age and character. The first of these was generally straightforward. In the English Orange junior rules it simply stated they be 'the Sons and Daughters of Orangemen and other Protestant Parents'.[76] The other jurisdictions had similar wording, as the idea was to attract children who were being raised as Protestants.[77]

When it came to the age criteria, there were some slight differences. The juniors in England were aged between four and sixteen. The Canadian Juvenile Orange Association of British America, as it was originally called, was for boys and girls aged from eight until sixteen. The boys' and mixed lodges were under the Grand Orange Lodge of British America, whereas girls only came under the separate Ladies' Orange Benevolent Association.[78] The renamed junior Orange lodges in Canada have both boys and girls (mixed lodges), and the ages range from six to sixteen. This top-end age of sixteen was fairly standard, although the Junior Orangewomen's Association of Ireland began with an end age of eighteen, before reducing it to sixteen by the 1950s.[79]

The issue of age was important as this determined the length of time juniors would stay in their lodges before moving to the adult lodges. The transition from the juniors to the adults did create some problems. A notable example was in New Zealand. Some members felt that the transition from the junior organisation to the adult one was challenging. This was due to going from a junior lodge with young people to one with much older members, and the activities in adult lodges were not organised with young people in mind. As a result, intermediate lodges were proposed in 1950, although this did not eventuate until Southern Cross Intermediate Lodge, No. 1 was founded on 5 March 1954.[80] These lodges catered for either sex, aged fifteen to twenty-one. In Canada and the United States, the Orange Young Britons and the Orange Young Americans were there to ease the transition from child to teenager to adult. In the case of the OYA they had an age range of twelve to twenty-three. They also had some 'other' rules. Just like their parent body, they would not admit a candidate if they were 'not of the white race'.[81] Once again, it was the local conditions that were a determinant in rule changes. This racial requirement meant the American junior Orange movement was an outlier compared to those in all the other jurisdictions.

Besides the rather tedious job of running lodge meetings, the other main focus was on the rituals. These formed the basis of inducting new members into the Orange Order. At the heart of these rituals was their Christian faith, with an emphasis on the Bible. The 'open Bible' was a key symbol within the Orange Order, which meant the Bible was available for everyone. The minute books do not record the details of the rituals as this was essentially the private or 'secret' aspect of lodge life. It is only through analysis of the ritual books that it is possible to get a true sense of how the rituals worked. In terms of the general structure and order of the junior Orange rituals, there were plenty of examples from other fraternal societies like the Independent Order of Rechabites or the Independent Order of Good Templars. These temperance societies also had juvenile sections complete with their own rituals.[82] Closer inspection of their rituals and the Orange ones shows surprising similarity in structure. Obviously, there are changes to their wording and focus, but the skeletal framework is still there.

The opening and closing ceremonies all have a pre-learned dialogue among the participants. The temperance initiates take the pledge to abstain from alcohol, whereas the Orange initiates pledge to uphold the Protestant faith. Another common element between these junior branches of fraternal organisations is the lodge layout.[83] Whether this is the English, Scottish or New Zealand Orange juniors, compared with their temperance or even friendly society counterparts, the lodge room layout is fairly uniform.[84] This layout is not just for a normal sense of order but is specifically designed to place the various officers in the lodge. It then leads on to the 'floorwork'. This is the movement around the lodge room taken by the participants in the various ceremonies. The hard part of any role playing by the participants is the mixture of movement and dialogue.

The danger for many of these junior lodges was that the ritual system would be too outdated and boring. The senior leadership in the various Grand Lodges were aware of this. For example, the Canadian Grand Lodge made constant revisions of their junior rituals. Even as early as 1928 in the Grand Lodge annual sessions, it was claimed that 'the ritual and unwritten work is along educational lines rather than partaking of the mystic lore characteristic of Senior Orders in general'.[85] This focus on education moved the juniors away from the more Masonic aspects of the rituals. The modern juvenile section of the Orange Order in the 1990s updated their ritual and introduced a 'badge' system. Like the previous example in Canada, the Scottish brethren focused on educating members 'about their culture, history, principles and Christian heritage'.[86]

While there was, and still is, a focus on the Orange ritual for these junior members, the Bible is still the core of their belief system. Many of the jurisdictions, like Ireland and Scotland, have Bible or Scripture quizzes and reading competitions.[87] These are grouped according to age. The rituals have lots of biblical references, and the lodge meeting also quotes the Bible at various points. A strong focus on general biblical knowledge therefore helps to underpin the additional activities of the junior members.

An advantage that present-day juniors or juveniles have in England, Ireland and Scotland over other parts of the Orange world are the links to historical sites and events that form a part of their history. For example, a fun day event in Scotland in 2015 saw a group of juveniles and juniors from the County Grand Lodge of Ayrshire, Renfrewshire and Argyll lay a wreath at a local memorial. This was a memorial to the Rev. Alexander Peden (1626–86), a major Covenanter.[88] This episode in Scottish history, that of the Covenanters, is one that the Scottish Orange Order weaves into its own history. The physical memorials and stories that go with them are part of the education that the younger members experience. In another instance, members of Samuel Johnson Memorial Junior LOL No. 137, Rutherglen, visited Carrickfergus Castle, the River Boyne in Drogheda, Schomberg House, Belfast, and Dan Winter's Cottage, Loughgall, the birthplace of the Orange Order.[89] The Scots Juveniles George Brown Memorial JLOL 18, No. 3 District, also visited Dan Winter's Cottage, Loughgall, in 2015. They were met by Hilda Winter, a direct descendant of Dan Winter.[90] All these visits tie into key Orange historical events.

Their Northern Irish counterparts take part in the historical re-enactments at Carrickfergus every year.[91] While the Northern Irish junior lodges do have a parade, there are junior lodges from England that travel each year as well. Again, this reinforces the notion of a shared history that crosses national boundaries. The Canadian juniors also take part in this shared heritage. Brooks Memorial Junior Orange Lodge No. 525 in Kendal, Ontario, as part of their thirtieth anniversary, raised money and went on a trip to Northern Ireland in 2011.[92] They met with their junior counterparts in Bangor and took part in parades. Interestingly, they were allowed to lead the Black parade in Scarva. This was because of Richard Lowery, the Grand Master of the Grand Black Chapter of Eastern Ontario.[93] The result of all these visits is that the lectures and stories from their lodge meetings are now rendered tangible through these shared experiences. They also go some way to emboldening the young people involved so that they can encourage others in their faith.

A more recent example of cooperation between Orange jurisdictions is the interjurisdictional meetings between representatives from England, Ireland and Scotland. There is also the interjurisdictional conference, with teenagers from England, Ireland and Scotland taking part. This is run every three years at Bonaly Camp, south of Edinburgh, with the first one held from 31 March to 2 April 2006. The activities were a mixture of discussions and vigorous assault courses to keep the participants well occupied.[94] This transnational cooperation indicates a desire on behalf of the Orange hierarchy to make a genuine effort to retain their younger members. Edward Hyde, Grand Secretary for Scotland, when giving his report at the Imperial Council in 2006, opened by claiming that their youth section, like other countries', was in free fall. Other youth organisations, not just the Orange ones, also experienced this.[95] Implicit in his message, therefore, was the imperative to do more with their young people to ensure the ongoing survival of the Orange Order.

The aspect of fundraising for charitable causes is indicative of the present-day juniors around the world. In Scotland, charitable causes are quite varied. Members of JLOL 25, Bridgeton, who were inspired by the adult lodges' 10 km run fundraiser that raised £650 for Erskine, organised their own events and raised £500.[96] This is a popular cause, as even small groups of quite young members visit the Erskine Hospital.[97] The Northern Irish juniors also have their charitable causes. One lodge in East Belfast which raised money for the Children's Hospice received a boost to their efforts by a donation of £250 from the Royal Black District Chapter.[98] The Canadians also have their causes, but sometimes they are more than mere charities. While these junior lodges carried out their fundraising for various causes, sometimes they combined their efforts. In 2011 juniors in England, Ireland and Scotland raised £20,000 for the National Society for the Prevention of Cruelty to Children (NSPCC) charity Childline.[99] The transnational nature of this enterprise reflects the parent bodies in these respective countries, which also cooperate across borders.

Today, a key determinant in keeping many of the Orange youth in the Orange Order would be their involvement in parades. Generally, the parades have tended to be all-male affairs, particularly in Ireland. Women only participated in certain countries. But with societal changes, more women and then children became involved. In the English context, the juniors have plenty of opportunities to parade, on Commonwealth Day, Reformation Sunday and the Twelfth of July. The juniors in Merseyside have long been a part of the marches. This is a family event, in contrast to other parades which are male or female, or even just adults. The

Figure 6.2 Loyal Orange Girls, No. 9, Philadelphia, USA, 1966 (*Philadelphia Evening Bulletin* © Special Collections Research Center, Temple University Libraries, Philadelphia, PA)

children at these parades dress up as King William and Queen Mary. The costumes are quite lavish as the parents attempt to get the historical look right.[100] Bands also form an important part of the parades. Many of the juniors are members of these.

DECLINE

The decline of the junior Orange movement was most noticeable at the meeting of the Imperial Orange Council held in Liverpool in 2015. All of the existing nine Orange jurisdictions gave their usual reports about their activities. The juniors are not always mentioned, even though these are country reports giving the other jurisdictions a glimpse into the state of the Orange Order in their respective countries. The Grand Secretaries from Australia, New Zealand, Togo and the United States all had to state there was no junior Orange movement in their countries. The Ghanaian Grand Secretary made no mention of juniors but had previously noted they had falling numbers. The Canadians could report on having had three lodges, one for girls and the other two mixed, with the total membership at thirty-nine. The English Grand Secretary had some optimism with reports of two new lodges, and his Scottish counterpart could also claim the same number of new lodges. The Irish Grand Secretary could report on five new and three more potential junior lodges.[101] The burning question is what happened to the junior Orange movement?

It was in the furthest-flung parts of the Orange diaspora that the death of the junior Orange movement first occurred. Australia and New Zealand both made attempts to stem the inevitable decline. The case of the intermediate lodges, introduced in New Zealand in 1954 to bridge the transition from junior to adult lodges, illustrates the issues. Despite their best intentions, the intermediate lodges only ever reached a high of five lodges in 1957, and this continued until 1962. The slow death of these lodges dragged on until 1982, when they ceased to exist. In a parallel with their junior counterparts, the lack of support from the adult membership was also apparent in the transition period from intermediate lodges to adult lodges. In a circular sent to all lodges in 1957 the then Grand Superintendent of Junior and Intermediate Lodges, C. P. Harris, noted a 'wrong impression' in regard to intermediate lodges. Some felt that they were not an official part of the Orange Order and, further, that they were undermining the functioning of junior lodges. Harris highlighted the function of intermediate lodges, as they were there 'to assist in maintaining interest in the Junior Lodges'.[102] He could speak with a sense of authority as he was a Past Grand Master (1948–54). He also oversaw the introduction of the intermediates, so this was, in essence, undermining the work he had brought about.

Despite this, the integration of the intermediates into the adult lodges was a difficult one. One member recalls the situation in the 1960s when a mixed intermediate lodge in Christchurch wanted to move on to the adult lodge system but wanted to retain their mixed-lodge status rather than separate into men's and women's lodges. The Grand Lodge of New Zealand did not allow this, so many members were lost. Also, when some young men did move to the male lodges, they were not made to feel welcome.[103] This anecdote received support from John Robinson, Grand Superintendent in 1964, who bluntly stated his own opposition to intermediate lodges when they were first introduced, but confirmed he now supported them. He felt the decline was due to both the intermediates themselves and the 'considerable opposition' from adult members. This opposition was now having an adverse effect on these lodges.[104] The opposition seems illogical as new members were needed, but some existing members may have felt the younger members were only delaying their shift to the adult lodges and by default the adult world.

This lack of support has been a constant theme throughout the Orange world. Sometimes it has been expressed as apathy. A perusal of Grand Master speeches across the Orange world testifies to the ongoing decline of the junior Orange movement, often expressed in terms of adult members not supporting their juniors. In the case of the Orange Order in Ghana, there was an acknowledgement of adults not supporting their lodges. This was seen as being not deliberate but a result of the severe economic hardship in the region.[105] The hardship was reflected in Togo, which has had political unrest and which reported on the demise of their junior lodges in 1994 as many of their members fled the country.[106]

A final outworking of the private sphere of the junior Orange movement has been the transnational cooperation between lodges. The New Zealand and Australian examples are now historic, but these ties did occur for many years through to the period of their eventual demise. The New Zealand juniors began having, from 1955, Junior Conferences every two years.[107] These were, in essence, mini versions of the adult conferences. They had all the same procedures like reports and remits. These remits were sent to the Grand Executive and then were 'subject to confirmation'.[108] In practice, this meant that anything that could genuinely be done did tend to happen. In 1973 a letter from the Grand Superintendent of Victoria, J. S. Davis, suggested holding a Pan-Pacific Conference in New Zealand in 1975. It would include delegates from Australia, New Zealand and Canada.[109] It is worth noting at this point that the Australians had had Junior Conferences since 1969.[110] The next couple of Trans-Tasman Conferences went very well. In 1977 Melbourne hosted and the New Zealand delegates also visited Canberra, Adelaide and Sydney.[111] The next conference in Auckland in 1979 also went well, with delegates from Victoria and New South Wales.[112]

Despite all the goodwill generated, this was to be the last Trans-Tasman Conference. At the New Zealand Junior Conference in 1984, it was put on record that these conferences ceased because of a lack of enthusiasm from members in both Australia and New Zealand.[113] Membership was also falling in these years, so finding willing adults and young people became more and more difficult, with the pool of talent to draw upon ever decreasing. By 1989 the 17th Junior Conference had to be cancelled.[114] The push for these conferences did initially demonstrate a shared heritage and a desire to form strong transnational links. However, like many well-intended initiatives, they faltered through a lack of support. A factor in this lack of support must surely be the dwindling membership, which meant that the personnel to carry on were now ageing or had other commitments. A diminishing pool of potential leaders also meant the same people did all the organisation, so once they did die or retire there was no one to replace them.

The slow decline of the Australian junior Orange movement has not been documented anywhere. The exception is a short sentence in a booklet for the New South Wales 150th celebrations of the Orange Order in 1995. It noted that their juniors came to a close in 1987, with their last lodge unable to continue because of a lack of numbers.[115] None of the other Australian states has juniors. The Orange Order in New Zealand had been attempting to maintain their juniors since the 1950s. Despite the best efforts of some members, it was to no avail. The annual reports continued through the 1950s onwards, to report on the general lack of interest by their youth. A contributing factor was the lack of support from adult members. Eileen Anderson, Grand Superintendent in 1970, was very critical of this lack of support. She lamented the fact that some junior lodges were being closed due to a lack of superintendents to carry them on.[116] Continued falling numbers were signalled by succeeding Grand Superintendents. This led to the eventual closing of the last junior lodge in 2001.[117] This lack of a younger membership means the current adult membership is slowly dying off as they age. Many of the current leaders of the Orange Order in New Zealand began in the junior Orange lodges.

Efforts to maintain membership levels among the Orange youth have presented major challenges to the Orange Order across the world. In Scotland from the year 2000, they saw a drop of 25 per cent from 1,600 to 1,200 members. In the same period, Northern Ireland had its junior membership fall by 20 per cent. The Scottish Grand Master at that time, Ian Wilson, compared their falling youth membership to similar organisations like the Boys' Brigade and the Scouts. The hierarchy of the Orange Order in Northern Ireland, Scotland and England, in response to falling youth numbers, decided to revamp their image. For instance, Tommy Ross, Grand Secretary of the Junior Grand Lodge of Ireland, worked with his British equivalents to update the Orange Order's image for current and prospective members. Meanwhile, Wilson stated that in Scotland they had modernised their junior ritual and were also trialling a badges awards system to retain and attract younger members.[118] Members from the other largest body of Orange members, Canada, noted in 1991 that they lacked 'a good vibrant Junior movement where both ladies' and men's lodges could enjoy the benefits of a young feeder organization to help bolster a declining membership'.[119] These comments by the Orange hierarchy indicate a realisation that without the younger members coming through, their organisation will die out. There is also a common theme of recognising that this lack of youth involvement is also present in other clubs and societies.

The Orange Order in Ireland has already made an attempt at reimaging themselves. In November 2007 they created an Orange superhero. Initially, he did not have a name, so the media were calling him Sash Gordon. The idea was he was committed to the Orange Order and the junior movement and was keen on recycling.[120] A competition to name him was won by seven-year-old schoolboy Steven Mitchell, who suggested 'Diamond Dan'. This was a clear nod to Dan Winter, one of the founders of the Orange Order, and the Diamond where the Orange Order was founded in 1795.[121] This was not without controversy as the image was similar to one posted on iStockphoto.com by Dan Bailey, a designer from Essex.[122]

While the media coverage was a mixture of derisive comments and the fallout over copyright, it did prompt the Grand Orange Lodge of Scotland to comment on the real story behind all of this. It was essentially the decline of the junior Orange movement. In a full-page article in their official organ, the *Orange Torch*, under the heading 'SUPERORANGEMAN', there was an acknowledgement of the falling numbers. The article noted the all-time high of membership for the juveniles and juniors in the 1970s to the falling numbers that have continued. The author mentioned that the general drift in numbers was also occurring in larger youth bodies like the Boys' Brigade and the Scouts. Interestingly, there was a comment about the restrictive legislation which followed the Dunblane school shootings and how this affected adult involvement in youth work. Some of the changes introduced to try to retain members were the modernisation of the lodge ritual, a badges system, a magazine called 'Olympia Kids' and the annual rally and fun day.[123] Also notable was that the attempt by the Irish at rebranding also influenced the Scots as they realised this was important for their future.

CONCLUSION

Why has there been such neglect of the junior Orange movement? Children's history, in general, has not often been a focus of historians. Just as women's history fought to gain recognition, so has history involving children struggled to find its place.[124] Therefore, it is not surprising that the junior Orange movement has been generally overlooked. Yet despite their dependency on the adult lodges for their guidance and leadership, the children of Orange members played an important role in maintaining the lifeblood of the Order. Another critical aspect that cannot be overlooked is the number of junior members who have gone into major leadership. The grounding and confidence they gained through the rituals and camaraderie of their junior years helped them as they dealt with the demands of running meetings and making public speeches.

The motivation for the junior Orange movement was initially quite simple in focus. There was a need for building a solid base for membership within the Orange Order. Women became more than bystanders as they formed their own lodges, and there was the natural progression to include the children. This was a loyalist organisation, so to maintain this, building an ongoing network of families helped to transition members in the lodge. Parallel with the Protestant churches from which members were recruited, there was a commonality. Many people became Christians as adults or joined other churches as adults. The Orange Order was no different. The core membership still came from adults, but the children of members needed a focus. As in many of the fraternal organisations that began in the eighteenth century, maintaining membership for the next generation has proven to be troublesome. Places like Australia and New Zealand are quite different societies, and fraternal organisations are no longer as relevant. Falling membership and a lack of support from adult members contributed to the eventual demise of the junior movement in New Zealand and also in Australia.

The junior Orange movement seems to have appealed to or been targeted at different age groups in different locations. In the case of Canada its appeal seems to have been greater for older adolescents. These differences can be explained by local conditions. Adult members had to organise their junior lodges while still being members of separate male or female Orange lodges. This impacted on their time. The mixed membership model is reflected in Protestantism being a blend of Church of England, Baptist, Presbyterian and many other denominations. There were competing organisations such as the Bands of Hope and the Boy Scouts. In addition, the early Orange Order was an adult organisation which only really considered the junior Orange movement once these adult lodges were established. In the Canadian context, young adults organising young adults meant the older members did not have to take part, whereas a junior Orange movement required willing adults to help with organisation, and these proved to be in short supply.

The junior movement has managed to stay alive in Canada, England, Ireland and Scotland. Some reasons for this include the greater numerical strength of the Orange Order in these countries and the heightened Old World sensitivities, with sectarian conflict still evident. Having more members means that families can take part in the activities, and the close proximity to historical sites of importance to the Orange Order helps to generate ongoing interest in the juniors' heritage. Also, these countries have been able to harness the lure of parades and bands, which provide children and young people with a chance to either dress up or play music. While children like to dress up and parade, the appeal for teenagers is weak. However, being in a band and learning an instrument is a drawcard for maintaining membership, especially as these teens can get to play at events other than parades. This community involvement, especially if families are involved, keeps the spirit of Reformation Protestantism and its combination with loyalism alive.

NOTES

1. *Juvenile LOL No. 1 Paisley, Minutes, March 1912–November 1916* (Olympia House, Glasgow, Scotland), 9 April 1916.
2. Muldoon later married in his hometown of Paisley in 1925 and then migrated to America in 1930, where he died in California in 1938.
3. Callum Brown, *The Death of Christian Britain* (London: Routledge, 2001), p. 12.
4. For the most recent examples see D. A. J. MacPherson, *Women and the Orange Order: Female Activism, Diaspora and Empire in the British World, 1850–1940* (Manchester: Manchester University Press, 2016); Patrick Coleman, '"In harmony": A comparative view of female Orangeism 1887–2000', in Angela McCarthy (ed.), *Ireland in the World: Comparative, Transnational, and Personal Perspectives* (London and New York: Routledge, 2015), pp. 110–36.
5. Eric Kaufmann, 'The Orange Order in Scotland since 1860: A social analysis', in Martin J. Mitchell (ed.), *New Perspectives on the Irish in Scotland* (Edinburgh: John Donald, 2008), pp. 176–8.
6. Donald M. MacRaild, *Faith, Fraternity and Fighting: The Orange Order and Irish Migrants in England, c. 1850–1920* (Liverpool: Liverpool University Press, 2005), pp. 139–41.
7. Brian Clarke, 'Religious riot as pastime: Orange Young Britons, parades and public life in Victorian Toronto', in David A. Wilson (ed.), *The Orange Order in Canada* (Dublin: Four Courts Press, 2007), pp. 109–27.
8. J. R. Fielding, *Loyal Orange Youth Association of Victoria: 1916–1976 Diamond Jubilee* (Melbourne: The Austral Printing, 1976).
9. Lilian Lewis Shiman, 'The Band of Hope movement: Respectable recreation for working-class children', *Victorian Studies*, 17:1 (1973), pp. 49–74; Annemarie McAllister, 'Onward: How a regional temperance magazine for children survived and flourished in the Victorian marketplace', *Victorian Periodicals Review*, 48:1 (2015), pp. 42–66.

10. McAllister, 'Onward', p. 44.

11. *Belfast News Letter*, 30 November 1874. Lisburn Juveniles No. 1 and Dunmurry Juvenile Little Blues held a soiree in Dunmurry.

12. Ibid., 22 November 1884. Kane was a Church of Ireland rector at Christ Church in Belfast.

13. Grand Orange Lodge of Scotland, *The Future Is Orange and Bright* (Glasgow: GOLS, n.d.), p. 38.

14. Adrian R. Bailey, David C. Harvey and Catherine Brace, 'Disciplining youthful Methodist bodies in nineteenth-century Cornwall', *Annals of the Association of American Geographers*, 97:1 (2007), p. 150.

15. William J. Smyth, *Toronto, the Belfast of Canada: The Orange Order and the Shaping of Municipal Culture* (Toronto: University of Toronto Press, 2015), p. 99.

16. Loyal Orange Association of British America, *Report of the Proceedings of the Twenty-Sixth Grand Annual Session of the Right Worshipful the Grand Lodge of the Loyal Orange Institution of British America: Held in the Court-House, Brockville, U.C., 17th to 25th June 1856* (Toronto: Printed for the Grand Lodge, by James Beaty, 1856), p. 31.

17. Loyal Orange Association of British America, *Report of the Proceedings of the Eighty-Sixth Meeting of the Most Worshipful Grand Orange Lodge of British America: Held in the City of Winnipeg, Manitoba, July 29th, 30th, and 31st 1915* (Toronto: Grand Lodge, 1915), p. 69.

18. *Report of the Fourteenth Annual Session of the Grand Orange Lodge of the United States of America Held in a P. Hall, Pittsburgh PA. June 12th, 13th, 1883* (Philadelphia: Protestant Standard Print, 1883), pp. 13, 19.

19. *Orange and Purple Courier*, November–December 1923.

20. William D. Moore, *Masonic Temples: Freemasonry, Ritual Architecture, and Masculine Archetypes* (Knoxville: University of Tennessee Press, 2006), p. 64.

21. *Minutes of Instituting Ceremonies and Journal Proceedings of First Biennial Session of Most Worshipful Grand Lodge Orange Young Americans, Pittsburgh, Pennsylvania August 12th and 13th 1936*, p. 10.

22. *Report of the Forty-Seventh Session of the Supreme Grand Orange Lodge Loyal Orange Institution of the United States of America Inc. Held in Rochester, N.Y. August 13, 14, & 15, 1938. And the Forty-Eighth Session Held in Wilmington, Delaware August 16, 17 & 18, 1940* (Pittsburgh: LOI, 1938–40), p. 14.

23. *Watchman*, 30 September 1905. Robilliard was the secretary of his lodge, LOL No. 57, Yarraville, Victoria, Australia. He was also Divisional Superintendent for this district's Independent Order of Rechabites (see *Werribee Shire Banner*, 11 March 1926) and one of the vice-presidents of the Victorian Protestant Defence Association (see *The Age*, 26 September 1908).

24. *Watchman*, 30 September 1905.

25. Ibid., 1 July 1909.

26. Hezekiah Evers (1845–1907). He was active in the Grand Lodge, and was Deputy Grand Master for three years. He was also a total abstainer, and in 1867 helped to form Dayspring Division, No. 1, Sons and Daughters of Temperance. He was active in this organisation as well, reaching the highest office of Most Worthy Patriarch. See *Watchman*, 29 August 1907.

27. *Watchman*, 8 July 1909. No. 17 LOL was the initiator of the ladies' lodges in New South Wales.

28. Ibid., 1 August 1912.

29. Fielding, *Loyal Orange Youth Association of Victoria*, pp. 10–16.

30. *Mercury*, 15 July 1924.

31. Ibid., 16 April 1925.

32. *Examiner*, 13 July 1925; 7 April 1926.

33. *Mercury*, 13 July 1921.

34. Loyal Orange Institution of New Zealand, *Report of Proceedings of the Grand Lodge of the Middle Island of New Zealand. Held on 27th and 28th December 1889* (Christchurch: James Caygill, Printer and Binder, 1889), p. 13. The rules are as appendices, pp. 28–32.

35. *Press*, 11 May 1893.

36. *JLOL Massey Boys' Lodge No. 1. 25th Anniversary and Installation of Officers. Orange Hall, Newton. 18th September 1954.*

37. *Manawatu Standard*, 24 April 1907; Grand Orange Lodge of New Zealand, North Island, *Forty-Second Annual Report 1908* (Wellington: W. J. Lankshear, 1908), p. 9.

38. *Report of the Seventh Grand Lodge of New Zealand. Held in the Oddfellows' Hall, Hastings 11, 13 and 14 April, 1914* (Christchurch: Frasers Ltd, Printers, 1914), 7.

39. This is evident in the experience across the Orange diaspora.

40. Ibid. p. 7. Hunter's father and mother were from Stirlingshire and Fife in Scotland.

41. D. A. J. MacPherson, 'Migration and the female Orange Order: Irish Protestant identity, diaspora and empire in Scotland, 1909–40', *The Journal of Imperial and Commonwealth History*, 40:4 (2012), p. 629.

42. *Report of Proceedings of the Grand Orange Lodge of Scotland at the Half-Yearly Meetings. Held in The Orange Hall, Glasgow, 8th December 1917 and The Chalmers Hall, Glasgow, 8th June 1918* (Glasgow: George Watt, 1918), p. 6.

43. Civil birth records give her birth name as Jane.

44. Rev. Ian Meredith, *A Short History of the Orange Order in Ghana* (Glasgow, c. 1990s), p. 3.

45. Grand Orange Lodge of Ireland, *Report of the Proceedings of the Grand Orange Lodge of Ireland at the General Half-Yearly Meetings, 1918 and 1925* (Belfast: GOLI, 1925).

46. *Association of Loyal Orangewomen of Ireland: 100th Anniversary 1912–2012* (Craigavon, County Armagh: Inhouse Publications, 2012), p. 12.

47. Billy Kennedy, *A Celebration: 1690–1990 The Orange Institution* (Belfast: GOLI, 1990), pp. 17–19.

48. Christi McCallum, 'Orangewomen show their colors: Gender, family, and Orangeism in Ulster, 1795–present' (PhD, Southern Illinois University Carbondale, 2011), pp. 209–10.

49. *Report of Proceedings of the Grand Orange Lodge of Scotland at the Half-Yearly Meetings. Held in The Chalmers Halls, Glasgow, 9th December 1911 and 8th June 1912* (Glasgow: George Watt, 1912), pp. 16–18.

50. *Report of Proceedings of the Grand Orange Lodge of Scotland at the Half-Yearly Meetings. Held in The Orange Hall, Glasgow, 9th December 1916 and 9th June 1917* (Glasgow: George Watt, 1917), p. 59.

51. Ibid. pp. 14–15.

52. *Report of Proceedings of the Grand Orange Lodge of Scotland at the Half-Yearly Meetings. Held in The Orange Hall, Glasgow, 13th December 1919 and 12th June 1920* (Glasgow: George Watt, 1920), p. 56.

53. *Report of Proceedings of the Grand Orange Lodge of Scotland at the Half-Yearly Meetings. Held in The Orange Hall, Glasgow, 9th December 1944 and The Orange Hall, Glasgow, 9th June 1945* (Glasgow: George Watt, 1945), p. 45.

54. David Bryce, email to author, 9 September 2016.

55. Grand Orange Lodge of Scotland Reports, 1904–2015.

56. Grand Orange Lodge of England Reports, 1887–2013.

57. Clarke, 'Religious riot as pastime', pp. 123–6.

58. Cecil J. Houston and William J. Smyth, *The Sash Canada Wore: A Historical Geography of the Orange Order in Canada* (Toronto: University of Toronto Press, 1980), p. 90.

59. *Constitution and Laws of the Loyal Orange Young Briton Association. As approved by the Most Worshipful Grand Orange Lodge of British America 1961* (Toronto: Britannia Printers, 1961), p. 33.

60. Loyal Orange Association of British America, *Report of the Proceedings of the Ninety-Eighth Meeting of the Grand Orange Lodge of British America: Held in the City of Edmonton, Alberta, July 25th, 26th 1928* (Toronto: Grand Lodge, 1928), p. 22.

61. Loyal Orange Association of British America, *Report of Proceedings of the One Hundred and Thirtieth Meeting of the Grand Orange Lodge of British America. Held at Toronto, Ontario, 13th and 14th July, 1960* (Toronto: Grand Lodge, 1960), p. 32.

62. Loyal Orange Association of British America, *Report of the Proceedings of the One Hundred and Third Meeting of the Grand Orange Lodge of British America: Held at Regina, Saskatchewan, July 21st and 22nd 1933* (Toronto: Grand Lodge, 1933), pp. 44–5.

63. MacPherson, *Women and the Orange Order*, p. 178.

64. Ibid. p. 153.

65. *Minutes of Instituting Ceremonies*, pp. 17–18.

66. Ibid. p. 16.

67. *Report of the Forty-Seventh Session of the Supreme Grand Orange Lodge*, p. 14.

68. *Sunday Mail*, 31 March 1929.

69. *Advocate*, 16 April 1927.

70. A. S. Russell, *Loyal Orange Institution of Queensland History 1865 to 1932* (Brisbane: Loyal Orange Institution of Queensland, 1933).

71. Grand Orange Lodge of New Zealand Reports, 1930–60.

72. *Report of the Thirty-Eighth Meeting of the Imperial Orange Council, 1867–1994. Held at Auckland, New Zealand, 26th, 27th, 29th & 30th September, 1994* (Auckland: LOI, 1994), p. 37.

73. *Report of the Twenty-Fifth Meeting of the Imperial Grand Orange Council of the World held at Liverpool, England, 14th–15th July, 1955* (Belfast: Northern Whig Ltd, 1955), pp. 24–5.

74. *Nation*, 10 August 1935.

75. Imperial Grand Council of the World, *Report of the Forty-Second Meeting of the Imperial Orange Council 1867–2006. Held at the Marriott Airport Hotel, Toronto, Canada, 17th–22nd July 2006* (Toronto: LOI, 2006), p. 39.

76. Loyal Orange Institution of England, *Rules and Ceremonies of the Junior Branch* (Liverpool: Rudham & Rowley, 1977).

77. Loyal Orange Institution of New Zealand, Grand Orange Lodge, *Constitution and Rules of the Juvenile Lodges* (Wellington: Wright & Carman Ltd, 1943), pp. 2–4.

78. Loyal Orange Association of British America, *Constitution and Laws of the Loyal Orange Association of British America: with rules of the Royal Scarlet Order, Juvenile Orange Association and Grand Lodge Benefit Fund* (Toronto: McCallum Press, 1947), pp. 120–1.

79. McCallum, 'Orangewomen show their colors', pp. 208–9.

80. *Report of Proceedings of the Thirty-Ninth Session of the Loyal Orange Institution of New Zealand (Inc.) and 24th Ladies' Conference. Held in Christchurch April 7th, 8th and 10th 1950* (Dunedin: Robertson McBeath Print, 1950), p. 40; Charles Ferrel, *Notes on the Early History of Wellington District Junior Lodges*, 10 September 1956.

81. *Orange Young Americans no. 3 Star of the East, Meeting minutes, 1949–53*, Collection D0462, M98-14, box 4 (Historical Society of Pennsylvania, Philadelphia, USA).

82. British-American Order of Good Templars, and James A. Barchard, *Juvenile Ritual: Containing the Opening, Initiation, Installation, Funeral and Closing Ceremonies, Together with the Constitution, By-Laws, and Rules of Order; with General Directions for the Organization of*

Juvenile Lodges of the British American Order of Good Templars, of the Dominion of Canada (Stratford, Ontario: J. A. Barchard, 1870); Independent Order of Rechabites, *Rules Governing Juvenile Section Independent Order of Rechabites: New Zealand Central District, No. 86 (Salford Unity) Friendly Society* (Wanganui, NZ: Hanton & Andersen, 1934); Independent Order of Rechabites Friendly Society, *Juvenile Tent Ritual* (Adelaide: South Australian District, 1932).

83. In the Rechabites this is called a 'tent', while in the Templars they are called 'temples'.

84. Loyal Orange Institution of England, *Rules and Ceremonies of the Junior Branch* (Liverpool: Rudham & Rowley, 1977); Loyal Orange Institution of England, *Rules and Ceremonies of the Junior Branch* (Liverpool: GOLE, 1995); Loyal Orange Institution of Scotland, *Juvenile Lodge Ritual. Adopted by Grand Lodge, 1905* (Glasgow: LOIS, revised 1957); Loyal Orange Institution of New Zealand, *Ritual for the Use of Juvenile Orange Lodges* (Dunedin: Crown Print Ltd, 1941).

85. Loyal Orange Association of British America, *Report of the Proceedings of the Ninety-Eighth Meeting of the Grand Orange Lodge of British America*, p. 22.

86. Grand Orange Lodge of Scotland, *The Future Is Orange and Bright*, p. 39.

87. The issues of the *Orange Standard* and *Orange Torch* report on these yearly competitions.

88. *Orange Torch*, July/August 2015, p. 8.

89. Ibid., April 2010, p. 6.

90. Ibid., June 2015, p. 7.

91. There are usually pictures and articles in the *Orange Standard*.

92. *The Sentinel*, 137:1 (Spring 2001), p. 16.

93. *The Sentinel*, 137:2 (Spring 2001), pp. 15–20.

94. *Orange Torch*, May 2006, p. 10.

95. Imperial Grand Council of the World, *Report of the Forty-Second Meeting of the Imperial Orange Council*, p. 51.

96. *Orange Torch*, February 2014, p. 7.

97. Ibid., May 2016, p. 7.

98. Ibid., February 2016, p. 11.

99. *Orange Standard*, April 2011.

100. Peter Day, 'Pride before a fall? Orangeism in Liverpool since 1945', in M. Busteed, F. Neal and J. Tonge (eds), *Irish Protestant Identities* (Manchester and New York: Manchester University Press, 2008), pp. 277–81.

101. Imperial Grand Council of the World, *Forty-Fifth Meeting of the Imperial Orange Council 1867–2015. Held at the Crowne Plaza Hotel, Liverpool, England, 6th–10th July, 2015* (Liverpool: LOI, 2015), pp. 23–57.

102. Loyal Orange Institution, *Grand Orange Lodge of New Zealand Circular To All Lodges 3rd March 1957*.

103. Beverley Buist, interview by Patrick Coleman, 11 January 2005.

104. Loyal Orange Institution of New Zealand, *Report of Proceedings of the Forty-Sixth Session of the Grand Orange Lodge of New Zealand and the 31st Session of Ladies' Conference. Held at Timaru, 27th to 30th March 1964* (Masterton: Printcraft Ltd, 1964), p. 13. Robinson reiterated his views many years later. John Robinson, interview by Patrick Coleman, 29 May 2005, transcript, OHA-5205. Patrick Coleman, *Oral History of the Loyal Orange Institution in the South Island 2004–2005.* OHColl-0791, Alexander Turnbull Library, Wellington, New Zealand.

105. *Report of the Thirty-Ninth Meeting of the Imperial Orange Council, 1867–1997. Held at the Stormont Hotel, Belfast, Northern Ireland, 15th, 16th, & 18th July 1997* (Belfast: LOI, 1997), p. 38.

106. *Report of the Thirty-Eighth Meeting of the Imperial Orange Council,* p. 45.

107. Loyal Orange Institution of New Zealand, *Report Book for the Year Ended 31st January 1955* (Wellington: LOI, 1955), p. 11.

108. Grand Orange Lodge, *Constitution and Rules of the Junior Lodges* (Wellington: LOI, 1971), pp. 10–12.

109. Loyal Orange Institution of New Zealand, *Report of Proceedings. Tenth Junior Lodges Conference held in Auckland 2nd–4th June 1973* (Wellington: LOI, 1973), p. 7.

110. Fielding, *Loyal Orange Youth Association of Victoria,* p. 36.

111. Grand Orange Lodge, *Report of Proceedings of the Fifty Third Session of the Loyal Orange Institution of New Zealand and 38th Session of Ladies' Conference. Held in Christchurch March 24th, 25th and 27th 1978* (Christchurch: LOI, 1978), p. 27.

112. Loyal Orange Institution of New Zealand, *Grand Orange Lodge. Report of Proceedings of the Fifty Fourth Session and 39th Session of Ladies' Conference of the Grand Orange Lodge of New Zealand, Wellington, April 4, 5 and 7, 1980* (Wellington: LOI, 1980), p. 33.

113. Loyal Orange Institution of New Zealand, *Report of Proceedings of the Fifteenth Conference of New Zealand Junior Lodges held in the Salvation Army Youth Complex, Constable Street, Wellington on 25th, 26th, 27th August 1984* (Wellington: LOI, 1984), p. 5.

114. Loyal Orange Institution of New Zealand, *Report of Proceedings Auckland Easter 1990 Grand Lodge 59th Sessions 44th Ladies* (Christchurch: G.B. Data Systems, 1990), p. 10.

115. Loyal Orange Institution of NSW, *Sesqui-Centenary of the Grand Orange Lodge of New South Wales. Supplement to Souvenir Book 1995* (Chipping Norton, NSW: Gowans & Son Pty, Ltd, 1995), p. 11.

116. *Report of Proceedings of the Forty-Ninth Session of the Grand Orange Lodge of New Zealand and the 34th Session of Ladies' Conference. Held in Invercargill, 27th to 30th March, 1970* (Wellington: Digest Print Ltd, 1970), p. 14.

117. *JLOL No. 2 Bluebird/Derry, Minutes 3 December 1988–4 May 2001* (Orange Hall, Christchurch, New Zealand), 4 May 2001.
118. *Belfast News Letter*, 14 February 2008.
119. *Imperial Orange Council 1867–1991. Held at the Golden Lion Hotel, Stirling, Scotland, 23rd, 24th, 26th and 27th September 1991* (Stirling: LOI, 1991), p. 30.
120. *Orange Standard*, April 2008.
121. *Orange Standard*, May 2008.
122. *Belfast Telegraph*, 19 July 2008.
123. *Orange Torch*, February 2008, p. 3.
124. For a recent discussion about the state of the history of children and childhood see Bengt Sandin, 'History of children and childhood – Being and becoming, dependent and independent', *The American Historical Review*, 125:4 (2020), pp. 1,306–16.

Conclusion:
Reflections on Key Findings

A central claim of this book is that the Orange Order across the world, despite its adaptations in new countries, has failed to shake off its negative public image. Why is this so? Part of the reason has been the media coverage of events in Northern Ireland around contentious parades and the constant references to past riots. Much of the literature on the Orange Order in the Orange diaspora has helped to fuel this distrust of the Order. Certainly, the focus on the political involvement of the Orange Order across these countries has contributed to its overall reputation as bigoted and violent. This book necessitated a shift in focus beyond the Orange Order's involvement in politics and riots to other research areas. Using a comparative and transnational framework enabled the highlighting of similarities and differences within Orangeism across a range of countries and revealed the transnational networks operating across space and time.

Many scholars of the Orange Order have slowly shifted the focus from Ireland and Northern Ireland to the diaspora. The Orange Order in Canada has continued to provide much of the focus for researchers, with scattered studies in other parts of the world. This book is an attempt to bring together these fragments and create a cohesive, holistic view of the global Orange Order while at the same time identifying gaps in need of further study.

One area that has stood out in the research is the gendered image of the Orange Order. It has long been portrayed as a male-dominated organisation, and this image persists despite more recent efforts to show the work and influence of Orangewomen.[1] The original framing of Orangewomen was largely as 'tea makers' and support for the men, who were the central focus of the Orange Order. Although there have been more recent studies to interrogate such assumptions, these end up focusing solely on Orangewomen. This book, in contrast, has integrated the role of Orangewomen throughout the chapters in an attempt to shift the narrative. Treating Orangewomen as equal in the overall history and practices of the Orange Order normalises their contribution rather than seeing them as aberrations or bit players.

This book has documented the spread of the Orange Order from Ireland to the British world in a way not previously done. It has found that the predominantly Irish soldiers in the British army were the impetus for this early spread. These soldiers were supported transnationally by Grand Lodges in England and Ireland. However, the sustainability of these lodges depended on the influx of new migrants. Again, there was an Irish element to this migration and initial set-up of Orange lodges across the world. The real exceptions have been in the small outposts of Orangeism in Ghana and Togo. While these countries had small groupings of lodges, they have been and still are dependent on transnational networks to support their ongoing work. Orangewomen were also vital in the spread of Orangeism. Their contribution to the Orange Order, besides increasing membership, was their involvement in benevolent activities. This form of activism showed a different side to the organisation, quite different from the harsher, more negative public image. The growth and decline in all Orange jurisdictions has not been uniform, occurring earlier or later in different areas, but all areas have shown a significant decline from the 1960s until the present day.

One of the overarching questions of this book has been how the Orange Order, given its localised origins, managed to spread across the British world and maintain its ongoing existence. Part of the answer lay in its structure and rituals. The Masonic-inspired structure enabled the Orange Order to move rapidly beyond the shores of Ireland. This tight structure was easily implemented and portable as members migrated or were deployed on military duty. However, a structure in itself is never enough. This book argues that the inner workings of the lodges or rituals bound members in thinking and practice. Again, while Masonic lodges inspired these rituals, they were not purely a Masonic invention. For the Orange Order the focus on the ritual was wholly biblically inspired and gendered. The men's rituals were there to create a brotherhood of believers bound by a Protestant faith and loyalist defenders against the 'encroachment' of the Roman Catholic Church. The Orangewomen's rituals emphasised a sisterhood through the emphasis on the biblical story of Naomi. The practice of these rituals helped to bind together members across countries as they shared their experiences in a transnational fashion. However, the Masonic origins of these rituals have dogged the Orange Order, as some evangelical churches from which members of the Orange Order are drawn have labelled these practices as satanic. This negative image has prevented potential members from joining, and in some cases members left because of this link. The rituals detracted from the core message of being Protestant; the strength of the Orange Order was when they were truly pan-Protestant. This embraced the diversity of Protestant members, who ranged from Anglican to Baptist and everything in between.

Armed with a solid organisational structure and bound by a brotherhood and sisterhood of believers, the Orange Order wanted to spread their message. They did this in several ways. Much of the political involvement by the Orange Order in the nineteenth and early twentieth centuries had an anti-Catholic element. The Orange Order also connected with Protestant associations in England, Australia and the United States to try and get 'suitable' candidates voted into various political positions. These efforts met with mixed success. While the names of these organisations were quite generic, many of the members were Orangemen. Some of the other activism by the Orange Order was more about the medium they used to propagate their message. The old-fashioned public meetings did draw crowds and in a pre-digital age were an effective means to generate publicity for their message. The flip side was that sometimes this led to sectarian clashes that only exacerbated the problem of the public perception of the Orange Order. This is an area of research that has not been fully explored, and there is plenty of scope for future researchers to build on the current work.

The benevolence of the Orange Order may not seem at first to be activism at all. However, this book has argued that the creation of orphanages and children's homes has been a successful area of outreach, particularly for Orangewomen. Jim MacPherson has been at the forefront of revealing this type of activity by Orangewomen. This book has expanded the focus from just a few countries to many of the countries where Orangewomen have lodges. Again, the importance of this is in how often Irish Protestant women and then local women from the Orange diaspora have created a new focus for the Orange Order. However, despite all of these endeavours, many members feel aggrieved that their efforts are ignored, and the dominant narrative of bigoted, violent Orangemen has prevailed.

This book argues that the belief system of the Orange Order was engendered in the lodges and the rituals, while the parades were the public displays of these beliefs. There have certainly been a number of studies on Orange parades that focus on Ireland, riots or both. The broader scope of this book has enabled a macro view of the parades. Two aspects stand out. First is the proliferation of legislation across the Orange world concerning parades. This impact on wider society has meant that the experience of the Orange Order shaped public parades for some countries. The legislation enacted, while having the Orange Order in mind, also affected other fraternal organisations. An example noted was the banning of parades in Australian cities like Melbourne. This meant that a parading tradition was not able to take form in the same way as in Toronto, Canada, which has had an unbroken tradition of parading. The visible presence of parades has kept the Orange Order in the public sphere, whereas for countries in the southern hemisphere, without parades, their presence is often forgotten. This book further argues that while the parades have continued in Northern Ireland and Scotland, they have done so at a cost to the present-day public image of the Orange Order. Drunkenness and sectarian clashes are still features that are highlighted in the media. While the Grand Lodges in present-day Ireland and Scotland have sought to improve their image, the negative perceptions persist. This has occurred despite evidence to the contrary. Membership of the Orange Order across the world has drastically declined, and many among the Orange diaspora no longer parade or do so with reduced numbers. The parades have led to an increased interest in band membership, especially in Northern Ireland and Scotland. However, while these new recruits are keen to express their Protestant heritage, this has not necessarily translated into increased membership of the Orange Order.

The material culture of the Orange Order woefully lacks research, particularly outside of Ireland. This book has tried to shift the focus on banners in Northern Ireland to include other material objects in order to understand and explain many of the ritualistic aspects of the Orange Order. Taking a global view, this book has argued that the material culture emanating from Ireland has generally been kept, with some exceptions and adaptations. The Orange Order is an organisation full of symbolism and rituals, and therefore the material objects they use are also a part of their identity. The famous Orange song 'The Sash My Father Wore' or, more commonly, just 'The Sash' embodies an emotional attachment to a material object. The song even gives a description:

It is old but it is beautiful, and its colours they are fine
It was worn at Derry, Aughrim, Enniskillen and the Boyne.
My father wore it as a youth in bygone days of yore,
And on the Twelfth, I love to wear the sash my father wore.[2]

This song has been used in research with a focus on its music and meaning. At the heart of the song is the 'sash'. This material object is a symbol of the Orangeman and all that he embodies. This book has demonstrated that material objects like sashes, badges and banners all represent vital aspects of Orange belief. This is rooted in the civil and religious liberty of King William III and the upholding of Protestantism.

This book concluded with the most neglected area of research on the Orange Order – the junior Orange movement. They provide a microcosm of the issues that are at the heart of the Orange Order. The juniors are, this book argues, a symbol of Orange vitality but also a lost opportunity. Like the Orangewomen and the advent of ladies' lodges, the juniors were late in starting their own organisation. However, they were there from the start, just like the Orangewomen. The juniors were part of the Orange family not just when they formed lodges but also as the children of members. The children still heard the stories and watched from the sidelines as they saw their fathers, brothers and older male friends march. This family inclusiveness differed in Ireland and the Orange diaspora. The marching of youngsters occurred early for the English and Scottish Orange Orders, while the American Orange Order was very late in including children.

Although the junior Orange movement was created for young people, adults heavily influenced its success and failure. The origins of the various lodges came from enthusiastic individuals, whereas the lack of enthusiasm killed off the juniors in many countries. This focus on the juniors is significant as it showed how a children's organisation, formed from its parent body, also had to adapt and change according to its environment. For instance, changes to the rituals to make them relevant had to happen, as the older ways were relics of a bygone era that were of no interest to the young. The transnational exchanges replicated those among adult members, with exchanges between Australia and New Zealand and England, Ireland and Scotland. There is further opportunity to explore the rise and decline of the junior Orange movement in more micro studies in Ireland and across the Orange diaspora.

The source material used to complete this book has by nature and necessity been wide-ranging and at times disparate. A study of any organisation should try to make sufficient use of the source material created by it. In the case of the Orange Order, this has proved to be problematic. The survival of some records has been more by luck than design. While there was a lot of record keeping and other materials printed, over the centuries so much has been lost. Fire, water and deliberate destruction of materials have been common themes. The historian by nature has to be resourceful and pragmatic in their choice and use of source materials.

This book has had to make decisions based on the availability of, access to and usefulness of source materials. The use of minute books and various annual proceedings has provided some of the insights into the day-to-day activities of the Orange Order across the world. Like all sources, they have limitations, particularly concerning what is not recorded. For example, a local Orange lodge or even Grand Lodge may vote on an issue. The issue and possibly the voting is recorded but not always the reason for this. To overcome this problem, insider knowledge from Orange members and newspapers was used to fill these gaps.

Newspapers are a common source for the historian. This book has made good use of these as they document events and sometimes speeches where no other records exist. Again, this is still an imperfect source, but sometimes this is all that is available. Despite some criticism of newspapers for not being accurate, a comparison of some Orange Order annual sessions with newspaper accounts of the same meetings shows reasonable likenesses. This is because many organisations supply the newspapers with information. The only addition might be a comment, but nineteenth-century newspapers tended to write verbatim the speeches at these events. This multiplicity of source material has been used to piece together the life of the Orange Order.

Overall, the potential for future researchers lies in increasing access to source materials. This recent development allows for tightly focused studies building on materials that previously were not readily available to the researcher. Indeed, it reflects an openness in an organisation that this book has identified as suffering from an image problem. So many loyalist and fraternal organisations have faded away, but the Orange Order has managed to outlive these organisations with similar ideals. Though not as numerically strong as they once were, the Orange Order has managed to survive in the modern age.

NOTES

1. See the work by D. A. J. MacPherson, who uses a comparative and transnational framework.
2. *Orange Standard* (Glasgow: Mozart Allen, 1936), pp. 6–7.

Appendix 1: Origins of Men's Lodges by Country

Ireland
1795 first lodge
England
1799 first military lodge
Scotland
1799 first military lodge
Canada
1799 first military lodge
United States of America
c. 1820s first documented lodges
New Zealand
1843 first lodge
Australia
1830 New South Wales – first military lodge 1832 Tasmania – first military lodge 1843 Victoria – first lodge c. 1849 South Australia – first lodge 1865 Queensland – first lodge 1886 Western Australia – first lodge
Ghana
1918 first lodge

Togo

1915 first lodge

South Africa

1821 first military lodge
1852 first formal lodge

Appendix 2: Origins of Women's Lodges by Country

Ireland

1801 Dublin – ladies' lodges
1887 Woman's Orange Association formed
1912 Revived Association of Loyal Orangewomen of Ireland

England

c. 1850 Lancashire – Female Protestant Association of Loyal Orangewomen attached to GPALO

Scotland

1872 ladies' lodges formed
1909 revived ladies' lodges

United States of America

1876 Philadelphia – Loyal Orange Ladies' Institution

Canada

1878 Montreal – Princess Louise Female Orange Lodge No. 1
1888 Hamilton, Ontario – Ladies' Protestant Association, name changed 1891
1894 Ladies' Orange Benevolent Association

New Zealand

1888 Wellington

Australia

1890 Queensland
1894 New South Wales
1901 Tasmania
1902 South Australia
1903 Victoria
1903 Western Australia

Ghana
1959 Keta – Ladies' Lodge Wycliffe No. 160

Togo
c. 1963 Lomé – Ladies' Lodge Morning Star No. 161

Appendix 3: Origins of the Junior Orange Movement by Country

Ireland

1870s boys' lodge
1918 formalised
1927 Junior Orangewomen's Association
1975 Junior Grand Orange Lodge of Ireland

Scotland

1875 boys-only juvenile lodges
1917 girls allowed to join existing juvenile lodges
1944 13–16 (juniors)

England

1887 mixed

United States of America

1923 Orange Young Americans – defunct
1933 Orange Young Americans revived
c. 1938 Junior Orange Order (included Loyal Orange Girls' Lodges)

Canada

1853 Orange Cadets
1869 Orange Young Britons
1884 restructured Orange Young Britons
1915 juniors – boys/girls/mixed

New Zealand

1907–14 – boys
1929 revived – boys
1929 – girls

Australia

1909 New South Wales – mixed
1911 Queensland – mixed
1916 Victoria – mixed
1921 South Australia – mixed
1925 Tasmania – mixed

Ghana

1959 Hope of Ghana JLOL No. 1

Appendix 4: Note on Sources

The Orange Order has been in existence for over 200 years and has generated a range of materials. In theory, this should mean that researchers have a wealth of source material to work with. However, access to materials has been problematic for a number of reasons, primarily because many materials were or are held either at Orange halls or by the secretary of local lodges or the Grand Secretary of Grand Lodges, and access is not always provided. In recent years the solution has been the creation of Orange archives or the depositing of Orange material in public archives.

The Grand Orange Lodge of Ireland (GOLI) has its headquarters at Schomberg House in Belfast. With European Union funding, they created the Museum of Orange Heritage in 2015. This includes two centres: one onsite and the other at Sloan's House in Loughgall, County Armagh.[1] On the Belfast site, they have a small library with archival materials. However, a lot of materials are still held by individual lodges. In Scotland, the Grand Orange Lodge of Scotland (GOLS) had archives at their headquarters of Olympia House, Glasgow. Olympia House was sold in December 2020.[2]

In Canada, the Orange Order has its own archive in Toronto but there is still plenty of material stored in libraries and museums scattered across the country. England also has the challenge of scattered resources in various libraries. Their Grand Lodge historian, who kindly assisted me in my research, had a large collection of materials. Following his death in 2019, these were deposited in the Richard Cameron Library at Olympia House, Glasgow, in the appropriately titled Michael Phelan Memorial Collection.[3]

In other parts of the world, a lot of Orange material has been destroyed by fire, such as in Victoria, Australia. David Fitzpatrick's excellent article on the Orange Order in South Australia used material that had been found at a recycling centre. This material is now in the state library.[4] This situation is also true of the Orange Order in New South Wales, with some recent deposits of materials in the Mitchell Library, State Library of New South Wales. Prior to this it was challenging for researchers to get access, as this was dependent on local members being available, which created time constraints. The source material in New Zealand has had a mixture of damage from leaking roofs, fire and deliberate destruction by a former Grand Secretary.[5] Further material was rescued and organised by the late Robert (Bob) Fenton, former Grand Master and Grand Secretary, when I was writing a Masters thesis many years ago. This is now stored by the local Christchurch Orange lodges. In Auckland, the Orange Order has a large collection in storage. Other Orange materials have found their way to local libraries, state libraries, university libraries and private archives across the world.

NOTES

1. Grand Orange Lodge of Ireland, 'Museum of Orange Heritage', <https://www.orangeheritage.co.uk/> (accessed 4 July 2023). Sloan's House is a joint project between the GOLI and the County Armagh Grand Orange Lodge.
2. *The Scotsman*, 23 May 2022.
3. *Orange Torch*, May 2019, p. 2.
4. David Fitzpatrick, 'Exporting brotherhood: Orangeism in South Australia', *Immigrants & Minorities*, 23:2–3 (2005), p. 299, n. 7.
5. Information supplied to the author by current Orange Order members in New Zealand.

Bibliography

PRIMARY SOURCES

Government Legislation/Publications

10 Vict. No. 1, An Act to prevent for a limited time Party Processions and certain other public Exhibitions in the Colony of New South Wales.

14 Vict. No. 49, 19 Vict. No. 1, 22 Vict. No. 68.

An Act to restrain Party Procession in certain cases 1843 (7 Vict c. VI).

Attwood, Sarah-Anne, *Orangefest 2017 Business Feedback & Event Report* (Belfast: Belfast City Centre Management, 2017).

Baber, Mary, *Public Processions in Northern Ireland, House of Commons Research Paper 98/11* (London: House of Commons, 1998).

Hansard HC Deb, 4 March 1897, vol. 46, cc 1580–1.

Heritage Council of Western Australia, *Register of Heritage Places-Assessment Documentation Protestant Hall* (Perth: Heritage Council of Western Australia, 2005).

Hong Kong Blue Book for the Year 1911 (Hong Kong: Norontha & Co., 1912).

Hong Kong Government Gazette, 28 April 1913.

Hong Kong Government Gazette, 7 June 1912.

Justice 2 Committee Official Report 14 November 2005: Police, Public Order and Criminal Justice (Scotland) Bill: Stage 1, <http://www.par liament.scot/parliamentarybusiness/report.aspx?r=2325> (accessed 1 December 2023).

Minutes of Evidence Taken Before the Select Committee of the House of Lords Appointed to Inquire into the State of Ireland: More Particularly with Reference to the Circumstances which May Have Led to Disturbances in that Part of the United Kingdom (London: House of Commons, 1825).

Orr, John, *Review of Marches and Parades in Scotland: A Report* (Edinburgh: Scottish Executive, 2005).

Parades Commission, *Parading in a Peaceful Northern Ireland: Forward View and Review of Procedures . . ., 2006–2007* (Belfast: Parades Commission, 2006).

Parades Commission Reports, <https://www.paradescommission.org/Publicati ons.aspx> (accessed 1 December 2023).

Party Processions (Ireland) Act 1832 (2 & 3 Will. 4 c. 118).

Party Processions (Ireland) Act 1850 (13 & 14 Vict. c. 2).

Party Processions Act (Ireland) Repeal Act 1872 (35 & 36 Vict. c. 22).

Party Processions Prevention Act 1846 10 Vic No. 1 (Repealed 1899 63 Vic No. 9 s 3 sch 3).

Party Processions Prevention Act Amendment Act 1857 20 Vic No. 6 (Repealed 1899 63 Vic No. 9 s 3 sch 3).

Report from the Select Committee Appointed to Inquire into the Origin, Nature, Extent and Tendency of Orange Institutions in Great Britain and the Colonies; with the Minutes of Evidence, Appendix and Index (London: House of Commons, 1835).

Rosie, Michael, *Independent Report on Marches, Parades and Static Demonstrations in Scotland* (Edinburgh: Scottish Government, 2016).

The Royal Ulster Constabulary, *The Chief Constable's Annual Report 1995* (Belfast: RUC, 1996).

The Unlawful Assemblies and Party Processions Statute 1865.

Unlawful Societies (Ireland) Act 1825 (6 Geo. IV c. 4).

Minute Books

28th Annual Session of State Grand Lodge of Maine No. 7, 9 June 1924, State Grand Lodge of Maine, Annual Session Minutes, 1923–1968, Collection D0462, 1993-103 (Historical Society of Pennsylvania, Philadelphia, USA).

American Protestant Association, *Minute of Proceedings of the Worthy Grand Lodge of the American Protestant Association of the State of Pennsylvania* (Philadelphia: Jared Craig, 1873).

The Everett LOL 108, Toxteth Park Liverpool, Minute Book 30 March 1882–5 July 1898 (Central Liverpool Library).

JLOL No. 2 Bluebird/Derry, Minutes 3 December 1988–4 May 2001 (Orange Hall, Christchurch, New Zealand).

Juvenile LOL No. 1 Paisley, Minutes March 1912–November 1916 (Olympia House, Glasgow, Scotland).

LOL No. 5 District Lodge, Christchurch, Minutes, August 1957–February 1983 (Orange Hall, Christchurch, New Zealand).

LOL No. 16 and LOL No. 17 True Blue, Southbridge, Minute Book, August 1892–February 1916 (Orange Hall, Christchurch, New Zealand).

LOL No. 24 Walkers Purple Heroes, Christchurch, New Zealand, Minute Book, 17 June 1901 (Orange Hall, Christchurch, New Zealand).

Minutes of Instituting Ceremonies and Journal Proceedings of First Biennial Session of Most Worshipful Grand Lodge Orange Young Americans, Pittsburgh, Pennsylvania August 12th and 13th 1936.

Orange Young Americans no. 3 Star of the East, Meeting minutes, 1949–53, Collection D0462, M98-14, box 4 (Historical Society of Pennsylvania, Philadelphia, USA).

Schomberg Loyal Orange Lodge, No. 2, Sydney, N. S. W. Minute Books, 1866–1872, MLMSS 7494 (Mitchell Library, State Library of New South Wales, Sydney, Australia).

Victorious Loyal Orange Lodge, No. 40, Dundas, N. S. W. Minute Books, 1870–1936, MLMSS 2064 (Mitchell Library, State Library of New South Wales, Sydney, Australia).

Annual Proceedings/Reports

Grand Orange Lodge, *Report of Proceedings of the Fifty Third Session of the Loyal Orange Institution of New Zealand and 38th Session of Ladies' Conference. Held in Christchurch March 24th, 25th and 27th 1978* (Christchurch: LOI, 1978).

Grand Orange Lodge of England, *Grand Lodge Sessions Portsmouth 12–13 September 1997* (Portsmouth: GOLE, 1997).

Grand Orange Lodge of Ireland, *Report of the Proceedings of the Grand Orange Lodge of Ireland at the General Half-Yearly Meetings, 1918 and 1925* (Belfast: GOLI, 1925).

Grand Orange Lodge of Ireland, *Report of the Proceedings of the Grand Orange Lodge of Ireland at the General Half-Yearly Meetings, Held in the Orange Hall, Lisburn, 1890* (Dublin: James Forrest, 1890).

Grand Orange Lodge of New Zealand, *Report of Proceedings for the Year Ending January 1884, Auckland, New Zealand* (Auckland: John Brame at the Free Press Office, 1884).

Grand Orange Lodge of New Zealand, Middle Island, *Report of Proceedings of the Thirty-Ninth Annual Session, 1905* (Christchurch: James Caygill, Printer and Binder, 1905).

Grand Orange Lodge of New Zealand, North Island, *Forty-Second Annual Report 1908* (Wellington: W. J. Lankshear, 1908).

Grand Protestant Association of Loyal Orangemen of England, *Report of the Proceedings of the Association in Extraordinary Grand Lodge assembled, on Tuesday 4th July 1876 at the Guildhall Tavern in the City of London* (Bradford: Squire Auty and Son, 1876).

Imperial Grand Council of the World, *Forty-Fifth Meeting of the Imperial Orange Council 1867–2015. Held at the Crowne Plaza Hotel, Liverpool, England, 6th–10th July, 2015* (Liverpool: LOI, 2015).

Imperial Grand Council of the World, *Report of the Forty-Second Meeting of the Imperial Orange Council 1867–2006. Held at the Marriott Airport Hotel, Toronto, Canada, 17th–22nd July 2006* (Toronto: LOI, 2006).

Imperial Grand Orange Council, *Report of the Triennial Meeting of the Imperial Grand Orange Council. Held at the Westminster Palace Hotel, London, July 19th, and 20th, 1882* (London: LOI, 1882).

Imperial Grand Orange Council of the World, *Thirty Second Triennial Conference. House of Orange, Belfast, Northern Ireland, 15th and 16th July, 1976* (Belfast: LOI, 1976).

Imperial Orange Council 1867–1991. Held at the Golden Lion Hotel, Stirling, Scotland, 23rd, 24th, 26th and 27th September 1991 (Stirling: LOI, 1991).

Loyal Orange Association of British America, *Report of Proceedings of the One Hundred and Thirtieth Meeting of the Grand Orange Lodge of British America. Held at Toronto, Ontario, 13th and 14th July, 1960* (Toronto: Grand Lodge, 1960).

Loyal Orange Association of British America, *Report of the Proceedings of the Eighty-Sixth Meeting of the Most Worshipful Grand Orange Lodge of British America: Held in the City of Winnipeg, Manitoba, July 29th, 30th, and 31st 1915* (Toronto: Grand Lodge, 1915).

Loyal Orange Association of British America, *Report of the Proceedings of the Ninety-Eighth Meeting of the Grand Orange Lodge of British America: Held in the City of Edmonton, Alberta, July 25th, 26th 1928* (Toronto: Grand Lodge, 1928).

Loyal Orange Association of British America, *Report of the Proceedings of the One Hundred and Third Meeting of the Grand Orange Lodge of British America: Held at Regina, Saskatchewan, July 21st and 22nd 1933* (Toronto: Grand Lodge, 1933).

Loyal Orange Association of British America, *Report of the Proceedings of the One Hundred and Twentieth Meeting of the Grand Orange Lodge of British America: Held at St John's, Newfoundland, 22nd and 23rd June 1950* (Toronto: Grand Lodge, 1950).

Loyal Orange Association of British America, *Report of the Proceedings of the Twenty-Sixth Grand Annual Session of the Right Worshipful the Grand Lodge of the Loyal Orange Institution of British America: Held in the Court-House, Brockville, U.C., 17th to 25th June 1856* (Toronto: Printed for the Grand Lodge, by James Beaty, 1856).

Loyal Orange Institution of British South Africa, *Report of the Annual Meeting of the Grand Orange Lodge. Held in the Freemason's Hall, Jeppestown, Johannesburg on Friday, December 16th, 1910* (Johannesburg: The Lodge, 1910).

Loyal Orange Institution of England, *Report of the Annual Meeting of the Grand Orange Lodge, 1907–1910* (Manchester: GOLE, 1907–10).

Loyal Orange Institution of England, *Reports of the Annual Meeting of the Grand Orange Lodge, 1940–48* (GOLE, 1940–48).

Loyal Orange Institution of Great Britain, *Proceedings of the Grand Lodge held at the Green Man Inn, Bacup, 3rd July 1854* (Liverpool: Bro. T. Davies, 1854).

Loyal Orange Institution of New South Wales, *Annual Report 1995* (Sydney: LOINSW, 1995).

Loyal Orange Institution of New South Wales, *Annual Report 1997* (Sydney: LOINSW, 1997).

Loyal Orange Institution of New South Wales, *Grand Lodge Report for the Year 1880* (Sydney: Samuel E. Lees, 1881).

Loyal Orange Institution of New Zealand, *Abridged Report Book for the year ended 31st January 1953 and containing Resume of Grand Executive Meetings, Wellington, 10–11 April 1953* (Napier: Swailes Print, 1953).

Loyal Orange Institution of New Zealand, *Fourth Annual Session of the Grand Orange Lodge of New Zealand. Held in Christchurch, April 15, 17, & 18, 1911* (Dunedin: Wallace's Crown Print, 1911).

Loyal Orange Institution of New Zealand, *Grand Orange Lodge. Report of Proceedings of the Fifty Fourth Session and 39th Session of Ladies' Conference of the Grand Orange Lodge of New Zealand, Wellington, April 4, 5 and 7, 1980* (Wellington: LOI, 1980).

Loyal Orange Institution of New Zealand, *Report Book for the Year Ended 31st January 1955* (Wellington: LOI, 1955).

Loyal Orange Institution of New Zealand, *Report of Proceedings Auckland Easter 1990 Grand Lodge 59th Sessions 44th Ladies* (Christchurch: G.B. Data Systems, 1990).

Loyal Orange Institution of New Zealand, *Report of Proceedings of the Fifteenth Conference of New Zealand Junior Lodges held in the Salvation Army Youth Complex, Constable Street, Wellington on 25th, 26th, 27th August 1984* (Wellington: LOI, 1984).

Loyal Orange Institution of New Zealand, *Report of Proceedings of the Forty-Sixth Session of the Grand Orange Lodge of New Zealand and the 31st Session of Ladies' Conference. Held at Timaru, 27th to 30th March 1964* (Masterton: Printcraft Ltd, 1964).

Loyal Orange Institution of New Zealand, *Report of Proceedings of the Grand Lodge of the Middle Island of New Zealand. Held on 27th and 28th December 1889* (Christchurch: James Caygill, Printer and Binder, 1889).

Loyal Orange Institution of New Zealand, *Report of Proceedings. Tenth Junior Lodges Conference held in Auckland 2nd–4th June 1973* (Wellington: LOI, 1973).

Loyal Orange Institution of New Zealand, *Reports for 1972–1973 Period* (Wellington: LOI, 1973).

Loyal Orange Institution of New Zealand, *Reports for 1975 Period* (Wellington: LOI, 1975).

Loyal Orange Institution of Queensland, *Annual Report and Balance Sheets of the Grand Orange Lodge of Queensland for the year 1886* (Brisbane: Queensland Evangelical Standard, 1887).

Loyal Orange Institution of the United States of America, *Official Directory Recognized and Constitutional Lodges of the Loyal Orange Institution U.S.A.,*

Inc. and the Loyal Orange Ladies' Institution, USA, Inc. (Philadelphia: The Supreme Grand Lodge of the United States, 1911–2014).

Loyal Orange Institution of Victoria, *Annual Report 1994* (Melbourne: LOIV, 1994).

Loyal Orange Institution of Victoria, *Report of the Annual Grand Lodge Meeting, held at the Protestant Hall, Exhibition Street, Melbourne, November 7th, 1890* (Melbourne: C. W. Burford, 1891).

Orange and Protestant Friendly Society, *Executive Committee's Report: to be submitted to Annual Meeting on October 4th, 1912* (Belfast: Thos. Brough & Cox, 1912).

Report of Proceedings of the 19th Annual Session of the Grand Orange Lodge of New Zealand. Also 5th Annual Session of Ladies' Grand Chapter, Invercargill, April 15th, 16th, and 18th, 1927 (Dunedin: Crown Print Ltd, 1927).

Report of Proceedings of the 22nd Annual Session of the Grand Orange Lodge of New Zealand. Also 8th Annual Session of Ladies' Grand Chapter. Held in Wellington, April 18, 19, 21, 1930 (Dunedin: Crown Print, 1930).

Report of Proceedings of the 25th Annual Session of the Grand Orange Lodge of New Zealand. Also 10th Annual Session of Ladies' Grand Chapter. Held in Wellington, March 25, 26, 28, 1932 (Dunedin: Crown Print, 1932).

Report of Proceedings of the 26th Annual Session of the Grand Orange Lodge of New Zealand. Also 11th Annual Session of Ladies' Grand Chapter. Held in Christchurch, April 14, 15, 17, 1933 (Dunedin: Crown Print, 1933).

Report of Proceedings of the 38th Annual Session of the Grand Orange Lodge of New Zealand Incorporated. 23rd Session of Ladies' Conference and Centenary Celebrations 1843–1943. Held in Auckland, March 25, 26, 27, 29, 1948 (Dunedin: Stanton Bros, 1948).

Report of Proceedings of the Annual Meeting of the Grand Orange Lodge of England. Held in the City of Birmingham, 7th and 8th July 1920 (Birmingham: GOLE, 1920).

Report of Proceedings of the Eighth Annual Session of the Grand Orange Lodge of New Zealand. Held in Wellington, April 22, 24 and 26, 1916 (Christchurch: Frasers Limited, 1916).

Report of Proceedings of the Eleventh Annual Session of the Grand Orange Lodge of New Zealand. Held in Ashburton, April 19, 21 and 22, 1919 (Wellington: Wright & Carman, 1919).

Report of Proceedings of the Fifteenth Annual Session of the Grand Orange Lodge of New Zealand. Held in Dunedin, March 31, April 2 and 3, 1923 (Palmerston North: Watson & Eyre, 1923).

Report of Proceedings of the Fifty Fifth Session and 40th Session of Ladies' Conference of the Grand Orange Lodge of New Zealand, Hastings, 9–12 April 1982 (Hastings: LOI, 1982).

Report of Proceedings of the Forty-Ninth Session of the Grand Orange Lodge of New Zealand and the 34th Session of Ladies' Conference. Held in Invercargill, 27th to 30th March, 1970 (Wellington: Digest Print Ltd, 1970).

Report of Proceedings of the Fourteenth Annual Session of the Grand Orange Lodge of New Zealand. Held in Auckland, April 15, 17 and 18, 1922 (Wellington: Wright & Carman, 1922).

Report of Proceedings of the Fourteenth Triennial Session of the Imperial Grand Orange Council of the Loyal Orange Association of the World. Held in the city of Toronto, Canada, July 16th, 17th and 18th, 1906 (Toronto: The Sentinel Print, 1906).

Report of Proceedings of the Grand Orange Lodge of Scotland at the Half-Yearly Meetings. Held in The Chalmers Halls, Glasgow, 9th December 1911 and 8th June 1912 (Glasgow: George Watt, 1912).

Report of Proceedings of the Grand Orange Lodge of Scotland at the Half-Yearly Meetings. Held in The Orange Hall, Glasgow, 9th December 1916 and 9th June 1917 (Glasgow: George Watt, 1917).

Report of Proceedings of the Grand Orange Lodge of Scotland at the Half-Yearly Meetings. Held in The Orange Hall, Glasgow, 8th December 1917 and The Chalmers Hall, Glasgow, 8th June 1918 (Glasgow: George Watt, 1918).

Report of Proceedings of the Grand Orange Lodge of Scotland at the Half-Yearly Meetings. Held in The Orange Hall, Glasgow, 13th December 1919 and 12th June 1920 (Glasgow: George Watt, 1920).

Report of Proceedings of the Grand Orange Lodge of Scotland at the Half-Yearly Meetings. Held in The Orange Hall, Glasgow, 9th December 1944 and The Orange Hall, Glasgow, 9th June 1945 (Glasgow: George Watt, 1945).

Report of Proceedings of the Ninety-Seventh Session of the M.W. Grand Lodge Ladies' Orange Benevolent Association of Canada. Centennial Edition. June 14, 15, 16, 17, 1994 Saint John, New Brunswick (Toronto: LOBA, 1994).

Report of Proceedings of the Seventeenth Triennial Meeting of the Imperial Grand Orange Council of the World. Held in Belfast, Ireland, 15th–16th July, 1920 (Belfast: LOI, 1920).

Report of Proceedings of the Sixteenth Annual Session of the Grand Orange Lodge of New Zealand. Held in Wellington, April 19, 21, and 22, 1924 (Dunedin: Crown Print, 1924).

Report of Proceedings of the Sixth Annual Session of the Grand Orange Lodge of Michigan Held in West Bay City, Michigan May 1, 2 and 3, 1894 (Saginaw: Jones & McCall Co., 1894).

Report of Proceedings of the Thirteenth Triennial Session of the Imperial Grand Orange Council of the Loyal Orange Association of the World (1903). Held in the city of Dublin, Ireland, July 15 and 16th, 1903 (Glasgow: Office of Imperial Grand Secretary, 1903).

Report of Proceedings of the Thirty-Ninth Session of the Loyal Orange Institution of New Zealand (Inc.) and 24th Ladies' Conference. Held in Christchurch April 7th, 8th and 10th 1950 (Dunedin: Robertson McBeath Print, 1950).

Report of Proceedings Wellington Easter 2000 Grand Orange Lodge 64th Sessions (Wellington: LOI, 2000).

Report of the Forty-First Meeting of the Imperial Orange Council, 1867–2003. Held at the Swallow Hotel, Glasgow, Scotland, 20th–25th July, 2003 (Glasgow: LOI, 2003).

Report of the Forty-Seventh Session of the Supreme Grand Orange Lodge Loyal Orange Institution of the United States of America Inc. Held in Rochester, N.Y. August 13, 14, & 15, 1938. And the Forty-Eighth Session Held in Wilmington, Delaware August 16, 17 & 18, 1940 (Pittsburgh: LOI, 1938–40).

Report of the Fourteenth Annual Session of the Grand Orange Lodge of the United States of America Held in a P. Hall, Pittsburgh PA. June 12th, 13th, 1883 (Philadelphia: Protestant Standard Print, 1883).

Report of the Proceedings of the Grand Orange Lodge of Ireland at a Meeting Held at No. 3, Stephen's-Green, North Dublin, on the 14th, 15th, 16th, 17th, 18th and 20th November 1848 (Dublin: LOI, 1848).

Report of the Proceedings of the Seventy-Second Biennial Meeting of the Supreme Grand Lodge Loyal Orange Institution of the United States of America Inc. Pittsburgh, Pennsylvania August 9 and 10 1988 (Pittsburgh: LOI, 1988).

Report of the Proceedings of the Sixty-Seventh Biennial Meeting of the Supreme Grand Lodge of the Loyal Orange Institution of the United States of America Inc. Pittsburgh, Pennsylvania August 15 and 16 1978 (Pittsburgh: LOI, 1978).

Report of the Second Annual Session of the Grand Orange Lodge of New Zealand. Held in Dunedin, April 10, 12, 13, 1909 (Dunedin: Wallace's Crown Print, 1909).

Report of the Seventh Grand Lodge of New Zealand. Held in the Oddfellows' Hall, Hastings 11, 13 and 14 April, 1914 (Christchurch: Frasers Ltd, Printers, 1914).

Report of the Thirty-Eighth Meeting of the Imperial Orange Council, 1867–1994. Held at Auckland, New Zealand, 26th, 27th, 29th & 30th September, 1994 (Auckland: LOI, 1994).

Report of the Thirty-Ninth Meeting of the Imperial Orange Council, 1867–1997. Held at the Stormont Hotel, Belfast, Northern Ireland, 15th, 16th, & 18th July, 1997 (Belfast: LOI, 1997).

Report of the Twenty-Fifth Meeting of the Imperial Grand Orange Council of the World held at Liverpool, England, 14th–15th July, 1955 (Belfast: Northern Whig Ltd, 1955).

Report of the Twenty-Sixth Meeting of the Imperial Grand Orange Council of the World. Held at Londonderry, Northern Ireland on the 16th July and 17th July, 1958 (Belfast: LOI, 1958).

Constitutions/Rituals/Rules and Regulations

American Protestant Association, *Address of the Board of Managers of the American Protestant Association, with the Constitution and Organization of the Association* (Philadelphia: American Protestant Association, 1843).

Anderson, James, *The Constitutions of the Free-Masons: Containing the History, Charges, Regulations, &c. of that Most Ancient and Right Worshipful Fraternity* (London: William Hunter, 1723).

Anderson, James, *The New Book of Constitutions of the Most Ancient and Honourable Fraternity of Free and Accepted Masons* (Dublin: Edward Pratt, 1751).

Australian Protestant Defence Association, *Constitution and By-Laws for the Use of Branches* (Sydney: W. M. Madgwick & Sons, 1904).

British-American Order of Good Templars, and James A. Barchard, *Juvenile Ritual: Containing the Opening, Initiation, Installation, Funeral and Closing Ceremonies, Together with the Constitution, By-Laws, and Rules of Order; with General Directions for the Organization of Juvenile Lodges of the British American Order of Good Templars, of the Dominion of Canada* (Stratford, Ontario: J. A. Barchard, 1870).

Constitution and Laws of the Loyal Orange Association of British North America (Toronto: Sign of the Golden Sun, 1859).

Constitution and Laws of the Loyal Orange Association of British North America Including the Act of Incorporation. Assented to, April 24th 1890 By an Act of the Parliament of Canada. Amended 1st Session 15th Parliament 16–17 George V, 1926. Laws and Rules relating to real Property of the Association (Toronto: Grand Lodge, revised 2015).

Constitution and Laws of the Loyal Orange Institution of the United States of America (Philadelphia: Protestant Standard Print, 1889).

Constitution and Laws of the Loyal Orange Young Briton Association. As approved by the Most Worshipful Grand Orange Lodge of British America 1961 (Toronto: Britannia Printers, 1961).

Constitution of the Loyal Orange Institution of New Zealand. Adopted by the Grand Orange Lodge of New Zealand March 1978 (Wellington: LOI, 1978).

Female Orange Association Laws and Ordinances in Connection with The Grand Lodge of the Middle Island of New Zealand (Christchurch: Caygill and Co., 1888).

Forms to be Observed by Dominion Grand Chapter and Private Preceptories for Invitation, Dedication, Installation of Officers and Diagrams of Halls (Christchurch: Cyril E. Rose, Printer, 1928).

Grand Orange Lodge, *Constitution and Rules of the Junior Lodges* (Wellington: LOI, 1971).

Grand Orange Lodge of Ireland, *Rules and Regulations for the use of all Orange Societies. Revised and corrected by a Committee of the Grand Orange Lodge of Ireland; and adopted by the Grand Orange Lodge, January 10, 1800* (Dublin: Printed by an Orangeman, 1800).

Grand Orange Lodge of New Zealand, *Ritual Book* (Wellington: Wright & Carman Ltd, n.d.).

Grand Orange Lodge of Scotland, *Ladies' Loyal Orange Association: Ritual of Introduction/Ritual Second Degree* (Glasgow: George Watt, Printers, 1955).

How, Jeremiah, *The Freemason's Manual; or, Illustrations of Masonry, containing, in addition to the rites sanctioned* (London: Simpkin, Marshall & Co., 1862).

Independent Order of Rechabites, *Rules Governing Juvenile Section Independent Order of Rechabites: New Zealand Central District, No. 86 (Salford Unity) Friendly Society* (Wanganui, NZ: Hanton & Andersen, 1934).

Independent Order of Rechabites Friendly Society, *Juvenile Tent Ritual* (Adelaide: South Australian District, 1932).

Ladies' Orange Benevolent Association of British America, *Constitution and Laws of the Ladies' Orange Benevolent Association of British America* (Toronto: W. E. Johnston & Co'y Limited, 1920).

Ladies' Orange Benevolent Association of British America, *Ritual: First Degree. Second Degree* (Toronto: The Sentinel Print, 1894).

Laws and Constitutions of the Loyal Orange Institution of Scotland (Glasgow: GOLS, 1986).

Laws and Ordinances of the Orange Institution of Ireland: Revised and adopted by the Grand Orange Lodge of Ireland, June 3rd, 1896 (Dublin: GOLI, 1896).

Laws and Ordinances of the Orange Institution of New Zealand (Auckland: Free Press, 1883).

Laws of the Protestant Alliance Friendly Society of Australasia: Adopted by the Grand Council of Representatives, at Thames, in the Colony of New Zealand (Thames, NZ: The Society, 1882).

Loyal Orange Association of Australia Felix, *Laws and Regulations of the Provincial Grand Lodge of the Loyal Orange Association of Australia Felix, on the registry of the Grand Lodge of Ulster* (Melbourne, 1854).

Loyal Orange Association of British America, *By-Laws of Strathroy Lodge, L.O.A., No. 537* (Strathroy: Dispatch Book and Job Office, 1867).

Loyal Orange Association of British America, *Constitution and Laws of the Loyal Orange Association of British America* (Toronto: The Sentinel Print, 1883).

Loyal Orange Association of British America, *Constitution and Laws of the Loyal Orange Association of British America* (Belleville, Ontario: Moore Printer to Grand Lodge, 1875).

Loyal Orange Association of British America, *Constitution and Laws of the Loyal Orange Association of British America: with rules of the Royal Scarlet Order, Juvenile Orange Association and Grand Lodge Benefit Fund* (Toronto: McCallum Press, 1947).

Loyal Orange Grand Council of Australasia, *Ritual–Female. For the Opening and Closing of Lodges and the Initiation of Members into the Orange Degree* (Adelaide: L. J. McBride Print, 1913).

Loyal Orange Institution, *Enniskillen Memorial Orphan Scheme, Rules and Constitution* (Dublin: James Forrest, 1888).

Loyal Orange Institution of England, *Female Branch. Rules for the Regulation of Lodges of Loyal Orangewomen including opening and closing ceremonies* (London: GOLE, 1922).

Loyal Orange Institution of England, *Laws and Constitution Enacted by the Grand Lodge of England at Corby 15 September 1995* (London: GOLE, amended 2015).

Loyal Orange Institution of England, *Laws and Ordinances Enacted by the Grand Lodge of England at Leicester, 5th and 6th July 1893. With Alterations and Additions to 1920* (London: Forbes & Co., 1921).

Loyal Orange Institution of England, *Rules and Ceremonies of the Junior Branch* (Liverpool: Rudham & Rowley, 1977).

Loyal Orange Institution of England, *Rules and Ceremonies of the Junior Branch* (Liverpool: GOLE, 1995).

Loyal Orange Institution of Ireland, *Laws and Ordinances of the Association of Loyal Orangewomen of Ireland* (Dublin: Brother James Forrest, Printers, 1888).

Loyal Orange Institution of New Zealand, *Laws and Ordinances of the Orange Institution of New Zealand* (Auckland: Free Press, 1883).

Loyal Orange Institution of New Zealand, *Ritual for the Use of Juvenile Orange Lodges* (Dunedin: Crown Print Ltd, 1941).

Loyal Orange Institution of New Zealand, Grand Orange Lodge, *Constitution and Rules of the Juvenile Lodges* (Wellington: Wright & Carman Ltd, 1943).

Loyal Orange Institution of Queensland, *Laws and Ordinances of the Loyal Orange Institution of Queensland (incorporated by Letters Patent) Passed As Revised by the Grand Lodge of Queensland, 1935 to 1940* (Brisbane: Rallings & Rallings, 1935).

Loyal Orange Institution of Scotland, *Juvenile Lodge Ritual. Adopted by Grand Lodge, 1905* (Glasgow: LOIS, revised 1957).

Loyal Orange Institution of the United States of America, *Constitution and Laws of the Loyal Orange Institution of the United States of America* (Philadelphia: Protestant Standard Print, 1889).

Loyal Orange Institution, Supreme Grand Lodge (U.S.), *Constitution–General Laws, Regulations and Rules: Supreme Grand Lodge of the Loyal Orange Institution of the United States of America, Inc. Adopted at 48th Session of the Supreme Grand Lodge August 1940* (Philadelphia: LOI, revised 1964).

Loyal Orange Institution, Supreme Grand Lodge (U.S.), *Constitution–General Laws, Regulations and Rules: Supreme Grand Lodge of the Loyal Orange Institution of the United States of America, Inc. Adopted at 74th Session of the Supreme Grand Lodge August 1972* (Philadelphia: LOI, revised 1992).

Loyal Orange Ladies' Institution, Supreme Grand Lodge (U.S.), *Constitution and By-Laws of the Supreme Grand Lodge of the Loyal Orange Ladies' Institution, Inc. Also Constitution for Subordinate Lodges with Rules of Order, 1996* (Philadelphia: LOLI, 1996).

New South Wales Protestant Political Association, Manifesto, *Rules and By-Laws of the New South Wales Protestant Political Association* (Sydney: Samuel E. Lees, 1872).

Orange Institution of Ireland, *Laws and Ordinances of the Orange Institution of Ireland* (Dublin: George P. Bull, 1830).

Orange Institution of Ireland, *Laws and Ordinances of the Orange Institution of Ireland. Revised and Adopted by the Grand Orange Lodge of Ireland* (Belfast: News Letter, 1872).

Orange Institution of Ireland, *Laws and Ordinances of the Orange Institution of Ireland. Revised and Adopted by the Grand Orange Lodge of Ireland, June 3rd, 1896* (Dublin: Br. James Forrest, 1896).

Protestant Defence Association of New Zealand, *Constitution and By-Laws* (Dunedin: Otago Daily Times, 1903).

Rules and Regulations of the Loyal Orange Institution of New South Wales, Adopted 25th August 1928 (Sydney: The Institution, 1928).

Rules and Regulations of the Orange Institution of British North America: Adopted by the Grand Lodge at its first meeting. Held in the Court House, Brockville, Upper Canada 1st of January 1830 (Brockville: Thomas Tomkins, 1830).

Rules of the Loyal Orange Institution: Adopted by the Grand Orange Lodge of Dominion of New Zealand, March 1910 (Wellington: Wright & Carman, 1910).

Rules of the Loyal Orange Institution Incorporated. Adopted by the Grand Orange Lodge of Dominion of New Zealand. April 1908. Revised to June 1916 (Dunedin: Crown Print Co., 1916).

Orange Publications

Association of Loyal Orangewomen of Ireland: 100th Anniversary 1912–2012 (Craigavon, County Armagh: Inhouse Publications, 2012).

Birmingham, A. H., County Master of Toronto, 1934, *How Orangeism Began in Canada*, <https://web.archive.org/web/20140624032544/http://canadi anorangehistoricalsite.com/index-152.php> (accessed 10 July 2023).

Bryce, David, *A History of Scotland's Orange Friendly Societies* (Glasgow: GOLS, 2004).

Bryce, David, *The Undaunted: A History of the Orange Order in Scotland from 1799 to 1899* (Glasgow: D. Bryce, 2012).

Ferrel, Charles, *Notes on the Early History of Wellington District Junior Lodges*, 10 September 1956.

Fielding, J. R., *Loyal Orange Youth Association of Victoria: 1916–1976 Diamond Jubilee* (Melbourne: The Austral Printing, 1976).

Grand Orange Lodge of Scotland, *The Future Is Orange and Bright* (Glasgow: GOLS, n.d.).

Hume, David (ed.), *Battles Beyond the Boyne* (Belfast: Schomberg Press, 2001).

Hume, David, Jonathan Mattison and David Scott, *Beyond Banners: The Story of the Orange Order* (Holywood, County Down: Booklink, 2009).

JLOL Massey Boys' Lodge No. 1. 25th Anniversary and Installation of Officers. Orange Hall, Newton. 18th September 1954.

Johnstone, R., *Behind Closed Minds: An Examination of the Book 'Behind Closed Doors'* (Grand Royal Arch Purple Chapter of Ireland, c. 2000).

Kennedy, Billy, *A Celebration: 1690–1990 The Orange Institution* (Belfast: GOLI, 1990).

Kilpatrick, Cecil (ed.), *The Formation of the Orange Order 1795–1798* (Belfast: GOLI, 1999).

Kilpatrick, Cecil S., David Cargo and William Murdie (eds), *History of the Royal Arch Purple Order* (Belfast: Royal Arch Purple Order Research Group, 1993).

Long, Samuel Ernest, *A Brief History of the Loyal Orange Institution in the United States of America* (Dromara, County Down: Samuel Ernest Long, 1979).

Loyal Orange Institution, *Grand Orange Lodge of New Zealand Circular To All Lodges 3rd March 1957.*

Loyal Orange Institution of New Zealand, *Centenary Celebrations 1843–1943: Brief History of the Institution Programme of Centenary Celebrations* (Wellington: Wright & Carman Ltd, 1948).

Loyal Orange Institution of NSW, *Sesqui-Centenary of the Grand Orange Lodge of New South Wales 1995* (Chipping Norton, NSW: Gowans & Son Pty, Ltd, 1995).

Loyal Orange Institution of NSW, *Sesqui-Centenary of the Grand Orange Lodge of New South Wales. Supplement to Souvenir Book 1995* (Chipping Norton, NSW: Gowans & Son Pty, Ltd, 1995).

Loyal Orange Ladies' Institution United States of America, *History of the Loyal Orange Ladies' Institution United States of America* (Philadelphia: LOLI, 1944).

McClure Watters, R. S. M., *A Report on the Socio-Economic Impact of the Traditional Protestant Parading Sector in Northern Ireland* (Belfast: GOLI, 2013).

Meredith, Rev. Ian, *A Short History of the Orange Order in Ghana* (Glasgow, c. 1990s).

Meredith, Ian, and Brian Kennaway, *The Orange Order: An Evangelical Perspective* (Meredith & Kennaway, 1993).

Orange Lodge of Ireland, *Applications for Warrants 1854 to 1890*, held at Schomberg House, Belfast, Northern Ireland.

Popery Proved Paganism (New Plymouth, NZ: Taranaki Daily News, n.d.).

Russell, A. S., *Loyal Orange Institution of Queensland History 1865 to 1932* (Brisbane: Loyal Orange Institution of Queensland, 1933).

Stewart, W. A. (compiler), *Early History of the Loyal Orange Institution N.S.W.* (Sydney: Grand Orange Lodge of New South Wales, 1926).

Vertigan, Tas, *The Orange Order in Victoria* (Melbourne: Loyal Orange Institution of Victoria, 1979).

Contemporary Works

Anon., *'Is the "escaped nun" a fraud?' Being a full report of the public discussion between Mr Fred Fulton and Miss O'Gorman (Mrs Auffray) at the Garrison Hall, Dunedin, 2 March 1886* (Dunedin: J. Powers, Smith & Co., 1886).

Baker, W., *Orangeism in the Cape: A Resume* (Belfast, 1905).

Cannon, Richard, *Historical Records of the British Army: The Sixth or Royal First Warwickshire Regiment of Foot* (London: William Clowes & Sons, 1837).

Carnahan, Joseph, *A Brief History of the Orange Institution in the North Island of New Zealand from 1842 to the Present Time* (Auckland: Star Office, 1886).

Carnahan, Joseph, *Life and Times of William the Third and History of Orangeism* (Auckland: Star Office, 1890).

Cleary, H. W., *The Orange Society* (Melbourne: Bernard King & Sons, 1897).

Cupples, S., *The Principles of the Orange Association* (Dublin: W. McKenzie, 1799).

The Cyclopedia of New Zealand [*Canterbury Provincial District*], vol. 3 (Christchurch: The Cyclopedia Company, 1903).

Desmond, Humphrey Joseph, *The APA Movement: A Sketch* (Washington, DC: New Century Press, 1912).

Gowan, Ogle R., *Orangeism; Its Origins and History* (Toronto: Lovell & Gibson, 1859).

Lewis, E., *Orangeism Exposed* (Melbourne: Advocate Office, 1900).

O'Gorman, Edith, *Trials and Persecutions of Miss Edith O'Gorman: Otherwise Sister Teresa de Chantal, of St. Joseph's Convent, Hudson City, N.J.* (Hartford: Connecticut Publishing Co., 1871).

Orange Standard (Glasgow: Mozart Allen, 1936).

Reid, Thomas, *Travels in Ireland, in the Year 1822* (London: Longman, Hurst, Rees, Orme, & Brown, 1823).

Shannon, William, *The United Empire Minstrel: A Selection of the Best National Constitutional and Loyal Orange Songs and Poems* (Toronto: Henry Rowsell, 1852).

Sibbett, R. M., *Orangeism in Ireland and throughout the Empire*, vols 1–2 (Belfast: Henderson & Company, 1914).

Smith, James (ed.), *The Cyclopedia of Victoria*, vol. 3 (Melbourne: The Cyclopedia Company, 1904).

Taxil, Léo, *Pie IX Devant l'Histoire: Sa Vie Politique et Pontificale Ses Débauches, Ses Folies, Ses Crimes* (Paris: Librairie Anti-Cléricale, 1883).

Newspapers

Advocate
The Age
The Argus
Auckland Star
The Banner
Belfast News Letter
Belfast Telegraph
Belfast Weekly News
Birmingham Daily Post
Brisbane Courier
Clarence and Richmond Examiner and New England Advertiser
Colonial Times
The Courier Mail
Daily Mail
Daily News
Daily Record
Daily Telegraph
Derby Mercury
Dublin Weekly Journal
Evening Public Ledger
Examiner
Fiery Cross
Glasgow Courier
Glasgow Herald
Globe and Mail
The Guardian
The Herald
Houlton Times
The Inquirer and Commercial News
Irish Times
Liverpool Chronicle
Liverpool Echo
Liverpool Mail
Lyttleton Times
Maitland Daily Mercury
Manawatu Standard
Melbourne Courier

Mercury
Nation
New York Times
New Zealand Herald
New Zealand Tablet
Newcastle Morning Herald and Miners' Advocate
News Letter
The Observer
Orange and Protestant Banner
Orange and Purple Courier
Orange Standard (Belfast)
Orange Standard (Bradford)
Orange Torch
The Orangeman
Otago Daily Times
Philadelphia Inquirer
Press
Preston Guardian
The Protestant Standard
Queensland Times
The Register
The Scotsman
The Sentinel
South Australian Chronicle and Weekly Mail
South Australian Register
Southport Visiter
The Straits Times
Straits Times Weekly Issue
Sunday Mail
Sunday Times
Sydney Morning Herald
The Telegraph
Toronto Star
The True Witness and Catholic Chronicle
Tuapeka Times Post
Victorian Standard
Watchman
The Week
Werribee Shire Banner
Western Mail

Emails and Interviews with Author

Bryce, David, 18 September, 1 November 2013; 23 July, 9 September 2016.

Buist, Beverley, Interview 11 January 2005, transcript, OHA-5201.

Coleman, Patrick, *Oral History of the Loyal Orange Institution in the South Island 2004–2005*. OHColl-0791, Alexander Turnbull Library, Wellington, New Zealand.

Ellis, Patricia, Interview 19 January 2005, transcript, OHA-5203.

Mattison, Jonathan, 27 March 2018.

Nolan, Ray, 10 May 2014.

Owens, Billy, 24 January 2016.

Phelan, Michael, 27 October 2013, 4 November 2013.

Rimmer, Gillian, 31 December 2015.

Robinson, John, Interview 29 May 2005, transcript, OHA-5205.

Wells, John, 13 June 2014.

SECONDARY SOURCES

Books

Amenumey, D. E. K., *The Ewe Unification Movement: A Political History* (Accra: Ghana Universities Press, 1989).

Belchem, John, *Irish, Catholic and Scouse: The History of the Liverpool-Irish, 1800–1939* (Liverpool: Liverpool University Press, 2007).

Bell, Desmond, *Acts of Union: Youth Culture and Sectarianism in Northern Ireland* (London: Macmillan, 1990).

Bew, Paul, *Ideology and the Irish Question: Ulster Unionism and Irish Nationalism, 1912–1916* (Oxford: Clarendon Press, 1994).

Blackstock, Allan, *Loyalism in Ireland 1789–1829* (Woodbridge: Boydell Press, 2007).

Blackstock, Allan, and Frank O'Gorman, *Loyalism and the Formation of the British World: 1775–1914* (Woodbridge: Boydell Press, 2014).

Brown, Callum, *The Death of Christian Britain* (London: Routledge, 2001).

Brown, Callum G., *Religion and the Demographic Revolution: Women and Secularisation in Canada, Ireland, UK and USA since the 1960s* (Woodbridge and Rochester, NY: Boydell & Brewer, 2012).

Bryan, Dominic, *Orange Parades: The Politics of Ritual, Tradition and Control* (London: Pluto Press, 2000).

Bullock, Stephen C., *Revolutionary Brotherhood: Freemasonry and the Transformation of the American Social Order, 1730–1840* (Chapel Hill: University of North Carolina Press, 1996).

Busteed, Mervyn, *The Sash on the Mersey: The Orange Order in Liverpool, 1819–1982* (Manchester: Manchester University Press, 2023).

Campbell, Malcolm, *Ireland's Farthest Shores: Mobility, Migration, and Settlement in the Pacific World* (Madison: University of Wisconsin Press, 2022).

Carnes, Mark C., *Secret Ritual and Manhood in Victorian America* (New Haven and London: Yale University Press, 1989).

Choquette, Robert, *Canada's Religions: An Historical Introduction* (Ottawa: University of Ottawa Press, 2004).

Clawson, Mary Ann, *Constructing Brotherhood: Class, Gender, and Fraternalism* (Princeton: Princeton University Press, 1989).

Cook, Christopher C. H., *Alcohol, Addiction and Christian Ethics* (Cambridge: Cambridge University Press, 2006).

Cunningham, Anne Elizabeth, *The Price of a Wife: The Priest and the Divorce Trial* (Spit Junction, NSW: Anchor Books Australia, 2013).

Davis, Richard P., *Orangeism in Tasmania 1832–1967* (Newtownabbey, County Antrim: Institute of Ulster-Scots Studies, 2010).

Dudley Edwards, Ruth, *The Faithful Tribe: An Intimate Portrait of the Loyal Institutions* (London: HarperCollins, 1999).

Farrell, Sean, *Rituals and Riots: Sectarian Violence and Political Culture in Ulster, 1784–1886* (Lexington: University Press of Kentucky, 2000).

Fitzpatrick, David, *Descendancy: Irish Protestant Histories since 1795* (Cambridge: Cambridge University Press, 2014).

Fraser, T. G. (ed.), *The Irish Parading Tradition: Following the Drum* (Basingstoke: Palgrave Macmillan, 2000).

Gibbon, Peter, *The Origins of Ulster Unionism: The Formation of Popular Protestant Politics and Ideology in Nineteenth-Century Ireland* (Manchester: Manchester University Press, 1975).

Gordon, Michael A., *The Orange Riots: Irish Political Violence in New York City, 1870 and 1871* (Ithaca and London: Cornell University Press, 1993).

Gould, Robert Freke, and revised by Frederick J. W. Crowe, *The Concise History of Freemasonry* (London: Gale & Polden Ltd, 1920; revised 1951).

Gray, Tony, *The Orange Order* (London: The Bodley Head, 1972).

Haddick-Flynn, Kevin, *Orangeism: The Making of a Tradition* (Dublin: Wolfhound Press, 1999).

Harland-Jacobs, Jessica, *Builders of Empire: Freemasons and British Imperialism, 1717–1927* (Chapel Hill: University of North Carolina Press, 2007).

Hastings, Gary, *With Fife and Drum: Music, Memories and Customs of an Irish Tradition* (Belfast: Blackstaff Press, 2003).

Hennessey, Thomas, Máire Braniff, James W. McAuley, Jonathan Tonge and Sophie Whiting, *The Ulster Unionist Party: Country before Party?* (Oxford: Oxford University Press, 2019).

Houston, Cecil J., and William J. Smyth, *The Sash Canada Wore: A Historical Geography of the Orange Order in Canada* (Toronto: University of Toronto Press, 1980).

Iriye, Akira, and Pierre Yves Saunier (eds), *Palgrave Dictionary of Transnational History* (London: Palgrave Macmillan, 2009).

Irving, Helen (ed.), *The Centenary Companion to Australian Federation* (Cambridge: Cambridge University Press, 1999).

Jacob, Margaret C., *Living the Enlightenment: Freemasonry and Politics in Eighteenth-Century Europe* (Oxford: Oxford University Press, 1991).

Jarman, Neil, *Displaying Faith: Orange, Green and Trade Union Banners in Northern Ireland* (Belfast: Institute of Irish Studies, Queen's University Belfast, 1999).

Jarman, Neil, *Material Conflicts: Parades and Visual Displays in Northern Ireland* (Oxford: Berg, 1997).

Jess, Mervyn, *The Orange Order* (Dublin: O'Brien Press, 2007).

Kaufmann, Eric, *The Orange Order: A Contemporary Northern Irish History* (Oxford: Oxford University Press, 2007).

Kaufmann, Eric, *Orange Order Membership Data, with a Focus on Ireland, Canada and Scotland, 1852–2002* (Colchester: UK Data Archive, 2004).

Kealey, Gregory S., *Toronto Workers Respond to Industrial Capitalism 1867–1892* (Toronto: University of Toronto Press, 1980).

Kenny, Kevin, *The American Irish: A History* (New York: Routledge, 2014).

Kenny, Kevin, *Diaspora: A Very Short Introduction* (Oxford: Oxford University Press, 2013).

Kinzer, Donald Louis, *An Episode in Anti-Catholicism: The American Protective Association* (Seattle: University of Washington Press, 1964).

Laffan, Tony, *How Orange Was my Valley? Protestant Sectarianism and the Loyal Orange Lodges of Australia's Hunter Valley, 1869–1959* (Singleton, NSW: Toiler Editions, 2009).

Lyon, David, and Marguerite Van Die (eds), *Rethinking Church, State, and Modernity: Canada between Europe and America* (Toronto: University of Toronto Press, 2000).

McCormick, W. J. McK., *Christ, the Christian and Freemasonry* (Belfast: W. J. McK. McCormick, 1977).

MacDonald, Darach, *Blood and Thunder: Inside an Ulster Protestant Band* (Cork: Mercier Press, 2010).

McFarland, Elaine, *Protestants First: Orangeism in Nineteenth-Century Scotland* (Edinburgh: Edinburgh University Press, 1990).

McGrath, Charles Ivar, *Ireland and Empire, 1692–1770* (London and New York: Routledge, 2016).

MacKenzie, John M., *The British Empire Through Buildings: Structure, Function and Meaning* (Manchester: Manchester University Press, 2020).

McLaughlin, Robert, *Irish Canadian Conflict and the Struggle for Irish Independence, 1912–1925* (Toronto: University of Toronto Press, 2013).

MacPherson, D. A. J., *Women and the Orange Order: Female Activism, Diaspora and Empire in the British World, 1850–1940* (Manchester: Manchester University Press, 2016).

MacRaild, Donald M., *Culture, Conflict and Migration: The Irish in Victorian Cumbria* (Liverpool: Liverpool University Press, 1998).

MacRaild, Donald M., *Faith, Fraternity and Fighting: The Orange Order and Irish Migrants in England, c. 1850–1920* (Liverpool: Liverpool University Press, 2005).

Malcomson, W. P., *Behind Closed Doors: The Hidden Structure within the Orange Camp* (Banbridge: Evangelical Truth, 1999).

Marshall, P. J., *The Making and Unmaking of Empires: Britain, India and America c. 1750–1783* (Oxford: Oxford University Press, 2005).

Miller, David W., *Queens Rebels: Ulster Loyalism in Historical Perspective* (Dublin: Gill & Macmillan, 1978).

Mirala, Petri, *Freemasonry in Ulster, 1733–1813: A Social and Political History of the Masonic Brotherhood in the North of Ireland* (Dublin: Four Courts Press, 2007).

Moore, William D., *Masonic Temples: Freemasonry, Ritual Architecture, and Masculine Archetypes* (Knoxville: University of Tennessee Press, 2006).

Neal, Frank, *Sectarian Violence: The Liverpool Experience, 1819–1914* (Manchester: Manchester University Press, 1988; revised 2003).

Neal, Frank, and Jonathan Tonge, *Irish Protestant Identities* (Manchester: Manchester University Press, 2008).

Parkinson, R. E., *History of the Grand Lodge of Free and Accepted Masons of Ireland, Volume 2* (Dublin: Lodge of Research, CC, 1957).

Patterson, Henry, and Eric Kaufmann, *Unionism and Orangeism in Northern Ireland since 1945: The Decline of the Loyal Family* (Manchester: Manchester University Press, 2007).

Putnam, Robert D., *Bowling Alone: The Collapse and Revival of American Community* (New York: Simon & Schuster, 2000).

Ramsey, Gordon, *Music, Emotion and Identity in Ulster Marching Bands: Flutes, Drums and Loyal Sons* (Oxford: Peter Lang, 2011).

Richard, Mark Paul, *Not a Catholic Nation: The Ku Klux Klan Confronts New England in the 1920s* (Amherst: University of Massachusetts Press, 2015).

Rooke, Patricia, and R. L. Schnell, *Discarding the Asylum* (Lanham, MD: University Press of America, 1983).

Schlereth, Thomas J., *Material Culture Studies in America* (Nashville, TN: Rowman Altamira, 1982).

Schrover, Marlou, and Eileen Yeo (eds), *Gender, Migration, and the Public Sphere, 1850–2005* (New York: Routledge, 2009).

See, Scott W., *Riots in New Brunswick: Orange Nativism and Social Violence in the 1840s* (Toronto: University of Toronto Press, 1993).

Senior, Hereward, *Orangeism: The Canadian Phase* (Toronto: McGraw-Hill Ryerson, 1972).

Senior, Hereward, *Orangeism in Ireland and Britain, 1795–1836* (London: Routledge & Kegan Paul; Toronto: Ryerson Press, 1966).

Sharpe, Kevin, *Rebranding Rule: The Restoration and Revolution Monarchy, 1660–1714* (New Haven: Yale University Press, 2013).

Sherling, Rankin, *The Invisible Irish: Finding Protestants in the Nineteenth-Century Migrations to America* (Montreal: McGill-Queen's University Press, 2016).

Smitley, Megan K., *The Feminine Public Sphere: Middle-Class Women and Civic Life in Scotland, c. 1870–1914* (Manchester: Manchester University Press, 2009).

Smyth, William J., *Toronto, the Belfast of Canada: The Orange Order and the Shaping of Municipal Culture* (Toronto: University of Toronto Press, 2015).

Spencer, Ian R. G., *British Immigration Policy since 1939: The Making of Multi-Racial Britain* (London: Routledge, 1997).

Stevenson, Brian, *'Stand Fast Together': A History of the Protestant Alliance Friendly Society of Victoria* (Brisbane: Boolarong Press, 1996).

Stewart, A. T. Q., *The Ulster Crisis: Resistance to Home Rule, 1912–14* (London: Faber & Faber, 1967, 1979).

Trocki, Carl A., *Singapore: Wealth, Power and the Culture of Control* (London: Routledge, 2006).

Urquhart, Diane, *Women in Ulster Politics, 1890–1940: A History Not Yet Told* (Dublin: Irish Academic Press, 2000).

Van Luijk, Ruben, *Children of Lucifer: The Origins of Modern Religious Satanism* (New York: Oxford University Press, 2016).

Walker, Graham, *A History of the Ulster Unionist Party: Protest, Pragmatism and Pessimism* (Manchester: Manchester University Press, 2004).

Walker, Graham, *The Labour Party in Scotland: Religion, the Union, and the Irish Dimension* (London: Palgrave Macmillan, 2016).

Webster, Joseph, *The Religion of Orange Politics: Protestantism and Fraternity in Contemporary Scotland* (Manchester: Manchester University Press, 2020).

Wilson, David A. (ed.), *The Orange Order in Canada* (Dublin: Four Courts Press, 2007).

Woodward, Ian, *Understanding Material Culture* (London: Sage Publications, 2007).

Zimmerman, Georges Dennis, *Songs of Irish Rebellion: Irish Political Street Ballads and Rebel Songs, 1780–1900* (Dublin: Four Courts Press, 1966, 2002).

Articles and Book Chapters

Bailey, Adrian R., David C. Harvey and Catherine Brace, 'Disciplining youthful Methodist bodies in nineteenth-century Cornwall', *Annals of the Association of American Geographers*, 97:1 (2007), pp. 142–57.

Bates, Christina, 'A wonderful syncretion: A Haudenosaunee (Iroquois) beaded Orange lodge crown', *Ornamentum* (2011), pp. 13–16.

Black, Eugene Charlton, 'The tumultuous petitioners: The Protestant Association in Scotland, 1778–1780', *The Review of Politics*, 25:2 (1963), pp. 183–211.

Blackstock, Allan F., '"A dangerous species of ally": Orangeism and the Irish Yeomanry', *Irish Historical Studies*, 30:119 (1997), pp. 393–405.

Bradley, Joseph M., 'Orangeism in Scotland: Unionism, politics, identity and football', *Eire-Ireland: An Interdisciplinary Journal of Irish Studies*, 39:1–2 (2004), pp. 237–61.

Brosnahan, Seán, 'The "Battle of the Borough" and the "Saige O Timaru": Sectarian riot in colonial Canterbury', *New Zealand Journal of History*, 28:1 (1994), pp. 41–59.

Brown, John, 'Orangeism in South Africa', in Donal McCracken (ed.), *The Irish in Southern Africa, 1795–1910* (Durban: Ireland and Southern Africa Project, 1992), pp. 110–19.

Brown, Kris, and Roger MacGinty, 'Public attitudes toward partisan and neutral symbols in post-agreement Northern Ireland', *Identities: Global Studies in Culture and Power*, 10:1 (2003), pp. 83–108.

Bryan, Dominic, 'Drumcree and "the right to march": Orangeism, ritual and politics in Northern Ireland', in T. G. Fraser (ed.), *The Irish Parading Tradition: Following the Drum* (Basingstoke: Palgrave Macmillan, 2000), pp. 191–207.

Bryan, Dominic, 'Parades, flags, carnivals and riots: Public space, contestation and transformation in Northern Ireland', *Peace and Conflict: Journal of Peace Psychology*, 21:4 (2015), pp. 565–73.

Bryan, Dominic, 'The right to march: Parading a loyal Protestant identity in Northern Ireland', *International Journal on Minority and Group Rights*, 4 (1997), pp. 373–96.

Buck, Jesse, 'The role of *Ne Temere* in the decline of an Irish custom regarding the religious affiliation of the children of mixed marriages', *Australasian Journal of Irish Studies*, 11 (2011), pp. 28–43.

Buckley, Anthony D., '"The chosen few": Biblical texts in the regalia of an Ulster secret society', *Folklife*, 24 (1985–86), pp. 5–24.

Buckley, Anthony D., '"On the club": Friendly societies in Ireland', *Irish Economic and Social History*, 14 (1987), pp. 39–58.

Buckley, Anthony D., 'Royal Arch, Royal Arch Purple and Raiders of the Lost Ark: Secrecy in Orange and Masonic ritual', in Trefor M. Owen (ed.), *From Corrib to Cultra: Folklife Essays in Honour of Alan Gailey* (Belfast: Institute of Irish Studies, Queen's University with Ulster Folk and Transport Museum, 2000), pp. 163–80.

Busteed, Mervyn, 'Resistance and respectability: Dilemmas of Irish migrant politics in Victorian Britain', *Immigrants & Minorities*, 27:2–3 (2009), pp. 178–93.

Byrne, Neil J., 'Edith O'Gorman, religious controversialist: The Australian lecture tour of 1886–1887', *Women Church*, 27 (2000), pp. 21–7.

Cahill, Gilbert A., 'Some nineteenth-century roots of the Ulster problem, 1829–1848', *Irish University Review*, 1:2 (1971), pp. 215–37.

Cairns, David, 'The object of sectarianism: The material reality of sectarianism in Ulster loyalism', *The Journal of the Royal Anthropological Institute*, 6:3 (2000), pp. 437–52.

Cairns, David, and Jim Smyth, 'Up off our bellies and onto our knees: Symbolic effacement and the Orange Order in Northern Ireland', *Social Identities*, 8:1 (2002), pp. 143–60.

Cargo, David, 'Part III: The Royal Arch Purple degree', in Cecil S. Kilpatrick, David Cargo and William Murdie (eds), *History of the Royal Arch Purple Order* (Belfast: Royal Arch Purple Order Research Group, 1993), pp. 171–202.

Cecil, Rosanne, 'The marching season in Northern Ireland: An expression of politico-religious identity', in Sharon Macdonald (ed.), *Inside European Identities: Ethnography in Western Europe* (London and New York: Routledge, 1993), pp. 146–66.

Chavura, Stephen A., and Ian Tregenza, 'A political history of the secular in Australia, 1788–1945', in Timothy Stanley (ed.), *Religion after Secularization in Australia* (New York: Palgrave Macmillan, 2015), pp. 3–32.

Clarke, Brian, 'Religious riot as pastime: Orange Young Britons, parades and public life in Victorian Toronto', in David A. Wilson (ed.), *The Orange Order in Canada* (Dublin: Four Courts Press, 2007), pp. 109–27.

Cline, Tyler, '"A clarion call to real patriots the world over": The curious case of the Ku Klux Klan of Kanada in New Brunswick during the 1920s and 1930s', *Acadiensis*, 48:1 (2019), pp. 88–100.

Cline, Tyler, '"A dragon, bog-spawned, is now stretched o'er this land": The Ku Klux Klan's patriotic-Protestantism in the northeastern borderlands during the 1920s and 1930s', *Histoire sociale/Social History*, 52:106 (2019), pp. 305–29.

Cline, Tyler, '"Orangeism, a great Protestant crusade": The nativist legacy of the Orange Order in the northeastern borderlands', *American Review of Canadian Studies*, 48:2 (2018), pp. 125–37.

Coleman, Patrick, '"A hotbed of Orangeism": The Orange Order in Canterbury 1864–1908', *Journal of Orange History*, 3 (2017), pp. 20–7.

Coleman, Patrick, '"In harmony": A comparative view of female Orangeism 1887–2000', in Angela McCarthy (ed.), *Ireland in the World: Comparative, Transnational, and Personal Perspectives* (London and New York: Routledge, 2015), pp. 110–36.

Coleman, Patrick, 'Orange parading traditions in New Zealand 1880–1914', *Australasian Journal of Irish Studies*, 10 (2010), pp. 81–104.

Coleman, Patrick, 'The Orange tartan: Scottish influences on the New Zealand Orange Order', *History Scotland*, 18:1 (2018), pp. 24–9.

Coleman, Patrick, 'Who wants to be a Grand Master? Grand Masters of the Orange Lodge of the Middle Island of New Zealand', in Brad and Kathryn Patterson (eds), *Ireland and the Irish Antipodes: One World or Worlds Apart?* (Sydney: Anchor Books, 2010), pp. 96–107.

Currie, Philip, 'Toronto Orangeism and the Irish question, 1911–1916', *Ontario History*, 87:4 (1995), pp. 397–409.

Day, Peter, 'Pride before a fall? Orangeism in Liverpool since 1945', in M. Busteed, F. Neal and J. Tonge (eds), *Irish Protestant Identities* (Manchester and New York: Manchester University Press, 2008), pp. 277–81.

Edwards, Jennifer, and J. David Knottnerus, 'The Orange Order: Parades, other rituals, and their outcomes', *Sociological Focus*, 43:1 (2010), pp. 1–23.

Edwards, Jennifer, and J. David Knottnerus, 'The Orange Order: Strategic ritualization and its organizational antecedents', *International Journal of Contemporary Sociology*, 44:2 (2007), pp. 179–98.

Fitzpatrick, David, 'Exporting brotherhood: Orangeism in South Australia', *Immigrants & Minorities*, 23:2–3 (2005), pp. 277–310.

Goheen, P. G., 'Parading: A lively tradition in early Victorian Toronto', in A. R. H. Baker and G. Biger (eds), *Ideology and Landscape in Historical Perspective* (Cambridge: Cambridge University Press, 1992), pp. 330–51.

Goheen, P. G., 'The ritual of the streets in mid-19th-century Toronto', *Environment and Planning D: Society and Space*, 11 (1993), pp. 127–45.

Hall, Dianne, 'Defending the faith: Orangeism and Ulster Protestant identities in colonial New South Wales', *Journal of Religious History*, 38:2 (2014), pp. 207–23.

Hamilton, Michael, and Dominic Bryan, 'Deepening democracy? Dispute system design and the mediation of contested parades in Northern Ireland', *Ohio State Journal on Dispute Resolution*, 22:1 (2006), pp. 133–87.

Harvey, David Allen, 'Lucifer in the city of light: The Palladium hoax and "diabolical causality" in fin de siècle France', *Magic, Ritual, and Witchcraft*, 1:2 (2006), pp. 177–206.

Heller, Michael, 'The National Insurance Acts 1911–1947, the approved societies and the Prudential Assurance Company', *Twentieth Century British History*, 19:1 (2008), pp. 1–28.

Houston, Cecil J., and William J. Smyth, 'The faded sash: The decline of the Orange Order in Canada, 1920–2005', in David A. Wilson (ed.), *The Orange Order in Canada* (Dublin: Four Courts Press, 2007), pp. 146–91.

Houston, Cecil J., and William J. Smyth, 'Transferred loyalties: Orangeism in the United States and Ontario', *American Review of Canadian Studies*, 14:2 (1984), pp. 193–211.

Ireland, Patrick R., 'Irish Protestant migration and politics in the USA, Canada, and Australia: A debated legacy', *Irish Studies Review*, 20:3 (2012), pp. 263–81.

Jarman, Neil, 'For God and Ulster: Blood and thunder bands and loyalist political culture', in T. G. Fraser (ed.), *The Irish Parading Tradition* (Basingstoke: Palgrave Macmillan, 2000), pp. 158–72.

Jarman, Neil, 'Material of culture, fabric of identity', in Daniel Miller (ed.), *Material Cultures: Why Some Things Matter* (Chicago: University of Chicago Press, 1998), pp. 121–45.

Jarman, Neil, 'The Orange arch: Creating tradition in Ulster', *Folklore*, 112:1 (2001), pp. 1–21.

Jenkins, Gareth, 'Nationalism and sectarian violence in Liverpool and Belfast, 1880s–1920s', *International Labor and Working-Class History*, 78:1 (2010), pp. 164–80.

Kaufmann, Eric, 'The decline of sectarianism in the West? A comparison of the Orange Order in Canada, Ulster and Scotland', in N. Singh and T. Vanhanen (eds), *Ethnic Violence and Human Rights* (Delhi: KIRS, 2002), pp. 1–19.

Kaufmann, Eric, 'The dynamics of Orangeism in Scotland: The social sources of political influence in a large fraternal organization', *Social Science History*, 30:2 (2006), pp. 263–92.

Kaufmann, Eric, 'The Orange Order in Ontario, Newfoundland, Scotland and Northern Ireland: A macro-social analysis', in David A. Wilson (ed.), *The Orange Order in Canada* (Dublin: Four Courts Press, 2007), pp. 42–68.

Kaufmann, Eric, 'The Orange Order in Scotland since 1860: A social analysis', in Martin J. Mitchell (ed.), *New Perspectives on the Irish in Scotland* (Edinburgh: John Donald, 2008), pp. 159–90.

Kealey, Gregory S., 'Orangemen and the corporation: The politics of class during the Union of the Canadas', in Victor Loring Russell (ed.), *Forging a Consensus: Historical Essays on Toronto* (Toronto: University of Toronto Press, 1984), pp. 41–86.

Kenny, Kevin, 'Diaspora and comparison: The global Irish as a case study', *The Journal of American History*, 90:1 (2003), pp. 134–62.

Kenny, Kevin, 'Irish emigration, c. 1845–1900', in Thomas Bartlett and James Kelly (eds), *The Cambridge History of Ireland* (Cambridge: Cambridge University Press, 2018), pp. 666–87.

Kilpatrick, Cecil S., 'Black, Scarlet, Blue, Royal Arch Purple or any other colour', *Ulster Folklife*, 42 (1996), pp. 23–31.

Kollar, Rene, 'An American "escaped nun" on tour in England: Edith O'Gorman's critique of convent life', *Feminist Theology*, 14:2 (2006), pp. 205–20.

Liagre, Guy, 'Protestantism and Freemasonry', in Henrik Bogdan and Jan A. M. Snoek (eds), *Handbook of Freemasonry* (Leiden and Boston: Brill, 2014), pp. 162–87.

Lineham, Peter J., 'Freethinkers in nineteenth-century New Zealand', *New Zealand Journal of History*, 19:1 (1985), pp. 61–81.

Lounsbury, Carl R., 'Architectural and cultural history', in Dan Hicks and Mary C. Beaudry (eds), *The Oxford Handbook of Material Culture Studies* (Oxford and New York: Oxford University Press, 2010), pp. 484–501.

McAllister, Annemarie, 'Onward: How a regional temperance magazine for children survived and flourished in the Victorian marketplace', *Victorian Periodicals Review*, 48:1 (2015), pp. 42–66.

McAreavey, Naomi, 'Building bridges? Remembering the 1641 Rebellion in Northern Ireland', *Memory Studies*, 11:1 (2018), pp. 100–14.

McAreavey, Naomi, 'Portadown, 1641: Memory and the 1641 depositions', *Irish University Review*, 47:1 (2017), pp. 15–31.

McAuley, James W., and Jonathan Tonge, '"For God and for the Crown": Contemporary political and social attitudes among Orange Order members in Northern Ireland', *Political Psychology*, 28:1 (2007), pp. 33–52.

McCracken, Donal P., 'Odd man out: The South African experience', in Andy Bielenberg (ed.), *The Irish Diaspora* (Harlow: Longman, 2000), pp. 251–71.

McFarland, Elaine, 'Marching from the margins: Twelfth July parades in Scotland, 1820–1914', in T. G. Fraser (ed.), *The Irish Parading Tradition: Following the Drum* (Basingstoke: Macmillan, 2000), pp. 60–77.

McGimpsey, Christopher D., 'Internal ethnic friction: Orange and green in nineteenth-century New York, 1868–1872', *Immigrants & Minorities*, 1:1 (1982), pp. 39–59.

McGreal, Chris, 'Ulster-by-the-Equator', *The Guardian*, 6 November 1999, <https://www.theguardian.com/uk/1999/nov/06/northernireland.books> (accessed 9 May 2024).

McKane, Pamela, '"No idle sightseers": The Ulster Women's Unionist Council and the Ulster Crisis (1912–1914)', *Studi Irlandesi: A Journal of Irish Studies*, 8:8 (2018), pp. 327–56.

MacPherson, D. A. J., 'The emergence of women's Orange lodges in Scotland: Gender, ethnicity and women's activism, 1909–1940', *Women's History Review*, 22:1 (2012), pp. 51–74.

MacPherson, D. A. J., '"Exploited with fury on a thousand platforms": Women, unionism and the *Ne Temere* decree in Ireland, 1908–1913', in Joan Allen and Richard C. Allen (eds), *Faith of Our Fathers: Popular Culture and Belief in Post-Reformation England, Ireland and Wales* (Newcastle: Cambridge Scholars Press, 2009), pp. 157–75.

MacPherson, D. A. J., 'Irish Protestant masculinities and Orangewomen in Scotland, Canada and England, 1890–1918', in Rebecca Anne Barr, Sean Brady and Jane McGaughey (eds), *Ireland and Masculinities in History* (Cham, Switzerland: Palgrave Macmillan, 2019), pp. 253–72.

MacPherson, D. A. J., 'Irish Protestant women and diaspora: Orangewomen in Canada during the twentieth century', in D. A. J. MacPherson and Mary J. Hickman (eds), *Women and Irish Diaspora Identities: Theories, Concepts and New Perspectives* (Manchester: Manchester University Press, 2014), pp. 168–85.

MacPherson, D. A. J., 'Migration and the female Orange Order: Irish Protestant identity, diaspora and empire in Scotland, 1909–40', *The Journal of Imperial and Commonwealth History*, 40:4 (2012), pp. 619–42.

MacPherson, D. A. J., 'Personal narratives of family and ethnic identity: Orangewomen in Scotland and England, c. 1940–2010', *Immigrants & Minorities*, 32:1 (2013), pp. 90–114.

MacPherson, D. A. J., and Donald M. MacRaild, 'Sisters of the brotherhood: Female Orangeism on Tyneside in the late nineteenth and early twentieth centuries', *Irish Historical Studies*, 35:137 (2006), pp. 40–60.

McQuaid, Sara, 'Parading memory and re-member-ing conflict: Collective memory in transition in Northern Ireland', *International Journal of Politics, Culture, and Society*, 30:1 (2017), pp. 23–41.

MacRaild, Donald M., '"The bunkum of Ulsteria": The Orange marching tradition in late Victorian Cumbria', in T. G. Fraser (ed.), *The Irish Parading Tradition: Following the Drum* (Basingstoke: Macmillan, 2000), pp. 44–59.

MacRaild, Donald M., 'Networks, communication and the Irish Protestant diaspora in northern England, c. 1860–1914', *Immigrants & Minorities*, 23:2–3 (2005), pp. 311–37.

MacRaild, Donald M., 'The Orange Atlantic', in David. T. Gleeson (ed.), *The Irish in the Atlantic World* (Columbia: South Carolina University Press, 2010), pp. 307–26.

MacRaild, Donald M., 'Transnationalising "anti-Popery": Militant Protestant preachers in the nineteenth-century Anglo-world', *Journal of Religious History*, 39:2 (2015), pp. 224–43.

Maddox, Neil P., '"A melancholy record": The story of the nineteenth-century Irish Party Processions Acts', *Irish Jurist*, 39 (2004), pp. 243–74.

Maunders, David, 'Awakening from the dream: The experience of childhood in Protestant orphan homes in Australia, Canada, and the United States', *Child & Youth Care Forum*, 23:6 (1994), pp. 393–412.

Millar, Stephen R., 'Musically consonant, socially dissonant: Orange walks and Catholic interpretation in West-Central Scotland', *Music and Politics*, 9:1 (2015), pp. 1–23.

Miller, David W., 'The Armagh troubles, 1784–95', in Samuel Clark and James S. Donnelly (eds), *Irish Peasants: Violence and Political Unrest, 1780–1914* (Madison: University of Wisconsin Press, 1983), pp. 155–91.

Miller, David W., 'The origins of the Orange Order in County Armagh', in A. J. Hughes and William Nolan (eds), *Armagh: History and Society* (Dublin: Geography Publications, 2001), pp. 538–608.

Moriaty, Gerry, 'Discontented Winters more concerned with local Orange history than elections', *Irish Times*, 20 May 1996.

Naylor, Rachel, 'The Orange Order in Africa', *History Ireland*, 14:4 (2006), pp. 7–9.

Neal, Frank, 'Manchester's origins of the English Orange Order', *Manchester Region History Review*, 4:2 (1990–91), pp. 12–24.

Ó Corráin, Daithí, '"Resigned to take the bill with its defects": The Catholic Church and the third Home Rule bill', in Gabriel Doherty (ed.), *The Home Rule Crisis 1912–14* (Cork: Mercier Press, 2014), pp. 185–209.

O'Kelly, Ciarán, and Dominic Bryan, 'The regulation of public space in Northern Ireland', *Irish Political Studies*, 22:4 (2007), pp. 565–84.

Pentland, Gordon, 'The indignant nation: Australian responses to the attempted assassination of the Duke of Edinburgh in 1868', *The English Historical Review*, 130:542 (2015), pp. 57–88.

Phoenix, Éamon, 'Catholic unionism: A case study: Sir Denis Stanislaus Henry (1864–1925)', in Oliver P. Rafferty (ed.), *Irish Catholic Identities* (Manchester and New York: Manchester University Press, 2013), pp. 292–304.

Pooley, Colin G., 'Housing for the poorest poor: Slum clearance and rehousing in Liverpool, 1890–1918', *Journal of Historical Geography*, 11:1 (1985), pp. 70–88.

Racioppi, Linda, and Katherine O'Sullivan See, 'Ulstermen and loyalist ladies on parade: Gendering unionism in Northern Ireland', *International Feminist Journal of Politics*, 2:1 (2000), pp. 1–29.

Radford, Katy, 'Drum rolls and gender roles in Protestant marching bands in Belfast', British Journal of Ethnomusicology, 10:2 (2001), pp. 37–59.

Radford, Katy, 'Red, white, blue and orange: An exploration of historically bound allegiances through loyalist song', *The World of Music*, 46:1 (2004), pp. 71–89.

Radforth, Ian, 'Collective rights, liberal discourse, and public order: The clash over Catholic processions in mid-Victorian Toronto', *The Canadian Historical Review*, 95:4 (2014), pp. 511–44.

Ramsey, Gordon, 'Playing away: Liminality, flow and *communitas* in an Ulster flute band's visit to a Scottish Orange parade', in Suzel Ana Reily and Katherine Brucher (eds), *Brass Bands of the World: Militarism, Colonial Legacies, and Local Music Making* (Burlington, VT: Ashgate, 2013), pp. 177–98.

Richard, Mark Paul, '"This is not a Catholic nation": The Ku Klux Klan confronts Franco-Americans in Maine', *The New England Quarterly*, 82:2 (2009), pp. 285–303.

Roberts, David A., 'The Orange Order in Ireland: A religious institution?', *The British Journal of Sociology*, 22:3 (1971), pp. 269–82.

Rooke, Patricia, and R. L. Schnell, 'The rise and decline of British North American Protestant orphans' homes as woman's domain, 1850–1930', *Atlantis*, 7:2 (1982), pp. 21–35.

Sahdra, Baljinder, and Michael Ross, 'Group identification and historical memory', *Personality and Social Psychology Bulletin*, 33:3 (2007), pp. 384–95.

Sandin, Bengt, 'History of children and childhood – Being and becoming, dependent and independent', *The American Historical Review*, 125:4 (2020), pp. 1306–16.

See, Scott W., 'The fortunes of the Orange Order in 19th century New Brunswick', in P. M. Toner (ed.), *New Ireland Remembered: Historical Essays on the Irish in New Brunswick* (Fredericton: New Ireland Press, 1988), pp. 90–105.

See, Scott W., '"Mickeys and demons" vs "bigots and boobies": The Woodstock Riot of 1847', *Acadiensis: Journal of the History of the Atlantic Region*, 21:1 (1991), pp. 110–31.

See, Scott W., 'The Orange Order and social violence in mid-nineteenth-century

Saint John', *Acadiensis: Journal of the History of the Atlantic Region*, 13:1 (1984), pp. 68–92.

Shiman, Lilian Lewis, 'The Band of Hope movement: Respectable recreation for working-class children', *Victorian Studies*, 17:1 (1973), pp. 49–74.

Smithey, Lee A., and Michael P. Young, 'Parading protest: Orange parades in Northern Ireland and temperance parades in antebellum America', *Social Movement Studies: Journal of Social, Cultural and Political Protest*, 9:4 (2010), pp. 393–410.

Urquhart, Diane, 'Unionism, Orangeism and war', *Women's History Review*, 27:3 (2016), pp. 468–84.

Vallance, Edward, 'Loyal or rebellious? Protestant associations in England, 1584–1696', *The Seventeenth Century*, 17:1 (2002), pp. 1–24.

Vella, Stephen, 'Newspapers', in Miriam Dobson and Benjamin Ziemann (eds), *Reading Primary Sources: The Interpretation of Texts from Nineteenth- and Twentieth-Century History* (London: Routledge, 2008), pp. 192–208.

Walker, Graham, 'The Orange Order in Scotland between the wars', *International Review of Social History*, 37 (1992), pp. 177–206.

Waters, Ian B., 'The first Australasian Catholic Congress: A mirror of the Australian Catholic Church in 1900', *Journal of the Australian Catholic Historical Society*, 21 (2000), pp. 9–23.

Webster, Joseph, 'From Scottish independence, to Brexit, and back again: Orange Order ethno-religion and the awkward urgency of British unionism', *Social Anthropology/Anthropologie Sociale*, 30:4 (2022), pp. 18–36.

Wilson, James, 'Orangeism in 1798', in Thomas Bartlett (ed.), *1798: A Bicentenary Perspective* (Dublin: Four Courts Press, 2003), pp. 345–62.

Witherow, Jacqueline, `Band development in Northern Ireland: Ethnographic researcher to policy consultant', *Anthropology in Action*, 13:1–2 (2006), pp. 44–54.

Witherow, Jacqueline, 'Parading Protestantisms and the flute bands of post-conflict Northern Ireland', in Jonathan Dueck and Suzel Ana Reily (eds), *The Oxford Handbook of Music and World Christianities* (Oxford: Oxford University Press, 2016), pp. 384–402.

Wolffe, John, 'Conclusion: Beyond Protestant-Catholic conflict?', in John Wolffe (ed.), *Protestant-Catholic Conflict from the Reformation to the Twenty-First Century* (London: Palgrave Macmillan, 2013), pp. 249–71.

Theses/Conference Papers/Unpublished Manuscripts

Butcher, Deborah, 'Ladies of the lodge: A history of Scottish Orangewomen, c. 1909–2013' (PhD, London Metropolitan University, 2014).

Carlyon, Jenny, 'New Zealand friendly societies, 1842–1941' (PhD, University of Auckland, 2001).

Coleman, Patrick, '"Irish Blackmen abroad": The Grand Black Chapter of New Zealand' (paper presented at 17th Australasian Irish Studies Conference,

'Transnational Ireland: Migration, conflict, representations', Queen's University, Belfast, 1–4 July 2010).

Coleman, Patrick J., 'Transplanted Irish institutions: Orangeism and Hibernianism in New Zealand 1877–1910' (MA, University of Canterbury, 1993).

Horn, Gerard Edward, '"A Loyal, united, and happy people": Irish Protestant migrants to Wellington Province 1840–1930: Aspects of migration, settlement and community' (PhD, Victoria University of Wellington, 2010).

Kaufmann, Eric, 'The demise of dominant ethnicity in English Canada: Orange Order membership decline in Ontario, 1918–1980' (full-length paper presented at the Institute of Commonwealth Studies conference on 'Canada and the end of empire', 26–28 April 2001).

McCallum, Christi, 'Orangewomen show their colors: Gender, family, and Orangeism in Ulster, 1795–present' (PhD, Southern Illinois University Carbondale, 2011).

McFarland, E. W., 'The Loyal Orange Institution in Scotland, 1799–1900' (PhD, University of Glasgow, 1986).

Moores, Harold S., 'The rise of the Protestant Political Association: Sectarianism in N.Z. during World War I' (MA, University of Auckland, 1966).

Phelan, Michael, 'Orange Order in Togo', 31 March 2014 (unpublished manuscript).

Thomson, Andrew, 'The Sentinel and Orange and Protestant Advocate, 1877–1896: An Orange view of Canada' (MA, Wilfred Laurier University, 1983).

Turner, Eric, '"Not narrow minded bigots": Proceedings of the Loyal Orange Institution of New South Wales, 1845–1895' (PhD, University of New England, 2002).

Wells, Cory, '"Tie the flags together": Migration, nativism, and the Orange Order in the United States, 1840–1930' (PhD, University of Texas, 2018).

Web-Based Materials

Adamson, Ian, 'The Ulster Accordion Band', <http://www.ianadamson. net/2011/06/04/the-ulster-accordian-band/> (accessed 1 December 2023).

Clement XII, *In Eminenti Apostolatus Specula* (Papal Bull) 28 April 1738, *Papal Encyclicals Online*, <https://www.papalencyclicals.net/Clem12/c12i nemengl.htm> (accessed 1 December 2023).

'Evangelical Truth', available at <www.evangelicaltruth.com> (accessed 5 November 2023).

Grand Orange Lodge of England, 'Marching bands', <https://web.archive.org/ web/20220529024048/https://www.gole.org.uk/bands> (accessed 20 July 2023).

Grand Orange Lodge of Ireland, <https://www.goli.org.uk> (accessed 10 April 2023).

Grand Orange Lodge of Ireland, 'Museum of Orange Heritage', <https://www. orangeheritage.co.uk/> (accessed 4 July 2023).

Grand Orange Lodge of Ireland, 'The Orange Standard Newspaper', <https:// www.goli.org.uk/orangestandard> (accessed 25 October 2023).

Grand Orange Lodge of Scotland, <https://orangeorderscotland.com> (accessed 23 August 2023).

Historic Places Canada, 'Royal City Christian Centre', <http://www.historic places.ca/en/rep-reg/place-lieu.aspx?id=16786> (accessed 23 August 2023).

Leo XIII, *Humanum Genus* (Papal Bull) 20 April 1884, *Papal Encyclicals Online*, <https://www.papalencyclicals.net/leo13/l13human.htm> (accessed 19 May 2023).

'Loyal Orange Institution of South Australia', <https://www.findglocal.com/AU/ Adelaide/423984171071340/Loyal-Orange-Institution-of-South-Australia> (accessed 30 November 2023).

'Ohahase Education Centre', <https://mbq-tmt.org/ohahase/> (accessed 14 December 2023).

'Orange History', <https://www.orangehistory.net/articles> (accessed 23 February 2024).

'OrangeNet', <https://web.archive.org/web/19990831053937/http://www.oran genet.org/about.htm> (accessed 19 May 2023).

Index